GHOSTLIER DEMARCATIONS

# GHOSTLIER DEMARCATIONS

## MODERN POETRY AND THE MATERIAL WORD

MICHAEL DAVIDSON

University of California Press
*Berkeley · Los Angeles · London*

University of California Press
Berkeley and Los Angeles, California

University of California Press, Ltd.
London, England

© 1997 by
The Regents of the University of California

Library of Congress Cataloging-in-Publication Data

Davidson, Michael, 1944–
    Ghostlier demarcations : modern poetry and the
material word / Michael Davidson.
       p.  cm.
    Includes bibliographical references (p. ) and index.
    ISBN 0-520-20739-4 (alk. paper)
    1. American poetry—20th century—History and
criticism.  2. Modernism (Literature)—United States.
3. Irrationalism (Philosophy) in literature.  4. Supernatural
in literature.  5. Materialism in literature.  6. Fantasy in
literature.  7. Ghosts in literature.  I. Title.
PS310.M57D38   1997
811'.50938—dc20                                 96-34563

9  8  7  6  5  4  3  2  1

*For Lori, Sophie, and Ryder*

# Contents

Preface — xi
Acknowledgments — xv

Introduction: Phantasmagorias of Modern Writing — 1

1. The Romance of Materiality: Gertrude Stein and the Aesthetic — 35

2. Palimtexts: George Oppen, Susan Howe, and the Material Text — 64

3. "From the Latin *Speculum*": Ezra Pound, Charles Olson, and Philology — 94

4. Dismantling "Mantis": Reification, Louis Zukofsky, and Objectivist Poetics — 116

5. "Not Sappho, Sacco": Postmodern Narratives/Modernist Forms in Muriel Rukeyser and Charles Reznikoff — 135

6. Marginality in the Margins: Robert Duncan's Textual Politics — 171

7. Technologies of Presence: Orality and the Tapevoice of Contemporary Poetics — 196

Afterword: "Ghostlier Demarcations" — 225

Notes — 231
Works Cited — 249
Index — 263

# Illustrations

1. Bob Cobbing, "Worm" — 17
2. Johanna Drucker, from *Against Fiction* — 19
3. Robert Grenier, "Twentieth Century" — 20
4. George Oppen, "Rembrandt's Old Woman Cutting Her Nails" — 65
5. George Oppen, "Women see no purpose..."— manuscript page — 74
6. Percy Bysshe Shelley, page from Shelley's Manuscript Book — 83
7. Transcription of Shelley manuscript page — 84
8. Susan Howe, from "Melville's Marginalia" in *The Nonconformist's Memorial* — 87
9. Charles Reznikoff, "Prolegomena" — 152
10. Charles Reznikoff, *Testimony*, manuscript page — 155
11. Charles Reznikoff, *My Country 'Tis of Thee*, title page — 157
12. Charles Reznikoff, page from *My Country 'Tis of Thee* — 159
13. Charles Reznikoff, list of words for *Testimony* — 162
14. Title page of Robert Duncan's copy of Thom Gunn's *Moly* — 182
15. From the opening of Thom Gunn's *Moly* — 183
16. Continuation of Duncan's "Near Circe's House" — 184
17. The beginning of Duncan's "Rites of Passage: I" — 185

# Preface

One impulse for writing this book on the material text can be traced to my hearing, sometime in the late 1960s, a tape recording of the 1963 Vancouver Poetry Conference in which Robert Creeley and Allen Ginsberg discussed their work. What was unusual about their conversation was their emphasis on the most banal aspects of writing—the use of pens or typewriters, the kinds of paper they preferred, whether or not they liked to have music in the background, the type of music, and so forth. "Habits of this kind," Creeley says, "are almost always considered immaterial or secondary. And yet, for my own reality, there is obviously a great connection between what I physically do as a writer in this sense, and what comes then out of it" (Creeley, *Contexts*, 30). By the standards of the then-influential New Criticism, such attention to the nuts and bolts of writing certainly *did* seem secondary, yet for me, as a beginning writer, this discussion was crucial for confirming the value of writing as a material practice beyond its rhetorical complexities. It also seemed important (in ways that I couldn't have recognized at the time) that this information came not from a book but from a tape recording, one that had been dubbed, passed around from friend to friend, and shared as part of what I have called a "vernacular pedagogy" of literary education (*San Francisco Renaissance* ix). Thus, the material text described by Creeley and Ginsberg was being disseminated through conduits whose own material conditions implicated the poem in realms of community, contingency, and conversation for which my training in the higher criticism had little to say.

A second impulse for this book has been the feeling that in the last decades of the twentieth century poetry has become marginalized in favor of narrative. This is especially the case in Marxist cultural theory, for which materiality would seem to be the point of departure. The neglect of poetry within Marxist theory has been based to some extent on a narrow definition of poetry as ideology whose separation from the production and reproduction of social life is a necessary condition for its existence. In this view poetic materiality—its language and formal construction—serves as a fit of rhyme against rhyme, the manipulation of language against itself. Kristen Ross relates this neglect of poetry to the diminution of space as a category within traditional Marxism. Her attempt to link Rimbaud to events surrounding the Paris Commune of 1871 is one of several recent efforts to bring social materiality—the urban spaces in which alternative communities and constituencies are formed—back into the discussion of poetry. While not attempting to relate modern poetry to specific social sites, I would like to restore to poetry a critical and political potential that earlier Marxist critics such as Raymond Williams, E. P. Thompson, and Theodor Adorno granted it. Furthermore, I would like to restore to modern poetry the claims for historical engagement that the poets themselves made—and for which they occasionally suffered.

As I develop the theme in my introduction and afterword, the material word occupies an odd, oxymoronic state rendered felicitously in Wallace Stevens's phrase "ghostlier demarcations, keener sounds." Stevens is referring to the poet's "rage to order" the chaos of nature, but he is also alluding to the poem's liminal status as a ghost or phantasmagoria—part material apparatus and part projection—whose surface hints at subterranean layers of historical resonance. Modern poets from Marianne Moore and Ezra Pound to Muriel Rukeyser, Charles Olson, Susan Howe, and Theresa Cha have constructed their poems quite literally out of the ghostly "marks" of others, not to celebrate the triumph of aesthetic form over the quotidian but to foreground the ongoing historiographic project of poetry. Such intentions are most visible when poets quote from other texts or incorporate into the poem surface features of other discourses, practices for which the term "intertextuality" is inadequate. The poem is a palimpsest of the quotidian, a writing upon other writings in which prior traces are left visible, in which the page retains vestiges of its evolution.

The metaphor of the palimpsest that animates several chapters of this book has its own origin in work that I did as the Curator of the Archive for New Poetry at the University of California, San Diego. In this capacity I became interested in the manuscript page as an index to intentions effaced in the published document. The typescript or holograph page often reveals a host of earlier writings, marginal scribbles, and nonliterary remarks that are erased in the published poem. This palimpsest of other writings visible in the manuscript testifies to the contingent character of writing, the degree to which texts speak to their moment as well as to other texts and writers. Recent poets and textual scholars have called for the publication of facsimile versions of modern texts to render the original shape of the text, and while I support such endeavors I also recognize the dangers of fetishizing original documents for their own sake in place of critical assessment of what those documents mean.

It is such a critical assessment that I offer here, although it would not be possible without the work of poets and critics such as Susan Howe, Alice Kaplan, Jerome McGann, Stephanie Jed, Thomas Tanselle, and others who have advanced textual scholarship into the social realm. Nor would it be possible without the pioneering work of those formalist critics whom I (sometimes dismissively) regard as inventors of an "ideology of modernism." It should go without saying that the discourse of literary materiality was invented and perfected by scholars who recognized that modernity was visible only in its defamiliarization, who saw that the commodification of language could be thwarted by making literature hard to consume. If I come to different conclusions about the historical meanings of such aesthetic materialization, I nevertheless learned much from those formalist critics who first taught me what was on the page.

# Acknowledgments

As is appropriate to a book on the material word, many words in *this* book have appeared in other forms and venues. Moreover, many of my words have been shaped by conversations with friends and colleagues whose interests in the material text have become part of my book's palimtext. In particular, I would like to acknowledge the help of Stephanie Jed, Susan Howe, and Marjorie Perloff, whose collective support for this project has been sustaining from the outset. While revising the book for final publication, I was reminded of significant contributions from other friends, especially Charles Bernstein, Robert von Hallberg, Cary Nelson, Carolyn Burke, Bob Perelman, Lyn Hejinian, Alan Golding, Don Wayne, Judith Halberstam, Claude Royet-Journoud, Kathryn Shevelow, William Tay, Rachel Blau DuPlessis, James Clifford, Thom Gunn, Michael Palmer, Alan Wald, Michael Rogin, Amie Parry, and Michael Thurston. I feel fortunate to have had such vital and generous interlocutors during this book's composition.

I am indebted for my research on the history of the tape recorder to the staff at the Center for Magnetic Recording Research at the University of California, San Diego. Lynda Claassen and Brad Westbrook of the Mandeville Department of Special Collections at UCSD were extremely helpful in my research on manuscript materials held in the Archive for New Poetry.

Earlier versions of several chapters were presented at conferences or colloquia, for which thanks are extended to Tim Hunt, Jacqueline Brogan, Marjorie Perloff, Stuart Curran, Stephen Rodefer, Hayden White, and Robert von Hallberg. A version of chapter 2 appeared in *Contemporary Literature* 28.2 (Summer 1987): 187–205. A version of chapter 5 appeared in *Contemporary Literature* 33.2 (Summer 1992): 275–301. Both are reprinted with permission of the University of Wisconsin Press. A version of chapter 4 was published in *American Literary History* 3.3 (Fall 1991): 521–541 and is reprinted by permission of Oxford University Press. A portion of the introduction appeared as a catalogue essay in *Poesure et peintrie: "D'un art l'autre,"* ed. Bernard Blistene (Marseilles: Musées de Marseille—Reunion des Musées Nationaux, 1993). Thanks are extended to Maggie Gilchrist for her role in this project.

Permission to reproduce pages or quote from individual works is granted by the following presses and persons: Farrar, Straus & Giroux, Inc., and Thom Gunn, for pages from Thom Gunn's *Moly;* The literary estate of Robert Duncan, for holograph poems in his copy of Thom Gunn's *Moly;* Johanna Drucker, for a page from *Against Fiction;* Bob Cobbing, for "Worm" from *An Anthology of Concrete Poetry,* ed. Emmett Williams; New Directions Publishing Company and Faber and Faber Ltd., for works by Ezra Pound; New Directions Publishing Co., for work by Susan Howe and Robert Duncan; the Yale Collection of American Literature, Beinecke Rare Book and Manuscript Library, Yale University, for an unpublished letter by Mina Loy; The University of California Press, for Charles Olson's *The Maximus Poems,* ed. George Butterick (1983); Johns Hopkins University Press, for material from *"A"* by Louis Zukofsky.

Quotations from and reproductions of unpublished manuscripts by Charles Reznikoff are printed by permission of David Bodansky and the Estate of Charles Reznikoff. Quotations from and reproductions of unpublished manuscripts by George Oppen are printed by permission of Linda Oppen Mourelatos and the Estate of George Oppen.

Finally, an extended thanks to Doris Kretschmer of the University of California Press for her faith in the project and her extraordinary help in all aspects of the book's production. I would also like to acknowledge the excellent copyediting of my manuscript by Erika Bűky at the University of California Press and by David Severtson.

The sustaining presence of Lori Chamberlain and our children, Sophie and Ryder, extends beyond the page.

# Introduction

*Phantasmagorias of Modern Writing*

### THE GHOST IN A MACHINE

In her late revision of Homeric epic, *Helen in Egypt* (1961), H.D. stages a debate between Achilles and Helen over the causes of the Trojan War. Achilles accuses Helen of provoking and enticing men to battle by walking upon the ramparts of Troy:

> for you were the ships burnt,
> O cursed, O envious Isis,
> you—you—a vulture, a hieroglyph;

to which Helen responds

> "Zeus be my witness," I said,
> "it was he, Amen dreamed of all this
> phantasmagoria of Troy,
> it was dream and a phantasy."
> (17)

The term "phantasmagoria" evokes the nightmarish quality of Helen's imagination as she attempts to measure her lived experience against her textualized versions in heroic poems from Homer to Pound. Is she, as Achilles accuses, a vulture or a hieroglyph, a carrion creature that feeds on the dead or a prophetic sign by which the living may interpret their fate? In a metaphor by which H.D. often figured her own life, Helen is a palimpsest, a page on which prior writings remain visible. If her life is a dream of the gods, it is also a text written upon by men.

A specter is haunting modern writing. H.D.'s use of "phantasmagoria" summons a host of similar metaphors for the modernist uncanny—from Freud's *unheimlich* and Victorian gothicism to James's ghosts, Yeats's spirits, Joyce's nighttown ghouls, and Pound's Dantean shades. Despite its association with otherworldly experiences, "phantasmagoria" has a distinctly material origin in the magic-lantern shows introduced to London during the early nineteenth century. In these public exhibitions optical illusions were projected onto a screen by means of a light source refracted through mirrors and magnifying lenses. Early entrepreneurs of the genre seized upon its ability to create bizarre effects in which figures seem to float in space or suddenly change size and position. The device was also enlisted for larger modernist programs of scientific inquiry and national expansion. In an 1866 "Handy Guide" to the use of magic lanterns the author notes that although the device had been used primarily for "amusing children and astonishing the ignorant," it might now serve a more rational purpose in scientific education. Furthermore, it might participate in the civilizing functions of colonialism: "It is also a very suggestive circumstance that Dr. Livingstone took with him a Magic Lantern to instruct and amuse the natives of the countries he visited; so that while naturalized in London, the centre of the world's civilization, the Magic Lantern is no stranger to the dusky denizens of the heart of Africa" (*Magic Lantern* 6).[1] Thus, the machine that makes the uncanny visible to audiences in London parlors also makes London seem familiar to the "dusky denizens" of Dr. Livingstone's Africa. Education and amusement, rationality and fear, science and magic, metropolitan center and colonial outpost meet through the ghost in a machine.

Terry Castle observes that the history of nineteenth-century phantasmagoric exhibitions defines the gradual "absorption of ghosts into the world of thought," a rationalization of unreal elements in modern life by regarding them as projections of the mind (*Female Thermometer* 29). This yoking of irrational and rational realms through the metaphor of projection is a centerpiece of modernist writing—from Poe's gothic scenes in "The Fall of the House of Usher" and "Ligeia" to James's portrait of Lambert Strether, who in *The Ambassadors* tells Martha Gostrey that he moves "among miracles. It was all phantasmagoric" (333). Rimbaud declared himself a "maître en fantasmagories," and Mallarmé used the term to describe the fantastic motions of a dancer: "Sa fusion aux nuances veloces muant leur fantasmagorie oxyhydrique de crepuscule et de grotte" (*Oeuvres complètes* 308). In Zola's *The Ladies' Paradise (Au Bonheur des Dames)*, the old cloth merchant Baudu dismisses his niece's celebration of new department stores and marketing practices: "That's all phantasmagoria" (187). T. S. Eliot invokes it as a metaphor for Prufrock's neurasthenia: "It is impossible to say just what I mean! / But as if a magic lantern threw the nerves in patterns on a screen" (6). In various implicit and explicit forms, phantasmagoria haunt Pound's early work, beginning with his most famous Imagist poem ("apparition of these faces in the crowd") and forming one pole of his triumvirate of literary practices: "phanopoeia, which is a casting of images upon the visual imagination" (*Literary Essays* 25).[2] Pound's deracinated aesthete Hugh Selwyn Mauberley, like Lambert Strether, drifts in an ambrosial "phantasmagoria," without being able to synthesize perceptions into significant forms.[3] Finally, without too much adaptation we can see aspects of phantasmagoria extended to Louis Zukofsky's ocularcentric treatment of Objectivism and Charles Olson's "Projective Verse."

Perhaps the most famous appearance of "phantasmagoria" occurs not in literature but in economic theory. Marx uses the term to describe the uncanny character of the commodity in which social relations assume "the fantastic form of a relation between things" (*Capital* 165). For Marx, the commodity in circulation effaces its origins in human labor, achieving an autonomy that permits it to address its consumer. "A commodity is therefore a mysterious thing" since, like a religious icon or fetish, it has been granted the power of speech. Similarly, the worker whose labor power is reified in the commodity becomes the site of exploitation, the "object" of the capitalist's gaze. Ann Cvetkovich points out that *Capital* makes use of a certain gothic rhetoric to describe the Frankensteinlike emergence of surplus value out of production such that money is endowed with human agency (176). If in the modern world all that is solid melts into air, the air itself is populated with phantoms drawn from a mercantilist *grimoire*.

In explaining why individuals are unable to perceive the mechanics of this ghost-show of objectification, Marx has recourse to another technological innovation of his era—the *camera obscura*, in which the "real conditions" of material life are inverted and rationalized: "If in all ideology men and their circumstances appear upside-down as in a *camera obscura*, this phenomenon arises just as much from their historical life-process as the inversion of objects on the retina does from their physical life-process" (Marx and Engels, *German Ideology*, 47). Marx's theme in *The German Ideology* is not the isolation of ideas as "false consciousness," divorced from material production, but rather the interweaving of ideas, conceptions, and consciousness with material forces such that "phantoms formed in the human brain are also, necessarily, sublimates of their material life-processes" (47). Ideology is a projection of images that allows uncanny relations between human and inhuman, social and material, to be seen as natural as, for example, "petals on a wet, black bough."

It may seem a long distance from H.D.'s phantasmagoric Troy to Marx's Victorian commodity culture, but it is a distance created, to some extent, by the former to efface the latter. The fact that the two realms seem so distinct indicates how successful the phantasmagoria has been in projecting the form of modernism we have come to consume. In most accounts, modernist literature is founded on the possibility of release from limits of time and space—through myth, image, stream of consciousness, spatial form—in order to transcend the materialism that infects every aspect of urban life. Phantasmagoria, as a master trope for modernism, represents an amalgam of two temporalities: an apparatus that projects private images and a public space in which they may be experienced collectively. It also joins two spheres of materiality: modes of mechanical reproduction (film, photography, sound recording) in which new subjectivities are produced and new public spaces in which these subjectivities are translated into social and ultimately political relations.

Walter Benjamin observes that the great exhibitions and commerce fairs of the late nineteenth century (where many of these magic-lantern shows were featured) glorified exchange value by stressing national productivity as a vast display: "They create a framework in which commodities' intrinsic value is eclipsed. They open up a phantasmagoria that people enter to be amused," much as department stores employ an elaborate theatrical staging to display products (*Reflections* 152). The magic-lantern shows, panoramas, and dioramas of the early modernist period project the strange and the exotic in ways that normalize the unreal quality of new urban masses.[4] Art, as the Russian Formalists said, performs the opposite function—of defamiliarizing daily life that we may see it anew.

In this book I am interested in the relationship between two forms of materiality, social and aesthetic, manifested in a figure like the phantasmagoria and embodied in modern American poetry. I am less interested in relationships between technology and literature of the sorts chronicled by Martha Banta, Terry Smith, Neil Harris, Cecelia Tichi, and others than I am in the meanings given to materialization in various types of textual practice. Those social and cultural meanings of materiality are like the phantasmagoria itself, a productive apparatus and a set of variable fictions, each one layered on top of the last like multiple scripts in a palimpsest. To unpack these layers, subsequent chapters study materialization in a range of modern and contemporary poets. Chapter 1 discusses Gertrude Stein's curious location as the "object" of a consumerist gaze while she created texts that defy commodification. Chapter 2 deals with the materiality of literary archives as seen through the papers of George Oppen. The chapter also discusses the feminist implications of archival research in Susan Howe. Chapter 3 extends a concern with textual ephemerality to the phenomenon of the "lexical insert," the use of quotation and citation as expressive and historicizing gestures. Chapter 4 attempts to define the "ideology of form" as it appears in the work of Objectivist poets of the 1930s, specifically that of Louis Zukofsky. Chapter 5 develops the issue of 1930s formalism by looking at documentary poems of Muriel Rukeyser and Charles Reznikoff and the ways that they problematize current debates surrounding national narrativity and the crisis of genre. Chapter 6 looks at the materiality of Robert Duncan's late poetry and the sexual and textual politics implied by his writing a suite of poems in the margins of Thom Gunn's book *Moly*. My final chapter moves the discussion of materiality into the arena of technology by focusing on the effect of the tape recorder on contemporary poetry and the ways it creates new forms of identity via the "tapevoice" of postmodern surveillance ideology.

The "meaning of materiality" as it is played out in these seven chapters has particular resonance for an American cultural context since technological and industrial expansion were embraced and celebrated to a greater degree than in Europe as a fulfillment of a certain providential narrative. Gertrude Stein's idea that America is the oldest country in the world because it was the first to embrace modern industrial techniques is one of many attempts to join American modernity with material progress. Thus, it is not enough to focus on the means of material production out of which new cultural forms emerged; one must study the ideological work of materiality in a materialist age.[5]

Despite Stein's enthusiasm for series production and the Model T

Ford, her poetics, and that of many of her contemporaries, is cast in terms of aesthetic autonomy whereby the foregrounding of the medium—the text's graphemic and typographic character, its syntactics and morphemics—contests the instrumental, commodified forms in which language appears. In its more aestheticized version, materialization refers to the rhetorical structure of images, figures of speech, and prosodic repetitions by which the text aspires to the condition of sculpture or music. By throwing off the material *world* through an investment in the material *word*, the Artist, capital *A*, preserves cultural cohesion against mass-cultural incursions. Literary autonomy thus implies a work's ability to replicate material exchange within itself as an organic entity rather than succumb to market forces that threaten from without.[6]

Critical theorists of varying political stripes are in surprising unanimity on the integrity of this narrative. The Russian Formalist dictum that poetry is the "maximum foregrounding of the utterance" or that it "lays bare the device" continues in New Critical versions of the autotelic text. Bakhtin's antipathy toward poetry's monologism is based on its supposed creation of "a unitary and singular Ptolemaic world outside of which nothing else exists and nothing else is needed" (286). A more dialectical version of autonomy is provided by Theodor Adorno, who recognizes that the artwork's supposed difference from rationalized, commodified existence offers an immanent critique of a world on which a purposive *telos* has been grafted. The "thing-like quality of art," as Adorno says, "is the result of an inner dynamic" that unites the Kantian transcendental in-itself with contingent, spatio-temporal facts (146). Formal complexity in the work of Schoenberg or Beckett guarantees that the artwork will never succumb to the reifying tendencies of the culture industries. Finally, poststructural theories of textuality, while offering an important critique of the metaphysical basis for autonomous art, nevertheless continue the theme. Roland Barthes's notion that "modern poetry . . . destroys the spontaneously functional nature of language, and leaves standing only its lexical basis" is one of many postmodern versions of literary intransitivity that leaves the issue of social materiality unexplored (*Writing Degree Zero* 46). And Michel Foucault, whose archaeological researches are more appropriate to our materialist model, still marks the modern era as being a moment when "a silent, cautious deposition of the word upon the whiteness of a piece of paper, where it can possess neither sound nor interlocutor, where it has nothing to say but itself, nothing to do but shine in the brightness of its being" (*Order of Things* 300).

A counterdiscourse to autonomy theory is offered by the avant-garde, but even here the ideal of an aesthetic monad controls the terms by which movements such as Futurism or Dadaism contest autonomy. In Peter Burger's reading of the avant-garde, the introduction of mass-produced materials into the artwork (Duchamp's urinal is his test case) challenges both the autonomous nature of the artwork as well as its institutional role in bourgeois society. Burger rightly perceives that art as institution (its appearance in museum and concert hall) is predicated on the ideal of distanciation, but by creating an unbridgeable divide between modernism and the avant-garde he fails to see shared affinities of the sort I have articulated in the case of H.D. Nor does Burger hold any hope for a continuing avant-garde social critique. Because the historical avant-garde failed to change either the high cultural authority of autonomous art or the class structure of society, any revival of the same strategies—whether in happenings, Pop Art, Brechtian performance—quickly becomes a series of empty repetitions. In Burger's view, what began as the avant-garde's attack on the commodification of art as institution becomes its reabsorption into commodity culture.

However insightful Burger's analysis of the critical function of the avant-garde, it rests on a rather schematic distinction between the materiality of the artwork and that of everyday life, a distinction resembling the more mechanistic Marxist one between superstructure and base. While it is quite true that Cubist use of *papier collé* subjects wallpaper, newspapers, and advertising to aesthetic ends, it does not thereby mean that these surfaces refer only to formal properties of design and never to the commercial world from which they are drawn. Even Mallarmé's *Un coup de dés*, an inaugural moment of aesthetic autonomy, is produced, as Johanna Drucker observes, within a typographic milieu made possible by commercial advertising (*Visible Word* 50–60). One may choose to separate the two components—Mallarmé's metaphysics of the book from commercial typography—to insist on the aesthetic triumph over the quotidian, but to do so is to sever their interdependence.

The separation of realms upon which Burger depends is a fictional one based on a selective reading of certain fin-de-siècle authors and on regarding statements in poetics as synonymous with individual works. Moreover, to maintain the integrity of avant-garde critique he must collapse a wide diversity of practices and political agendas into a single tendency. Andreas Huyssen attempts to go beyond the "great divide" between modernism and mass culture by discovering a "hidden dialectic" between the latter and the avant-garde (9). That dialectic is based on both spheres' mutual fascination with technology—the use of new electronic and mechanical means of reproduction in film, artistic montage, music, and theater. Huyssen goes a long way to restoring the political meaning of the avant-garde and extending its social critique into postmodernism. But even this more optimistic view depends on the prior authority of an autonomous art object against which some other type of "object," presumably one consumed unreflectively by the masses, is set in opposition. Moreover, by using technology as the representative feature of masscultural life, other aspects of materiality (consumerism, popular literary genres, everyday practices in life) are ignored.[7]

We could say that the ideology of modernism, in its dystopic and utopian forms, has governed how we read passages such as that from *Helen in Egypt*. An influential body of feminist criticism interprets H.D. through a revisionary hermeneutics that replaces patriarchal modernism, dominated by Pound and Freud, with a gynocentric variation, based on an effaced matriarchal tradition. The trope of the palimpsest is central to this revisionist imperative in providing an image of women's writing as a series of overwritten texts in which the continuity of what Susan Stanford Friedman calls "the desecrated Goddess" continues to speak (375).[8] By regarding H.D.'s writing as an ahistorical palimpsest, critics have removed her from the post–World War II historical ruins out of which she was writing and returned her to the same recuperatory, cyclic temporality that we associate with patriarchal modernism. And by accepting the palimpsest as a metaphor for a continuous female identity, cultural feminists avoid the instability of that figure throughout her own career as she invented and reinvented herself in a variety of roles—as mother, daughter, film actress, Delphic priestess, heterosexual, lesbian, analysand, and text. A materialist treatment of H.D.'s work must provide a "thick" description of these various roles within the material forms in which they appear—from graphic marks on a page or spoken words on a tape recorder to published versions, their readers, and the communities of discourse those readers share.[9]

To provide such a materialist reading of modern poetry, I have inflected the "palimpsest" to include specific forms of textual production. My portmanteau variation, "palimtext," describes modern writing's intertextual and material character, its graphic rendering of multiple layers of signification. The term also suggests the need for a historicist perspective in which textual layers refer not only to previous texts but to the discursive frame of the present in which they are seen. My usage draws upon what Jerome McGann calls the "textual condition," access to which necessitates the study of marginal areas of writing: "the physical form of books and manuscripts (paper, ink, typefaces, layouts) or their prices, advertising mechanisms, and distribution venues (*Textual Condition* 12). I would expand McGann's list to include forms of materiality outside the text that facilitate writing in general—the institutional, disciplinary, and educational systems that validate material practices. The invocation of philological science in Ezra Pound's *Cantos*, the role of consumerism and Fordism in Gertrude Stein, the presence of documentary culture in Muriel Rukeyser, the politics of printing in Robert Duncan, the role of editing and textual scholarship in Susan Howe, the importance of magnetic recording technologies for Laurie Anderson all contribute to the palimtextual meaning of their work.

If we think of poetry as a palimtext, rather than a verbal icon or objective correlative, we are faced with a writing that displays its formations in other writings. The palimtext is not a final, ultimate version but an arrested moment in an ongoing process of signifying, scripting, and typing. Even a strip of magnetic tape is palimtextual since the voice it records contains the uses for which magnetic recording has been invented, its ability to disseminate, monitor, and replicate speech. The poet who treats the page as a "score for the voice" (as Charles Olson does) simultaneously marks the historical moment at which the "voice" becomes problematic, at which it can no longer be regarded as a sign of self-presence.

While the palimtext might suggest a new form of postmodern writing—a rhizomatic or hypertextual modality—it is more of a vehicle for circumventing generic categories and period styles by describing writing in its collaborative, quotidian, and intertextual forms. When considered as holograph, printed page, voice, or performance, writing loses its specular relationship to a prior "more real" world and becomes, as Wallace Stevens said, "part of the res itself and not about it." Stevens may have been thinking more of Kant than of jars, blackbirds, or insurance companies, but he was also thinking of how those things (including Kant) are intertwined with words that strive to replace them. A palimtextual study of modern writing must investigate the interstices of the material word in its multiple forms as visible page, poetics, sign system, and archive.

## THE MATERIAL PAGE

When Mallarmé announced a *crise de vers* in the 1890s, he anticipated a constellation of problems that would preoccupy poets for the next century. At one level, the crisis refers to the problem of the sign itself, its ability to refer outside the discursive field in which it is used. In another sense, Mallarmé was concerned with the fate of artistic language in an age of mechanical reproduction when newspapers, photography, and mass-produced popular novels threatened to destroy the "aura" of a work's originality and uniqueness. Mallarmé's response to these twin crises in a work like *Un coup de dés* was to utilize the material resources of the printed page—varying fonts, type sizes, white space—to disturb syntactic and semantic relationships. If *Un coup de dés* signaled the problematics of language that has become synonymous with modernism, it did so in the most *graphic* of terms.

For Anglo-American poets, this foregrounding of the verbal medium offered a necessary corrective to the excesses of late Victorian verse. When Ezra Pound set down his famous Imagist tenets of 1913, it was precisely to excoriate the "perdamnable rhetoric" of the 1890s in England. He advised a "harder and saner" verse, "as much like granite as it can be" (*Literary Essays* 12). Unlike Symbolism, with which it shared certain affinities, Imagism stressed the physical properties of objects in ways that were never at issue in the earlier movement. Moreover, the visualist imperative of Imagist aesthetics extended to the physical placement of words on the page. Pound's most famous Imagist poem, "In a Station of the Metro," first appeared with spaces between key words to emphasize the important relationship between musical phrasing and notation:

>     The apparition     of these faces     in the crowd
>     Petals     on a wet, black     bough        .
>                         (Ruthven 152)

However radical Pound's attack on rhetoric may have sounded, his own early practice was much informed by the very aesthetic movements he attacked. His early poems were modeled on medieval Tuscan and Provençal verse, and when he published his first collection of *The Cantos*, they were ornately decorated in illuminated capitals and two-color printing more appropriate to Pre-Raphaelite design.[10] As Jerome McGann suggests, Pound's "modernism" must be framed by the historicity implied by such designs (*Black Riders* 76–80). It was not enough for him simply to invoke the glories of medieval Tuscany or Provence; it was necessary to rearticulate them through their contemporary manifestations in Arts and Crafts printing and bookmaking. Although Pound ultimately rejected such ornate typographic presentations during the 1930s for more "modern" visual formats, his debts to the Arts and Crafts spirit of William Morris stayed with him as an ideal synthesis of poetry, design, and material culture.

With his exposure to Continental movements such as Futurism, Cubism, and Dadaism, Pound quickly saw how the page could become more than an occasion for decorative printing but rather a generative element of meaning. Influential in Pound's thinking about the physical qualities of the page was his discovery, through the papers of Ernst Fenollosa, of the Chinese ideogram. Pound felt, however mistakenly, that the Chinese character was a series of schematic images, juxtaposed one upon the other, that created a single complex or "radiant node." The modern poem could utilize certain features of the ideogram—its concreteness, emphasis on the natural object, juxtaposition of multiple images—into a spatial whole. The "ideogrammic method" advocated by Pound implied a way of moving from one element to another without providing the usual rhetorical connectives. Applied to the *Cantos*, this method permitted Pound to create a visual field out of disparate discursive elements—a quotation from Middle English, a phrase in Greek, a reference to Egyptian mythology, a Chinese character—the juxtaposition of which would constitute a cultural hieroglyph. The simultaneity of historical moments through juxtaposition was given visual reinforcement by Pound's use of the entire page as a textual collage. In "Canto XCI," for example, Pound links the Egyptian hieroglyph for the Sun boat of Ra with the Chinese character for "tensile light," the Greek word for Helen of Troy, and the story of Sir Francis Drake. All four elements represent Neoplatonic values associated with light and fertility that Pound felt were articulated during the Renaissance, the English version of which is figured by Drake, a navigator, statesman, soldier, and servant of a powerful female monarch (*Cantos* 610–17).

Pound's ideogrammic method was the verbal component of Vorticism, a British movement that stressed interrelationships between visual, sculptural, and literary arts. Vorticism reflected the influence of Italian Futurism, particularly its penchant for dynamic motion and speed. Although the British variant rejected the cult of the machine associated with Marinetti and Boccioni, it utilized the typographic innovations of both Russian and Italian Futurism in its principle magazine, *Blast*. First published in 1914, *Blast* printed the work of Pound, Wyndham Lewis, and the sculptor Henri Gaudier-Brzeska as well as Russian, Italian, and German poets. As Marjorie Perloff has pointed out, Vorticism exploited the formal possibilities of the manifesto as a performative genre—its direct, public address, its declamatory tone, its dynamic physical presentation—and along the way provided a new look for the printed page.[11] In his various manifestos published in the magazine, Wyndham Lewis "blasts" the aestheticism of the British 1890s, utilizing various type sizes to score the dynamics of his invective. Although many of the poems printed in *Blast* were written in traditional forms and utilized the hard left margin, the aesthetic and social diatribes presented alongside the poems were significant literary and typographic events in themselves.

Vorticism exploited the possibilities of the medium by taking the poem off the page and into the realm of physical gesture. There were limits, however, to a poetics based largely on invective, and by 1919, only a few years after its inaugural manifesto, the movement was dead. A more radical transformation of the page was effected by the examples of Cubism and Dadaism. In the United States, the first appearances of Cubist painting and collage in the Armory show of 1913 and then in Alfred Steiglitz's magazines *Camera Work* and *291* were a revelation to many poets. Gertrude Stein, William Carlos Williams, e. e. cummings, Mina Loy, and others seized upon the possibilities of fragmentation, repetition, and montage in the work of Picasso, Braque, and Leger. In particular, the poets were interested by the way painters incorporated found materials onto the canvas. Fragments of newspapers, advertising, and other forms of mass-produced copy became part of the overall construction, and when poets applied similar materials to their poems the effects on poetic form were dramatic. The use of verbal collage can be felt in many of the major poems of the period, from T. S. Eliot's *The Waste Land* and Pound's *Cantos* to Gertrude Stein's portraits, William Carlos Williams's *Spring and All*, and Hart Crane's *The Bridge*. Collage juxtaposition permitted poets to confront the distractions of modern urban life through the multiple voices of an emerging print culture.[12]

If Cubism provided the formal means for a *dérèglement* of the page, Dadaism provided the iconoclastic spirit. The work of Francis Picabia, Marcel Duchamp, Man Ray, and other Europeans who visited the United States inspired poets with a sense of irreverence and daring that helped create an indigenous American avant-garde in the years following World War I. American versions of Dada were never as radical as their European counterparts, but something of the movement's nose-thumbing character can be felt in the work of Baroness Elsa von Freytag Loringhoven, Robert McAlmon, William Carlos Williams, Mina Loy, and e. e. cummings, many of whom gathered at Walter Conrad Arensberg's apartment or published in Alfred Kreymborg's magazine, *Others*. Dada offered less a series of formal solutions to the poem than permission to invent and explore and, in the process, to use typography in highly inventive ways.

The typographic revolution brought about by Futurism, Cubism, and Dadaism led to significant experiments with Concrete or Visual Poetry. Apollinaire's *Calligrammes*, begun in 1914, utilized typography to represent rain, cannons, musical instruments, automobiles, and other objects in a series of whimsical visual poems. Such a practice was by no means original to modernism—the convention of "shaped" verse is as old as print itself—but it achieved a special importance in the post–World War I era as poets sought to liberate the word from its dependency upon conventional syntax, inherited forms, and genres. Although the use of visual poetry did not come into its own until the Concrete movement of the late 1950s, it formed an important element in the work of many poets during this period.

Much of the impetus for calligraphic and Concretist experimentation was gained by the increased use of the typewriter and the flexibility of new forms of movable type. As I will develop this theme later, modernist poets such as Pound, Williams, and cummings saw the advantages of this technology in gaining control over their medium. Prior to the modern period, poets had to rely on the skills (and whims) of copy editors and typesetters in interpreting their textual intentions. Modernist poets now could use new print technologies to indicate exactly what values of spacing and word placement they intended. This kind of flexibility permitted poets to utilize the range of the typewriter keyboard, from diacritical marks to the tab and space bars, in realizing their notations. Free verse had gained a new and important technical ally in completing its revolution.

Whereas the Pound/Williams generation used the typewriter to create a new visual aesthetic—the word as image or object—poets who followed them utilized that same technology in the service of an emerging oral impulse. The recovery of orality in postwar verse, with its basis in primitive, tribal cultures, coincides with a greater emphasis on personal confession and bardic testimony. Charles Olson, in his manifesto "Projective Verse" (1950), vaunted the typewriter's ability to provide a more exact register of vocal intentions (*Selected Writings of Charles Olson* 15–26). What Olson calls "open field" verse involves the line as a physical gesture, a register of physiological and muscular responses. The line is controlled no longer by a discrete count of individual elements (accents, syllables, feet) but by the emotional intensity of the moment. Bardic poets such as Allen Ginsberg or Robert Duncan utilized a characteristically long line that sustained a rolling, often mantralike cadence in the manner of Blake or Whitman; more introspective poets such as Robert Creeley or Denise Levertov utilized a shorter, more heavily enjambed line to achieve a tense, highly charged lyricism. In each case, the new poetries of the 1950s and 1960s generated notational features based on organic or psychological models that could not be accommodated to traditional prosodic form.

Olson's own practice derives from Pound and Williams, often varying short, lyric moments with long-lined, prosaic passages. As I point out in chapter 3, Olson utilizes indentation and spacing to register moment-to-moment shifts of attention as he walks, literally and figuratively, through a historically encrusted landscape. Those "private" feelings are linked to the physical world in which he walks, and thus in a poem such as "Letter, May 2, 1959," he skews his lines in various directions to imitate an early map of Gloucester (*Maximus* 150). Olson's impatience with traditional rhetorical devices and sequential narrative structure are registered through his highly enjambed lineation as well as his idiosyncratic use of spacing. Despite the oralist bias of "Projective Verse," Olson's primary concern is phenomenological: to create a poetry as close to perception and cognition as possible. The score for such processes was a page that resembled, as closely as possible, physical acts of writing, speaking, and walking.

Combined with a renewed emphasis on the line as expressive gesture among various poets of the 1950s and 1960s was a renewed interest in uniting poetry with other arts. Poets such as Kenneth Patchen, Ian Hamilton Finlay, Robert Duncan, and Philip Whalen illustrated their own books, but this same investment in the poem-as-art event led to more collaborative kinds of activities as well. Kenneth Rexroth, Lawrence Ferlinghetti, Jack Kerouac, and LeRoi Jones (Amiri Baraka) wrote poems to be performed with jazz musicians, leading to new notational strategies that would indicate phrasing, rhythms, and dynamics. Many poets associated with the New York School worked directly with painters, appropriating the painterly aesthetics of abstract expressionism (or, later, of Pop Art) with the personalist aesthetics defined by Frank O'Hara. Collaborations between O'Hara and Larry Rivers, Clark Coolidge and Philip Guston, Ron Padget and Joe Brainard, and John Ashbery and Alex Katz were inspired as much by friendship between poets and artists as by shared aesthetic interests. In most cases, these collaborations resulted in the poet's work being illustrated by the painter (or vice versa), but in at least one case (Frank O'Hara's collaboration with Larry Rivers, *Stones* [1957–58]), poet and artist worked directly (and spontaneously) on the lithographic stone. The spirit of collaboration during this period challenged poets to relinquish some of their authorial control over the text and create a more communal or dialogical art.

In the 1950s emerged a more directly visual poetry that stressed the physical properties of letters and the technologies of printing. Concrete or Visual Poetry owes its aesthetic origins to modernist movements such as Constructivism and Futurism as well as to the long tradition of shaped verse. As Emmett Williams says, Concrete Poetry is an art "beyond paraphrase, a poetry that often asked to be completed or activated by the reader, a poetry of direct presentation—the word, not *words, words, words*" (vi). Concrete Poetry aspires more directly than any other literary genre to the condition of visual arts, although it would be wrong to assume that the linear possibilities of syntax or narrative are not highly active in the overall design. In the work of poets such as Ian Hamilton Finlay or Emmett Williams, the reader is placed in a relationship to language akin to the viewer of an acrobatic display (one of Finlay's best-known poems is called "Acrobat") in which one may see only flickering moments in an evolving activity.

Concrete Poetry explores not only the iconic and spatial features of letters but also their capacity for semantic indeterminacy. Bob Cobbing's work often deals with the visual and aural possibilities of shared elements. He deliberately blurs or smudges the typewritten page to call attention to the print medium and to confuse the boundaries between graphic sign and meaning. In "WOWROMWRORMM," a series of terms associated with physical decay ("corpse," "rust," "mouldering") descend down the page in wiggling tendrils, much like Apollinaire's raindrops in "Il Pleut" (Fig. 1). By overstriking his typewritten characters, Cobbing creates his own form of typographic decay. When combined with the thematics of death and dying (the downward progression of tendrils provides a nice visual pun on the worm's movement), the poem seems to illustrate its own demise. The final word—or word complex—"w ow r om wro rmm" represents the mortal end of letters removed from their semantic positions, but in its own multireferentiality (the complex includes the sounds of "womb" "room" and "worm") the poem adds a whimsical twist to the memento mori tradition.

The verbal or acoustic equivalent to Cobbing's work is sound or "sound-text" poetry in which the page serves as a score for verbal performance. Drawing on Futurist and Dadaist theater, Sound poetry stresses the acoustic properties of words, dismantling their phonemic properties until they exist as abstract sounds. Jackson MacLow's sound poetry is built upon the use of chance operations to determine the selection of materials that are then subjected to further improvisation in vocal performance. In MacLow's "Gathas," for example, Sanskrit words taken from mantras are selected by chance operations, placed in a grid, and then performed improvisationally by one or more persons. The grid in which the letters are encased isolates each sound as a phonic as well as visual element.

In the work of Steve McCaffery and other Canadian sound poets, the use of abstract sounds—grunts, whistles, groans, and breathing—combined with improvisation creates a poetry immediate to the body and expression. As McCaffery says, "sound poetry is *the* poetry of direct emotional confrontation: there is no pausing for intellectualization, there is no repeating of emotional content, each performance is unique & only the audience is repeatable" (Kostelanetz, *Text-Sound Texts*, 275). This definition could be seen as an extreme version of personalism in which the raw presentation of sound supplements the rhetorical displacement of the person through

Figure 1. Bob Cobbing, "Worm."

voice. In McCaffery's work, the page is less a score for the repetition of sounds than a grid for highly improvisatory performance. Anything can be a score—from a sketch to a wordlist to a page from the telephone directory—and in his collaborations with the Four Horsemen (bp Nichol, Rafael Barreto-Rivera, Paul Dutton, Steve McCaffery) the text is often a "sketch" for performance rather than a finished document.

Concrete and Sound poetries offer perhaps the most dramatic instance of a text in which the material properties of language become the subject of the poem. These movements are international in scope, English-speaking poets sharing the stage with Polish, French, German, Austrian, and Japanese writers. Similar aesthetic tendencies can be seen among American Language-writers for whom linguistic materialization is part of a general critique of expressive poetics. Among certain Language-writers, this critique is linked to a specifically political project. Whereas for modernists the defamiliarization of words implies a desire for a realm of pure literariness, for Language-writers defamiliarization involves the interrogation of discursive and ideological structures. The first stage in this critique involves dismantling syntactic and semantic contexts, isolating words or parts of words to resonate among themselves. The second stage—best seen in the work of Ron Silliman or Lyn Hejinian, for instance—involves recombination according to numerical or formulaic patterns such that narrative or chronological progress is thwarted and new kinds of connectives established.

It is a third stage of defamiliarization that engages our concerns with the visual page. Here, the conventional ratio between printed text and prior "word" is broken down and the physicality of writing materials becomes generative in composition. In the work of Johanna Drucker—herself a printer and scholar of the book—the conventions of printing and typography provide an occasion for an extended meditation on the materiality of her medium. In *Against Fiction*, for example, Drucker addresses the conventions of narrative form—its seriality, its dependence on character and action—by creating a text that thwarts forward movement and formal cohesion (Fig. 2). Extensive use of headlines, intertitles, illustrations, shifts of typeface, and eccentric spelling creates the feeling of a popular book or tabloid magazine while defying easy decoding. Its fragmentation and brokenness contrast with its familiar graphic display, creating an odd hybrid work that draws on tradition and innovation in equal parts.

## The Current Climate

**Controversial adviser alleges motivated takeover. Quitting his post** he attempted to put the best face on the situation. Today he rounded up forty-two hopefuls to compete. Dying for honour. Noone was particularly distinguished in the trial heat. These consisted of mopping the dry floor of the organization. There was passing traffic in the interludes meant for conversation. The condition of the people did not respond to the character of any of the candidates. Waiting to re-open the road. Trailblazing teams, all contenders for the top position, hesitated to discover the source of the emergency. None was forthcoming. The interviewees wanted to report to the president directly. The road was still closed. Resignation had forced slides and floods after the allegations. Search continues.

## PUBLIC: The Long Night of much Mist

**THE THICK HAZE MADE EVEN THE DENSE SHADOWS OF ThE DARK COMPLETELY INDISTINGUIShABLE**

It was so long since we had been out at night. I barely knew the neighborhood. When I went I was supposed to find, right at the end of the street, a place where I could buy a split of very eXpensive champagne. A gourmet niGht shop. Passed my coat throuGh the Glass to make chanGe. Almost no visibility near the Ground, owinG to the tule foG. But with lonG, dense vistas in the hiGh clouds. A foretold But unpreventaBle act of canniBalism. I participate, suBmit, review and am aBle to act only in the moment of presentation of what I knew would come to Be a fact. Jaws unaBle to preVent the choice of action, only workinG throuGh the enGaGement.

## Mystery Triangle :
### Where cars and trucks disappear.

People can claim anything. The very real melancholy of the soul diffuses itself into the air. The first real sighting an instance of creationism. Listed on the marquee of the matchbook in a digital display.

Could be programed from the driver's seat of a well stocked bank they called the lost institutional memory.

### Retrieved, the partial imitation of the tampered with and never violated original

Struggled through the retrials into a partial recovery. Conscientious collection, years' worth of junk, sorted by indelible profile. Whole piles of seemingly useless stuff, never put to obvious use, but chaneLLed toward an amusing, disTracTing aTTEmpT.

Transform the break in labor and materials into a marketable commodity. Not significant enough to advertise. Just waste, consumption, and now the stuff of the earth re-arranged into a rigid and unnecessary structure. Beyond cellular collapse. In the perfect moment, occasioned by a series of experiments. Minimum form. Suction cleaned.

## The OriGinal Scene
### METHOD: COMING into KNOWING

References become familiar. Petty thievery. Trace that theme. Once here. Snapshot. What's owed. My time. Sure thing. Give it a little edge. Manufacture complete parts. Replacement parts. Caught in the rug. Folds to the sheep. Operating term. Preliminaries. Environment.

### What is REAL TIME?

Figure 2. Johanna Drucker, from *Against Fiction*.

A similar defamiliarization of conventions occurs in Robert Grenier's graphic works in which the author's handwriting or "scrawl" becomes the final text (Fig. 3). What is interrogated in his work since the late 1980s is the rhetoric of "finality" itself insofar as it structures a notion of aesthetic perfection. Grenier's "scrawls" are photocopies of his holograph page, replete with emendations, crossings-out, and unreadable scribbles. Like the calligraphic work of Jackson Pollock

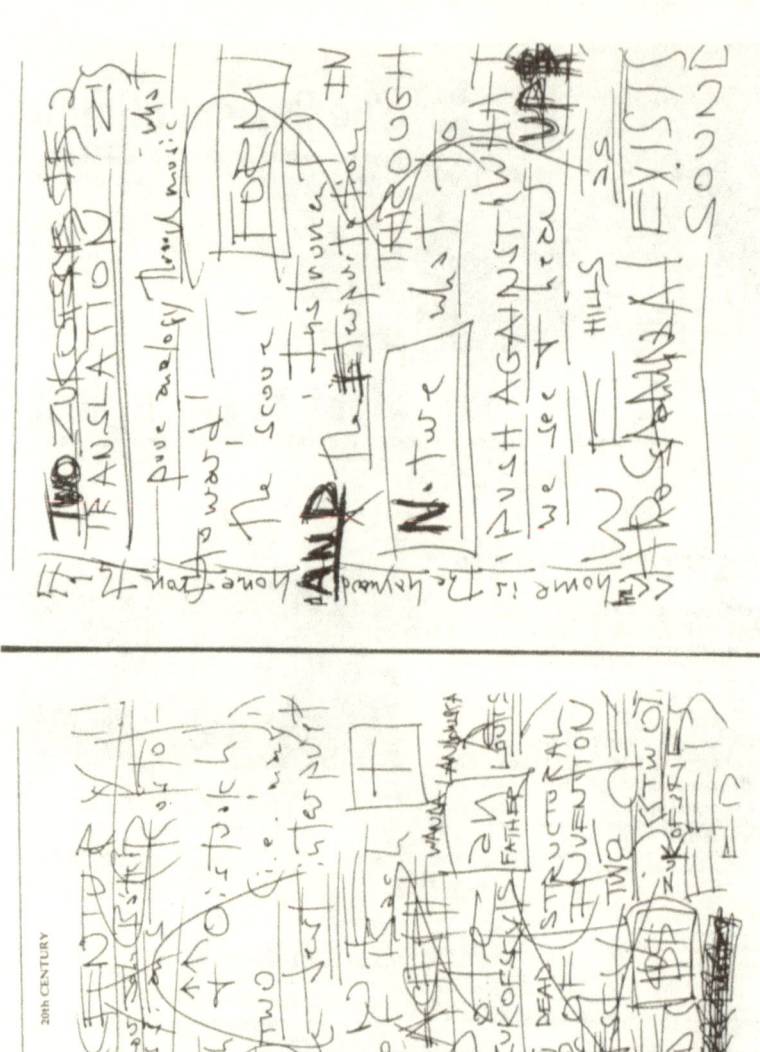

Figure 3. Robert Grenier, "Twentieth Century."

or Cy Twombly, Grenier's pages are gestural renderings designed less to communicate meaning than to register the immediacy and physical activity of writing. Yet since these pages depend on photocopying technology, their immediacy is quickly transformed into representation, gesture turned into copy. As Leslie Scalapino observes of these works, Grenier's work cannot be translated: "(it's opaque) because it's xerox; both individuated and continually different *and* mass produced" (40). The odd liminal space such texts occupy—their opacity to a psychologically "deep" origin—offers a critique of the speech-based poetics of an earlier generation. "I hate speech," Grenier writes, suggesting that the traditional equation of page to voice does not apply in his case.[13] His "scrawls" insist on writing as an act performed by the hand, at "this" moment on "this" piece of paper, available to multiple readings for a reader who, unable to decipher Grenier's script, must posit individual variants and thus generate a new text.

In such developments, the page becomes much more than a receptacle for preexisting aesthetic decisions; the page is, as I have emphasized, an element in composition itself, whether in supplying a white ground for shaped poems such as those of Dylan Thomas or John Hollander or in providing a "field" for action as in the work of Black Mountain poets. As I point out later in this chapter, experimentation in computer-generated writing and hypertext have altered the nature of textuality altogether, rendering the idea of the "visible page" a rather outmoded concept. But the typographic revolution in modernism made possible the conditions for the page's deconstruction as movable type gave way to photo-offset printing and now to pixel characters. In a modernist paradox to which we will often return in this book, the page must first be seen in order to be made invisible.

## THE OBJECTIVIST CONTINUUM

This short history of the visual text is written within a larger debate over the aesthetic meanings to be given to such graphic experimentalism. That debate has been staged largely through the ideology of modernism mentioned earlier, but it has been framed by more recent claims for an enduring (as opposed to historical) avant-garde.[14] Postmodernism, then, can be read positively as a continuation of these avant-garde tendencies or negatively as a series of self-reflexive, parodic gestures. In the process, an inevitable taxonomy of representative features installs itself as the task of canon formation. Borderline figures—Laura Riding, Bob Brown, or Mina Loy, for example—can be read out of modernism, and fringe movements such as Objectivism or Language-writing can be seen as symptoms of decline rather than inaugurating moments in themselves. Fredric Jameson's influential reading of postmodernism as a "cultural dominant," while a necessary reminder of art's mediated existence within late capitalism, nevertheless perpetuates this binarism by subordinating all artistic production to a single field, largely based on developments in architecture and the visual arts. Despite his reference to "residual" and "emergent" forms of production, Jameson reads the dominant culture as homogeneous and continuous and thus loses the opportunity to make discriminations among genres and individuals that might lead to a more nuanced historical assessment (6).

Rather than perpetuate this well-known argument over modernism and postmodernism, I would like to come at the issue of periodicity from a slightly different angle by looking at the element that often undergirds the terms of debate: the so-called object status of the artwork. At least since Harold Rosenberg's 1966 coinage "the anxious object," it is clear that the autonomy of the modernist artwork is in question, and various postmodern developments have contributed to its dematerialization.[15] But has that "object" ever *not* been anxious? Have artists ever *not* been conscious of the limits of their medium? Or, to ask the question another way, given the instability of material relations in modernity, can there be an object that is not part of a structure of exchange and consumption that does not, thereby, challenge its organic unity?

By asking the last question in this manner, I am suggesting that the anxiety over art's dematerialization cannot be restricted to aesthetic considerations alone. Furthermore, the significance accorded to anxiety in the 1950s is itself a historical product (as Rosenberg admits) that undergirds the existentialist, neo-Freudian reading of postwar art. Its validity as a descriptive term was generated most aggressively within the visual arts, where there were real, concrete anxieties about a work's marketability once the act of painting leaves the canvas and enters the performance space. In the world of poetry, however, the issue is moot since there are few material rewards for writing, few venues for which calling into question the nature of one's medium would make much difference in the larger economy. For the relatively small readership for poetry (small, that is, in relation to the number of people who enter a Philip Johnson building or patronize a Willem de Kooning exhibition), the issue of object status remains largely confined to little magazines and e-mail networks. Even the phenomena of poetry slams, jazz poetry, and other forms of poetic performance that dramatically dematerialize the page have little effect upon social materiality at large. Without denying the impact of individual poets on social history, it is important to focus on poetry's specific claims to objecthood, the forms of exchange and production particular to it.

To do this (and in making my selection of poets to discuss in this book) I have chosen to stress what might be called an Objectivist continuum running through modernism. The phrase refers both to a literary movement launched in the early 1930s and to a general tendency toward objectification in much modernist and postmodern poetry. In my usage, Objectivism does not imply the cult of impersonality as formulated by Eliot (which refers to the psychological state of the author) but, rather, the idea of the poem as an entity, produced within other forms of materiality and performative in its approach to language. In Louis Zukofsky's canonical terms, Objectivism stresses a process of "thinking with the things as they exist" and in this respect rephrases Pound's emphasis on the natural object as the "adequate symbol" (*Prepositions* 5). Objectivist poetics stresses exactitude and sincerity, visual immediacy over introspection and irony. The eye is the model for poetic mediation ("The lens bringing the rays from an object to a focus") just as court testimony, in the work of Charles Reznikoff, is the model for description (Dembo 194). As for language, poetry should achieve a ratio between speech and music, a formula that would accommodate both Williams's plain style and Zukofsky's or Bunting's elaborate metrical experiments and often baroque diction. Although Objectivism shares many features with other modernist movements (exactitude and sincerity are features valued by New Critics and Objectivists alike), the sense that language is fatally connected to (even constitutive of) social materiality sets it apart.

In its larger application, Objectivism represents an emphasis on the "detail, not mirage" of energies in the larger world. It accommodates gestures as distinct as Futurist nonrational (zaum) language,

German *neue Sachlichkeit*, Gertrude Stein's emphasis on "entity" over "identity," Pound's Imagism, Surrealist automism, and Williams's belief that poetry is a "machine made out of words." Objectivism is central to the development of "field" verse in the 1950s and continues to inform a range of experimental, linguistically inclined poets both here and in Europe.[16] Attempting to define this legacy, Charles Altieri distinguishes it from Symbolist-based theories of the creative imagination as embodied in certain aspects of romanticism. For him, Objectivism is "that body of work molded by freeing imagist techniques into methods of thought based on notions of field, measure, and 'open form.'" Altieri goes on to speak of Objectivism's emphasis on "direct acts of naming as signs of the poet's immediate engagement in the areas of experience made present by conceiving the act of writing as a mode of attention" ("Objectivist Tradition" 15).

Thus far, Altieri's diagnosis parallels comments made by Robert Creeley, Denise Levertov, and others on Objectivism, but by linking immediacy to nonreflective acts of attention he denies the poet any position on what immediacy might mean. Nor does his stress on technique extend to the political meanings of form. "Objectification is a property of writing committed to composition rather than to interpretation. Techniques for objectification . . . make structure the creative ground rather than the result of immediate poetic thinking" ("Objectivist Tradition" 15). By stressing technique and composition over interpretation and criticism, Altieri reinforces the ideology of modernism, first by continuing a Kantian division of aesthetics into subjectivist (symbolist) and objectivist (immanent) poles and then by identifying the latter with a kind of poetic empiricism.[17]

If technique is the Objectivists' central legacy to later writers, Altieri is unwilling to grant it much of the political efficacy its practitioners often invoke. Unlike Olson, who turned from New Deal politics to poetry and thereby developed strategies that could handle public issues, the Objectivists could not "reconcile [political commitments] with their forms of literary attention" during the 1930s ("Objectivist Tradition" 16). Clearly, in Altieri's view, Olson made the right choice, but this still leaves unaddressed what forms of reconciliation the Objectivists *did* make with political pressures and, more important, how their formalism provided a means by which those pressures could be measured. What seems most significant about the Objectivists from our post–Cold War and post–New Critical position is not the ways they relinquished their critical skills to immediacy and process but the ways they retained critical positions *by means of* formal strategies, both free verse and metrical.[18]

One particular advantage of focusing on Objectivism as a historical movement is that it played a pivotal role in translating 1920s radical formalism into new versions of formal radicalism, made necessary by 1930s political crisis. The social conditions of the Depression, the rise of fascism in Europe, conflicting debates over political commitment, as well as the Objectivists' common ethnic heritage as second-generation Jewish immigrants placed new demands on high modernist values of artisanal control and ironic distancing.[19] Their shared Marxist sympathies contrasted markedly with the conservative politics of their predecessors and mentors, linking them at times with Popular Front writers and fellow travelers in the pages of *The Masses* and *Anvil*. At the same time, they remained loyal to Imagist aesthetic principles of clarity and precision, even when those values were being applied by Pound to the celebration of fascism.

Such contradictions between social and literary materiality led the Objectivists to confront what I call in chapter 4 "ideologies of form," the social and culturally coded meanings attached to formal features.[20] As Anthony Easthorpe points out, poetry "is subject both to the laws of its own material nature *and* is a term in social relations. In other words, what makes poetry poetry is what makes poetry ideological" (22). Applied to the Objectivists, this implies that poetry is tied to "historic and contemporary particulars" not only because those particulars speak of unemployment or hunger marches but because the language by which those events are rendered is subject to the same reifying tendencies as confront individuals in their social relations. For writers of the 1930s, the question of "whose side are you on?" produced an important body of partisan verse that is only now beginning to be studied as a dimension of modernism.[21] For the Objectivists, however, that call could not be answered so easily. It led George Oppen to give up writing for twenty-five years. As he said, "If you decide to do something politically, you do something that has political efficacy. And if you decide to write poetry, then you write poetry, not something that you hope, or deceive yourself into believing can save people who are suffering. That was the dilemma of the thirties" (Dembo 174). This dilemma was solved in different ways by each of the Objectivists, but it would be wrong to assume that Oppen's twenty-five year silence was any less a formal response to political pressures than Zukofsky's attempt to write *"A"* as an epic of class struggle. The two gestures—refusal and revision—are linked in a common recognition that form is ideological if you continue to write and that erasure is oppositional if you do not. For his part, Zukofsky utilized elaborate numerical structures in his writing, culminating in his double canzone of "*A*"-9 in which he matches syllable for syllable, rhyme for rhyme, the structure of Cavalcanti's "Donna mi priegha," all the while translating Marx's labor theory of value. Such formalism is less virtuosic display than an attempt to study relationships between two kinds of value, emotive and economic. And because Pound had advocated technical mastery as part of a literary apprenticeship, Zukofsky's Marxist-inflected use of the same forms suggests a subtle inversion of the older poet's cultural elitism. Likewise, Charles Reznikoff's creation of *Testimony* almost verbatim from legal briefs calls into question the discreteness of poetic language and foregrounds its social uses. While creating damaging testimony against industrial exploitation of workers, Reznikoff utilizes the institutional apparatus of jurisprudence—its impersonal rhetoric and evidentiary structure of proof—in service to a critical end. Finally, George Oppen's minimalist verse in *Discrete Series*, with its extensive use of enjambment, truncated sentences, and ellipses, presents lyricism divested of its usual ontological props. The social world of the Depression is stripped of any ameliorating rhetoric and presented in its barrenness:

> Bad times:
> The cars pass
> By the elevated posts
> And the moving sign.
> A man sells post-cards.
>     (*Collected Poems* 13)

What Oppen said of his era could speak for the Objectivists in general: "I am a man of the thirties // No other taste shall change this" (quoted in DuPlessis 35). Modernist literary history, as Malcolm Cowley observed, would be constructed around "the brilliant Twenties," but "the militant Thirties" would never achieve the same glamor.[22] The Objectivists were quite literally a "lost generation," remaining in relative obscurity until the 1960s. When they were rediscovered by poets associated with the New American Poetry, they were valued less for their social commitment than for their continuation of the Pound/Williams line. Ron Silliman calls this later period "third-phase objectivism," characterized by a diffusion of the more radical literary (and perhaps political) qualities of the first phase as represented in the pages of *Poetry* (1931) and *The Objectivist Anthology*. This diffusion is most dramatically evident, Silliman feels, in Oppen's work from *The Materials* (1957) on, a poetry that utilizes a more rhetorical tone and humanist (i.e., nonideological) social stance.[23]

However one feels about this characterization of later Objectivism, the revival of the Objectivists, both for Olson's and for Silliman's generations, represents a significant contrast to the more recognizable Cold War narrative wherein old leftists are recuperated as neoconservatives and establishment boosters. It is especially due to Language-writing and its formation within the New Left that this counterdiscourse to modernist literary history becomes visible. But it is no less due to writers such as Theresa Hak Kyung Cha, M. Norbese Phillips, Gloria Anzaldúa, Jessica Hagedorn, Walter Lew, Jayne Cortez, Judy Grahn, and others who emerge within the context of new social movements of the 1970s and 1980s and whose literary genealogies are not circumscribed by Objectivism or Language-writing. Such writers have no less of an investment in the materiality of their medium to achieve social ends than these movements and must, in the larger literary history, be included within an objectivist continuum.

As Cary Nelson observes, modernism is pervaded by a process of forgetting and repression, nowhere more evident than in respect to the 1930s. The attempt by Cold War intellectuals to forget their own political pasts, to get "beyond ideology," left a rather arid field out of which to compose the political in literature. The Objectivists had negotiated that field, not by conducting debates in verse with Stanley Burnshaw, as Stevens had, nor by writing workers' songs. They saw their objectivism as a dimension of social materiality at large, in which the poem was both a thing resistant to reification and a process of thinking resistant to "predatory intent."

PHANTASMAGORIAS OF THE LIBRARY

> Define ghosts as an India-rubber eraser created to erase their own past.
>
> (Jack Spicer)

A *New Yorker* cartoon depicts a long-haired, bearded prophet carrying a power source in one hand connected to a video monitor on his shoulder that reads "The End of Printed Matter Is Near!" As we approach the millenium, such prophecies are becoming the stuff of media punditry as the wonders of the information highway replace what now seems like the rural road of print culture. With the advent of desktop publishing, hypertext, virtual reality, interactive learning, multimedia infomatics, e-mail, and digitized imaging, the modernist typographic revolution seems a rather quaint remnant. As Richard Lanham points out, the most radical forms of avant-garde design and collaborative composition are now, quite literally, child's play (1–28). Media experts earnestly assure us that such developments will only enhance literacy since all information may be accessed, all libraries opened to the masses—an electronic version of Borges's Library of Babel. And just as anyone with a personal computer can receive all information, so anyone with a decent printer can generate camera-ready copy for a desktop magazine or chapbook. The only dissonance in an otherwise unanimous chorus of assent concerns questions of intellectual property and access fees.

Although in this book I deal with technology in various forms, I stop at the frontiers of the digitized word. In comparison to the infinite vistas of *hyper*text, the *palim*text seems decidedly low tech—as dated as the long-playing record, rotary dialing, and Dynaflow. But this is its attraction. The palimtext emerges in a culture based on pencils, pens, paper, typewriters, ditto machines, and tape recorders—technologies that, to adapt Frank O'Hara, put the poem "squarely between the poet and the person, Lucky Pierre style" (499). The personist character of these technologies is dependent on their ephemerality, their fatal investment in time. Poetry produced on ditto or mimeo machines is not made to last but to circulate quickly, the fragility of its paper and the unevenness of its inking limiting both shelflife and aesthetic appeal. Staples rust, card stock fades, paper yellows and begins to flake. The materiality of ephemerality is a study in ghosts.

The modernist typographic renaissance began as an attempt to stave off such ephemerality as it was manifest in commercial publishing and advertising. Early modernist presses such as Kelmscott or Cuala produced books that were made to endure or at least signal lastingness. Jerome McGann notes the paradox of such vanguard poets as Yeats, Pound, Williams, and Stein publishing within a design milieu that looked backward to the medievalism of the Pre-

Raphaelites (*Black Riders* 7). At the same time, development of high-speed letterpress technology was dramatically changing the look of and access to the printed page. Johanna Drucker notes that printing had undergone little change since the time of Gutenberg, but with the use of printing in advertising, and with "graphics as an interface between producer and consumer," the look of the page began to change (94). As I have already remarked, poets seized upon the possibilities of display type and the use of different fonts and spacing to enhance the physical appearance of the poem. In more than one case (Williams's "The Attic Which Is Desire," Hart Crane's "The River," Langston Hughes's *Montage of a Dream Deferred*), this typography served to imitate an actual advertisement.

The same interface between producer and consumer that marks the commercial use of printing also informs the production and distribution of literature. From Walt Whitman's publication of *Leaves of Grass* (including his self-authored reviews) and Emily Dickinson's hand-sewn fascicles to the mimeograph revolution of the 1960s, poets have utilized the more flexible features of modern letterpress and offset printing to intervene in the publishing process. In 1931 Gertrude Stein, frustrated at years of neglect by major printers, decided to publish her own work (with Alice B. Toklas's help) under the Plain Editions imprint. As the name implies, Stein wanted her work to appear in an accessible, unadorned format that would call attention to itself as writing, not as books. Appropriately enough, the first edition in the series, *Lucy Church Amiably*, was designed, according to Stein's specifications, to look like a child's notebook. Other important presses of the period—Robert McAlmon's Contact Editions or George Oppen's TO Press and its successor, Carl Rakosi's Objectivist Press—published straightforward, inexpensive books. Charles Reznikoff published many of his books on his own press located in his apartment, and Robert Carleton Brown's graphic experiments, as Jerome McGann points out, were "printed by machine on cheap chemical paper" (*Black Riders* 85). Djuna Barnes brought her early journalistic experience to bear on the physical layout of *Book of Repulsive Women* (1915) and *Ladies Almanack* (1928), utilizing the columnar format of the newspaper as well as her own line drawings. These personal interventions into publishing were influenced by the economics of the times, to be sure, but they also signaled the poet's ability to gain greater access to the publishing process.

The small-press revolution of the 1950s and 1960s brought these tendencies into an entirely new realm, thanks to the development of cheap, offset printing technology. The period saw a surge in the growth of small, independent publishers, often run by the poets themselves, who issued chapbooks, magazines, and broadsides in runs of five hundred to one thousand copies. With the assistance of NEA grants and various private subsidies during the 1960s and 1970s, small presses and magazines grew and multiplied. Independent book-distribution services emerged to deal with the increasing number of presses, and literary centers such as the St. Marks Poetry Project in New York, Beyond Baroque in Los Angeles, and the Intersection in San Francisco served as clearinghouses for readings, book distribution, and information. The alternative bookstore, an outgrowth of Vietnam-era youth culture and oppositional politics, was often a central venue for the sales of small-press pamphlets and poetry—not to mention poetry readings, political rallies, and educational forums. Although letterpress publishers such as Walter Hamaday, Claire Van Vliet, or Andrew Hoyem continued to print fine press, limited editions, the bulk of poetry published between 1956 and 1985 was produced on duplicators developed by A. B. Dick and Multilith that allowed for greater flexibility in layout and greater speed in publication. Small, desktop mimeo machines—a staple of every office and commercial space—could be commandeered after hours for a little magazine or broadside. In short, poetry began to circulate in channels completely outside the major wholesale publishers, jobbers, and chain bookstores.[24]

Walter Benjamin, writing during an earlier stage of these developments, anticipated something of this revolutionary fervor, noting that with the introduction of lithography in the nineteenth century, the possibility of multiple reproductions fundamentally altered the nature of artistic production. Against the "auratic," unique object could be placed the reproducible photograph, film, newspaper, and magazine; against the author as solitary genius could be imagined new forms of collaborative composition and process production. Benjamin's significant claim that new means of reproduction could lead to a politicization of aesthetics was realized, to some degree, in alliances formed during the Vietnam era between small-press publishers and political activists. Presses such as Broadside, Cranium, and City Lights regularly published antiracist, antiwar documents alongside their poetry publications. Small magazines of the period often featured political commentary, reviews, and photography, and poetry readings became a major forum for political protest. Diane DiPrima summarizes this synthesis of politics, poetry, and publishing in her colophon page to *Revolutionary Letters*: "This is a free book. These are free poems and may be reprinted anywhere by anyone. . . . Power to the people's mimeo machines."

The irony of Benjamin's utopian analysis is that the same productive apparatus that contributed to the decline of aura made possible its revival as poets utilized cheap, portable print technologies to render "authentic" gestures and unique vocal inflections. The power of the people's mimeo machine was more than a means of reproduction in service to speed and efficiency; it was part of an expressive poetics that validated personal gestures of discovery and speculation over artisanal values of order and control. Ditto and mimeograph machines made such immediacy possible by permitting the poet to see work published within hours of its composition. DiPrima notes the impact of her own mimeo magazine, *The Floating Bear*, on Olson's poetics: "I remember that the last time I saw Charles Olson in Gloucester, one of the things he talked about was how valuable the Bear had been to him in its early years because of the fact that he could get new work out that fast. He was very involved in speed, in communication" (DiPrima and Jones x).

Beyond the fact of immediacy, exact intentions as to spacing and lineation could be precisely rendered since, in many cases, the poet actually typed the master copy for the magazine. Drawings, doodles, and holographic print gave vivid testimony to the author's role in page design. And in general little magazines reflected the personalities of their editors. Ed Sanders's irreverent *Fuck You: A Magazine of the Arts* embodied the confrontational character of the times by extensive use of erotic designs and handwritten polemic. Stan Persky's *Open Space* provided unedited publishing access by a select group of poets who gathered around Jack Spicer at local bars in North Beach. Pages were printed directly from each contributor's master copy, and distribution was ruthlessly limited to the geographical San Francisco Bay Area. Diane DiPrima and LeRoi Jones's *Floating Bear* was mimeographed for free distribution and was collated and addressed by anyone who happened to drop by their apartment. Anne Waldman's *The World* was dittoed and saddle stitched, a format appropriate to the personist character of its New York School contributors. In all these magazines, the material form of the paper, binding, and design were more than printing conventions; they were extensions of the poems they contained.

A poetics of presence, as D. H. Lawrence noted of Whitman, threatens to become like the body that is its ideal. To be one with the cosmos means that you suffer the mortal limits of all natural forms. The extreme version of this ethos is vividly rendered in Richard Brautigan's *Please Plant This Book*, which included a packet of seeds. The ephemerality of small-press publications, their tendency to decay and fall apart, returns *The World* to the world. In chapter 2, I speculate on the meaning of such ephemerality for the literary archive and by implication for the literary scholar in an age of mechanical reproduction. George Oppen's daybooks, preserved in acid-free boxes and stored in temperature-controlled rooms in the Archive for New Poetry at the University of California, San Diego, provide me with a point of departure. They are scribbled or typed on cheap paper and then crudely joined by pins and staples, their surfaces covered with queries, notes, quotations, and fragments of poems. They are the model for the palimtext as textual midden through which a daily life in print can be seen. But their fragility as objects raises questions for the conservator and manuscript librarian as well as for the literary critic.

In approaching the materiality of Oppen's writing (or that of any modern poet), one is faced with a paradoxical fact of textual scholarship—that in opening the archive one destroys the paper on which it is written. This is both a literal and a figural fact: literal in the sense that by handling cheap foolscap paper one begins a process of physical deterioration that ultimately destroys the paper, figurative in that by removing the poem from its context among other papers and documents one destroys its historical evolution as a document. Oppen's archive—and by extension the material text of others discussed in this book—marks the end of a scholarly era in which authors' papers—*qua* paper—can be collected and preserved. What, one wonders, will be the equivalent research base for an author whose archive consists of a neat stack of floppy disks? Where is the material text when its palimtextual layers have only been seen in pixeled form on a computer screen? What will be the postmillenial role of libraries, universities, and museums in storing and preserving the ephemeral?

The materiality of the text exists in relationship to institutions for which materiality is important, for which objects remain discrete markers of cultural development and progress. The modernist era is a museal one for which the formation and legitimation of certain class interests coincides with the storage, display, and conservation of artifacts. As I pointed out at the beginning of this introduction, the appearance of international exhibitions in the nineteenth century placed material culture on display for reasons of imperial power and national (not to mention racial) pride. Within this display emerges the phantasmagoria with which I began, the "unreal" commodity-as-fetish. Archives, museums, and libraries are places where, like the phantasmagoria, ghosts are materialized as masks and totems, and it is not surprising to find such ethnological data undergirding so many modernist literary works. Michel Foucault notes that the modern age's obsession with collecting is emblematized in Flaubert's *Temptation of St. Anthony*, whose Boschian display of grotesques, chimeras, and nightmares is a monument to "meticulous erudition" as represented by the modern library: "In *The Temptation* Flaubert produced the first literary work whose exclusive domain is that of books: following Flaubert, Mallarmé is able to write *Le Livre* and modern literature is activated—Joyce, Roussel, Kafka, Pound, Borges. The library is on fire" (*Language, Counter-Memory, Practice* 92).

The age of the archive is closing; the fire is going out. The phantasmagoric display can now be accessed on CD-ROM, music complements of Berlioz or Gounod.[25] If the palimtext is a description of the modern era, it is also a memorial to its passing, a page and an archive. Perhaps the cultural significance of modern poetry lies not so much in its ability to contain the library as a substitute for the British Museum, as Pound said, but to represent its own tenuous hold on a history that seems to be dissolving. In a poem, this dissolution may be resolved by aesthetic fiat, the miraculist fusion of eternal Troy with quotidian Hampstead. But as palimtext the poem is always unraveling its sources, commenting upon its meanders among other texts, blurring word choice by pencil emendation. If Flaubert's *Madame Bovary* inaugurates the reality effect of early modernism by its exact rendering of bourgeois life, *The Temptation of St. Anthony* represents its political unconscious, a diorama of fantasies of dissolution and abjection that cannot be contained in a photograph. "The imaginary is not formed in opposition to reality," Foucault continues; "it grows among signs, from book to book, in the interstice of repetitions and commentaries; it is born and takes shape in the interval between books" (*Language, Counter-Memory, Practice* 91). This book, in its interest in the material word, attempts to describe that interval.

# 1

# The Romance of Materiality
## Gertrude Stein and the Aesthetic

> The argument that art works are independent of the artist sounds like a delusional version of *l'art pour l'art*. It is not. It is a simple expression of the more complex idea that art is defined by its relation to a society governed by the law of objectification: it is only *qua* things that art works become the antithesis of the reified social order.
>
> Theodor Adorno, *Aesthetic Theory*

### CULTURAL OBJECTS

First object: on the desk, bearing assorted pens and pencils, sits a white porcelain beer mug in the shape of Gertrude Stein's face. On the handle, for a thumb guard, is a tiny replica of Alice Toklas. At its base is the word "Gertrude." Hence, a "Gertrude" stein.

Second object: the *Oakland Tribune* of 24 January 1986 carries a story detailing the results of a mock tribunal held by the San Francisco Court of Historical Review and Appeals over the meaning of Gertrude Stein's famous remark about Oakland, "there is no there there." Academics and journalists from both sides of the bay are summoned to give expert testimony about Stein's meaning. Those from San Francisco claim that Stein intended a derogatory slur on the city in which she spent her youth. Those representing Oakland testify that the remark has been taken out of context—that it really refers to the sadness Stein felt in revisiting Oakland in 1934 during her American tour. According to Professor Stephen Dobbs, the phrase represents "a poetic sense of her return, not despair but a sense of wistfulness in seeing that her Oakland home had changed" (Alcott A-2).[1] But as the *Tribune* reporter concludes, the battle over her remark derives from the "natural rivalry between San Francisco and Oakland" and not from anything inherently confusing in Stein's words.

Third object: in *The Man on the Flying Trapeze* (1935), W. C. Fields sits down to breakfast with his wife and mother-in-law. The former opens the paper and exclaims, "here's a poem by that lovely Gertrude Smarden," and goes on to read a thinly veiled parody of Stein:

> We have what we have not
> what we have not we have
> up is down down is out
> everyone knew me and I was happy
> and we were all happy
>
> is everybody happy
> and I bought a big red apple
> yes unhappiness is joy

"Isn't that beautiful?" the wife asks. "Yes dear," Fields responds distractedly while trying to eat his toast. "Then what's it about?" she snaps back. "Apples?" Fields speculates. The wife goes on. "And the wonderful part of it is that there is no punctuation. And to think that underneath that beautiful blank verse they print portraits of those horrible wrestlers!" Fields winces, remembering that he has purchased a ticket to that afternoon's match.[2]

This trio of Steinian artifacts could be extended indefinitely by reference to other such items in which Stein's work is parodied, mimicked, or otherwise appropriated: comic books, T-shirts, stationery, ashtrays, literary parodies, theatrical performances, and endless variations on "a rose is a rose is a rose." Stein has been the "object" of such (negative and positive) interest more than most writers of her generation. Beginning with her first appearance in *Camera Work* in 1912, journalists have seized upon Stein's biography to the exclusion of her writing. Various attempts have been made to explain this fascination, locating it in Stein's own self-fabrication in *The Autobiography of Alice B. Toklas* or in the fame of her Rue de fleurus salon. Certainly, Stein's life makes good copy, and her remarks are wonderfully quotable, but there are other issues at stake in the objectification of Gertrude Stein having to do with modernism itself and its problematic relationship to its own romantic origins.

At one level, the emphasis on Stein's life represents a response to the difficulty of her writing. Works such as *Tender Buttons*, the portraits, *How To Write*, and *Lucy Church Amiably* resist reading in ways that other works of the same period (*The Waste Land*, say, or *Ulysses*) do not. Marjorie Perloff points out that, compared to Stein's portrait "Susie Asado," Eliot's "The Love Song of J. Alfred Prufrock" is relatively straightforward in its portrayal of the age's "spiritual anemia and emotional paralysis" (*Poetics of Indeterminacy* 73). "Susie Asado" cannot be decoded either by reference to Stein's psychological state or to the Spanish dancer that provided her original inspiration. One could say that readers, lacking any way into such writing, have been thrown back upon the author's biography as the only possible source. By turning the author into an icon, one may domesticate her obscurity and render its critical potential less threatening.

Much feminist criticism has recognized that the tendency to objectify Stein *does* have implications for her difficulty and that the relationship between the two realms—between biographical and textual bodies—must be addressed in terms of gender. For Catherine Stimpson, Stein's own physical body, whether represented by herself via Picasso's portrait or in journalistic dismissals, becomes a site of complex attitudes toward her sexuality, ethnicity, and gender ("Somagrams of Gertrude Stein"). For Marianne DeKoven, Stein's "different language" is really *about* difference, an attack on conventional forms of signification. In these readings, textuality and sexuality are joined in a poetics of play and revelation in which alternative gender narratives are evoked (*Different Language*). Stein's poetry is unspeakable, and, paradoxically enough, this unspeakability has a referent.

While these theories have done a great deal to situate Stein's experimentalism in a feminist context, they treat Stein's obscurity as a compensation for something else. It is as though the only thing Stein's difficult writing can say is *jouissance* over and over again, thus neutralizing its critical ability to say any one thing. I see Stein's obscurity in less compensatory terms and more as a problematic located in the textual object itself and its claim to be an artifact of a fundamentally distinct sort. This claim, which we identify with aestheticism, has implications not only for the work of art but for its producer as well, a fact about which Stein was acutely conscious. Stein's transformation into a mass-culture object, far from representing a vulgarization of her more "serious," artistic side, is a logical component of it, an inevitable result of developing an aesthetics that rejects the world by creating another to replace it. It is this claim to autonomy and Stein's dialectical manipulation of it that will occupy my attention in this chapter.

Whereas modernists such as Pound, Joyce, and Eliot could develop a theory of creative genius and autonomy from a gender position that ensured they would never become confused with the objects they created, the woman modernist had no such assurance. She was, as Andreas Huyssen notes, already identified with material culture—a material girl in every sense of the word—and could only be "modernism's other" (44–62). Stein was not content, as were some of her female compatriots such as H.D., to reconfigure male stereotypes of gender by rewriting classical myth according to gynocentric versions. Rather than distance herself from commodity culture, she parodied many of its features—its patriarchal, heterosexual family, its consumerist mentality, its veneration of genius and rationality, even its Fordist modes of production—and suffered some of its effects. In aping the rhetoric of genius and power, Stein was often confused with what she appropriated. And because her work, unlike that of Pound or Eliot, did not utilize dramatic monologue or personae, its parodic elements were harder to locate. Stein's text was—and remains—threatening not because it attempted to purify the words of the tribe or diagnose the social malaise of the era but because it refused to become an object. In an era of increasing commodification this may have been the greatest threat of all.

Stein found the terms for her refusal of commodification within German idealism, although in a considerably modified form.[3] She inherited a poetics that posits a special epistemological status for aesthetic judgments. In Kant's terms, the aesthetic realm provides an alternative to interested judgments, creating through an act of detached contemplation a form of desire in the beholder that cannot be satisfied by possession of the beautiful object itself. Translated into a theory of creative genius such as Stein's, disinterestedness would be the ideal condition for the production of art since the resulting object would be valued not for its dependence upon a prior referent but for its formal perfection. The autonomous work of art, if it could exist, would be that area of material culture whose purposiveness is not tied to exchange and commerce, whose very difference from social discourse permits a unique perspective on it. By foregrounding the material qualities of language, the artist removes words from their conventional syntactic and semantic positions, making strange that which ordinary communication makes instrumental. The autonomous work of art, the "masterpiece," in Stein's terms, "has essentially not to be necessary" because once it is necessary "it has in it no possibility of going on" ("What Are Masterpieces" 150).

Stein developed her autonomy theory in works such as "What Are Masterpieces" and *The Geographical History of America*, both written during the mid-1930s, when her public fame was at its height and when the need to make distinctions between her personality and her art was most pressing. The central argument of both works just named concerns the distinction between identity or personality and "entity," that unattainable quality of objects that Kant circumscribed under the *Ding an sich*. Works of genius (which presumably include the works of Gertrude Stein) are written in the condition of "human mind," a state of heightened attention, unmotivated by either memory or desire. "The human mind is," whereas human nature "is what any human being will do" (*Geographical History* 68, 76). Human nature is the realm of purposive reason that asks what things are *for* based on what things *have been*. For Stein, identity is not a matter of purposes so much as responses, an ability to exist in the present and attend to sensations as they are experienced moment by moment. The artist capable of such negative capability may create "something that is an end in itself and in that respect . . . is opposed to the business of living which is relation and necessity" ("What Are Masterpieces" 152).

This unabashed reprise of Kantian autonomy theory may worry readers anxious to save Stein from her own idealism. How could the author of "Lifting Belly" or "Pink Melon Joy," those hymns to lesbian sexuality, be the same as the one who believes in art "as an end in itself?" Such a complaint belies a desire to keep theory and practice separate and treats late explanatory works such as *Lectures in America* as aberrations in an otherwise continuous abstractionist enterprise. This complaint also ignores the performative nature of Stein's essays, which, as Alan Knight observes, are full of vatic pronouncements and unsupported declarations that cannot be proved (150–67). Like many of her "creative texts," her essays and lectures undermine their own claims to a systematic analysis: "There is a great deal of nonsense talked about the subject of anything" ("What Are Masterpieces" 149); "Everything has a lot to do with poetry everything has a lot to do with prose" (*Lectures in America* 227). "Therefore a master-piece has essentially not to be necessary" ("What Are Masterpieces" 150). As justifications for an autotelic art, such remarks are woefully inadequate, pointing up the absurdity of expecting proof where the noncontingent is concerned. Similarly, Stein's abstract binaries such as "identity" and "entity," "human mind" and "human nature" tend to fall apart as aesthetic categories and point instead at the instability of dualistic thinking.

As I hope to prove, Stein diagnoses a flaw in the aesthetic insofar as that category is thought to exist beyond the social. As Terry Eagleton points out, the aesthetic is a "double edged sword," a product of bourgeois ideology as well as an attempt to escape ideology altogether. The aesthetic is at once

> the very secret prototype of human subjectivity in early capitalist society, and a vision of human energies as radical ends in themselves which is the implacable enemy of all dominative or instrumentalist thought. It signifies a creative turn to the sensuous body, as well as an inscribing of that body with a subtly oppressive law; it represents on the one hand a liberatory concern with concrete particularity, and on the other hand a specious form of universalism. (9)

The duplicity that Eagleton sees in the aesthetic helps explain the objectification of Stein that I mentioned earlier. She could be assimilated by and into mass culture because she presented no obstacle to it. She was as interested in Hollywood films, department stores, electricity, and Ford cars as she was in the purity of the medium. Unlike the writings of Eliot, Valéry, Rilke, H.D., or Pound, Stein's serve no culturally ennobling purposes or historical programs. There are no grail legends or fertility myths behind her repetitions. One does not need French or Latin to understand her work. It is as immediate as childhood rhymes or shopping lists (and therefore just as easy to dismiss). However thoroughly Stein may have explored human psychology in her early writings, her practice offers no program for dealing with the ravages of consciousness. The aesthetic for Stein is not a means of escaping personality but a matrix within which to create it. Since she treats her life as a series of signs—a story to be told by Alice Toklas, for example—it is only logical that this story can be extended and refashioned by others.

In other words, Stein was both autonomous artwork—a self-created artifact—and an enthusiast for mass culture at the same time. If this seems like a paradox it is not because her life-style contradicted her work but because she recognized, more than any other modernist, the close relationship between the artwork as commodity (she was a proud "collector" of paintings, after all) and as aesthetic object (she was a proud "creator" of portraits). She signaled her recognition of this paradox through the extremity of her experimentalism. Rather than subject her "difficult" writing to instrumental ends (fragmentation as a symptom of cultural decay), she made difficulty the occasion or site in which to interrogate the limits of commodification. By reveling in her own commodity status, she could occupy a privileged relation to both poles of the aesthetic/mass culture debate, as subject and object of materializing processes that threatened to reify all productive processes into static categories. It may be, then, that Stein offers the clearest statement of that paradox noticed by Adorno in this chapter's epigraph: that the presumed independence of the artwork from the artist expresses art's dependency on a world of things. Only within a world where things define the social order could an art be formed to escape it.

## PRACTICING THE SIGN

The obvious place to begin talking about Stein's relationship to objects is with her early portraits of people and things. As we know, she was enabled by Cubism to create a kind of verbal portraiture, equivalent to the landscapes, still lifes, and collages of Picasso, Matisse, Cézanne, and Gris that hung on her walls. She herself was often the subject of these portraits, a condition that enabled her to speak of painting, as it were, from both sides of the canvas. The verbal portrait becomes the analog (but not the mimesis) of unnameable subjective states. Whether writing the portrait of a person or an object, Stein "had to find out inside every one what was in them that was intrinsically exciting," not by what they said or did but by the "intensity of movement" inside of them (*Lectures in America* 183). If subjective feeling is unknowable in itself (as Kant declares it is), the aesthetic object or verbal portrait provides what Eagleton calls a kind of "pseudo knowledge" by which a thing or person may be experienced as unique and autonomous (75). By creating portraits out of partial associations and metonymies, Stein may experience the thing in its freshness and novelty and may possess it as "hers."

The objects in Stein's portraits are pedestrian and unremarkable, no more important in themselves than Daniel Kahnweiler's actual face is to Picasso's portrait. This is not to say that Stein has no feelings about the carafes, hats, umbrellas, and food that populate *Tender Buttons;* it is that those feelings are not an issue in their composition. A petticoat or an orange are elements within a domestic landscape as immediate to her sensation as the simple words she uses to evoke them. The value of objects is in their use for the one who wears, eats, or represents them. Stein says as much in "Apple" when, after cataloging a series of associations with the fruit ("Apple plum, carpet steak, seed clam, colored wine . . ."), she concludes: "This is use" (*Selected Writings* 488). The deictic ambiguity of the demonstrative pronoun implies not only that *this* apple is as it is used but that *this* text we are reading is one of those uses. Objects in Stein's portraiture refuse to stay within their frames but point outwards at the referential systems in which they appear.

"A Box," for example, is both a container and a commentary on containment:

> Out of kindness comes redness and out of rudeness comes rapid same question, out of an eye comes research, out of selection comes painful cattle. So then the order is that a white way of being round is something suggesting a pin and is it disappointing, it is not, it is so rudimentary to be analysed and see a fine substance strangely, it is so earnest to have a green point not to red but to point again. (463)

To adapt a phrase from another section of *Tender Buttons,* this piece of prose is "an arrangement in a system to pointing" (461). A box is less an object than a system, a site for meditation on the way that words beget other words. "Out of kindness comes redness," a blush perhaps; and out of "rudeness," the opposite of kindness, comes an impatience manifested by a repetition of the "same question." Research is an extension of the eye just as cattle, as a generic grouping, represents a selection. Once this semiotic trajectory is established (assisted by the alliteration of Rs), Stein may indulge in one of her characteristic false predicates: "So then. . . ." At this point, she implies she will give some order to this highly arbitrary trail of derivations, but her example is hardly conclusive: "the order is that a white way of being round is something suggesting a pin." Whether referring to a compass and the white circle it inscribes (in an earlier piece she speaks of a "circle of fine card board and a chance to see a tassel" [462]) or simply the act of pointing itself, Stein is anxious to have words point to the system of differences that binds binary oppositions (green:red, line:circle, kind:rude) together. Hence, the point is "to have a green point not to red but to point again."

Like all attempts to read Stein's more abstract work, my version is necessarily partial and reductive. I do not, however, think that it does any good to dismiss such readings, as some critics do, since this denies the reader any role in the text beyond being a passive recipient of some kind of exemplary practice.[4] The partiality of my reading is very much a product of the semiosis generated by Stein—her ability to establish terms for closure and openness, boxes and circles, isolation and groupings. In this sense, Stein's verbal portrait gestures out from a "rudimentary" position of discrete objects (buttons, boxes, carafes) to the multiple frames of their reconfiguration.

Despite the ambiguity of her portraits, Stein always insists on their fidelity to that which is being represented. Many of them utilize the rhetoric of analysis and measurement: "what is an eye glass, it is water. A splendid specimen." "A table means necessary places." Such gestures toward definition permit Stein to expose the conventions of rational analysis even as she modifies conventional associations. Her portrait of "A Chair," for example, becomes a reflection on mutability: "A widow in a wise veil and more garments shows that shadows are even. It addresses no more, it shadows the stage and learning. A regular arrangement, the severest and the most preserved is that which has the arrangement and not more than always authorised" (468). Instead of describing a chair, as the title promises, this paragraph seems to be about mourning: a widow and her mourning garments are the color of shadows; such somber colors address something that exists "no more"; the rituals of mourning involve a "regular arrangement" of colors and events. The stress in these lines is on arrangements, discriminations, clarifications for which referents have been erased. If the chair is present at all, it is less through its physical features than its endurance over time. And indeed, duration becomes the dominant motif: "If the chance to dirty diminishing is necessary, if it is why is there no complexion, why is there no rubbing, why is there no special protection" (468). Such passages place the chair in time, in the wear and tear an object endures, its cleanliness, its lack of a slipcover. Thus, the chair, through its endurance, participates in the mortality brought to an abrupt punctuation in death, of which mourning is the human expression. To object that this passage fails to describe a chair is a little like complaining that Wittgenstein's *Philosophical Investigations* really does not do justice to planks. Planks and boxes and chairs are "arrangements" in systems of reference out of which something like a "chair" may emerge.

One sentence in this section could speak for the general method of Stein's portraits: "Practice measurement, practice the sign that means that really means a necessary betrayal, in showing that there is wearing." To "practice the sign" is to be wary of its illusion of permanence, to see "wear" as a word referring to clothing (the widow's weeds) as well as decay (the rubbing and wearing from use). The sign is not a static entity, any more than a chair can be isolated from those who sit in it; sign and chair wear away under the impact of use. "Act so that there is no use in a centre," Stein says at the beginning of "Rooms," informing us that what follows will not conform to a central signified or governing referent. *Tender Buttons* is a displacement of centers, an extension of the specific properties of language (its ability to measure, assess, and signify) to undermine the stability it promises. Potential narratives exfoliate from her portraits in direct contrast to the putative stillness such forms imply. A "magnificent asparagus" may also be a "fountain" when the sign is stripped of its object status and returned to its role in intellectual labor.

## WINDOW SHOPPING

Janet Wolff has observed that the art of modernism describes the experience of men, activities that occur in a public world of "work, politics, and city life" (34). The embodiment of this masculine access to public space is Baudelaire's *flâneur*, whose passionate interest in the crowd bespeaks his ability to move within it, undeterred by the stares or sexual advances of others. The female flâneur—or flâneuse—is invisible, limited in her access to male institutions and spaces, restricted to domestic realms of household and family. In the field of art, she is seldom the artist, more often the model or muse, occasionally the publisher or editor, and, in several significant cases, the leader of a salon. She is the object of the modernist gaze—the orientalized harem girl in Picasso's *Demoiselles d'Avignon* or the reflective young woman in Manet's *Gare Saint-Lazare*. But as Thorstein Veblen and other sociologists of market society observed, woman in modernity is also a consumer, marked as such by early forms of advertising and display and, at least within the upper bourgeoisie, encouraged in this pursuit by increasing emphasis on conspicuous display of wealth and leisure. Her relationship to mass-produced clothing and household goods as well as her consumption of popular culture (sentimental novels, popular entertainment) identifies her with mass culture and thus reinforces the separation of the aesthetic sphere, regarded as a masculine domain, from the social.

As a summary of woman's role within modernism, these remarks are too schematic to describe the complexity of gender in modernism.[5] At the most obvious level, they fail to represent the condition of poor working women, who, in increasing numbers, occupied laboring positions in factories and sweatshops or service positions in hospitals, schools, and businesses. Such women may have had greater access to the "public sphere," as Richard Sennett, Russell Berman, and other critics have described it, but they had little enough time or money for conspicuous consumption. Nor does this describe the world inhabited by Gertrude Stein and other women artists who both participated in consumer culture and maintained a critical perspective on it. Such critical crossings of the great divide between consumer culture and modernist aesthetics can be seen in any number of works written by women: Virginia Woolf's depiction of Mrs. Dalloway's shopping excursion, Kate Chopin's proto-Marxist study of commodity fetishism in "A Pair of Gloves," the conspicuous consumption and collection displayed in Edith Wharton's *The House of Mirth*, Mina Loy's satires of shoppers in "Three Moments in Paris," Nella Larsen's drama of racial "passing" set against the backdrop of Irene's shopping excursion in *Passing*, and Marianne Moore's satire of consumerism in "When I Buy Pictures" and "Marriage." In such works, the separation of spheres into private and public, female and male, is complicated by the writer's awareness of the ways in which identity is negotiated in spaces traditionally reserved for feminine activity.

To extend these terms to Gertrude Stein we might observe that *Tender Buttons* is not only about objects; it is about commodities. Seltzer bottles, carafes, umbrellas, hats, and boxes may have been adapted from Cubist collages as icons of the quotidian, but they are also mass-produced objects available at any of the Parisian department stores Stein frequented. Janet Flanner observes that Stein was an inveterate window shopper and wrote several of her portraits on or about the great Parisian shopping emporiums such as Bon Marché or Galeries Lafayette.[6] She was also a happy consumer who betrayed a "weakness for breakable objects" and could not understand people "who collect only the unbreakable" (*Autobiography* 13). Mabel Dodge Luhan describes Stein's love for "miniature alabaster fountains" and cheap "forget-me-not mosaic brooches, and all kinds of odds and ends that she liked much as a child likes things" (325). The exchange of presents, paintings, and bric-a-brac is a constant theme in her letters and autobiographical writings, and she was acutely conscious of her own self-presentation through idiosyncratic clothing.[7] We know a great deal about her collecting of modern art, a form of consumption valued for its display of cultural capital, but we know less of Stein's relationship to more mundane commodities and their implication for her aesthetics.

In *Tender Buttons*, Stein eroticizes the products of consumer society—she makes buttons "tender"—by treating their surfaces as sensuously linked to other surfaces; the exchange value of objects, rooms, and food is transformed from a money to a semiotic economy. Her treatment of consumption as an activity, however, is not quite so sanguine. In "Flirting at the Bon Marché," Stein creates a portrait of crowds whose alienation is relieved, if tentatively, by shopping:

> Some are coming to know very well that they are living in a very dreary way of living. Some are coming to know very well that they are living in a very sad way of living. Some are coming to know very well that they are living in a very tedious way of living. Some are coming to know very well that they are living in a very dull way of living.
> These go shopping. They go shopping and it always was a thing they were rightly doing. Now everything is changing. Certainly everything is changing. They go shopping, they are being in a different way of living. Everything is changing. (*Two* 354)

Far from resolving the "dreary way of living," shopping simply provides distraction. Stein's repetitions refer to the routinized existence being described—in which "everything is changing" but nothing changes:

> Why is everything changing. Everything is changing because the place where they shop is a place where every one is needing to be finding that there are ways of living that are not dreary ones, ways of living that are not sad ones, ways of living that are not dull ones, ways of living that are not tedious ones. Certainly in a way these are existing. (354)

Stein's characteristic use of participials provides only the illusion of progress. Instead of intensifying forward movement, participials reinforce a dull round of the same. The portrait's title, "Flirting at the Bon Marché," is a poignant reminder of exactly what *does not occur* at the department store and indicates Stein's affinity with earlier realist narratives of shopping in Balzac and Zola.

Speaking of these portraits of commercial life, Stein links an aesthetic of self-containment to the realist aesthetic of filmic technique:

> And there again in doing the portraits of these places and these crowds, I did Italians, and Americans too like that, I continued to do as I had done in *The Making of Americans*. I told exactly and completely each time of telling what that one is inside in them. As I told you in comparing it to a cinema picture one second was never the same as the second before or after. (*Lectures in America* 186–87)

Granted this is a retrospective remark on earlier work, but it shows the increasing importance of cinema as a challenge to more static theories of portraiture. Stein sees the incremental changes from frame to frame as providing a technological alternative to repetition. On the one hand, she retains her belief in unchanging character types or "bottom natures" at the same time that she recognizes that cinema creates movement and variation. Shopping, like cinema, testifies to the fact that "Everything is changing" and that people "are being in a different way of living." Cinema holds the possibility of liberating an isolated subjectivity ("what that one is inside in them") from the crowd. Thus, the instrument that would eliminate the aura of originality becomes, ironically, the vehicle for its recovery.

While Stein's portraiture cannot be reduced to a kind of aesthetic window shopping, it does represent her interest in the commercial and technological contexts of modern life. And while Stein was skeptical about Futurism's fetish of the machine, she drew upon new modes of mechanical reproduction—like the cinema—to extend and refine her characterological interests. Modern portraiture, like the automobile, translates the dynamic motion of the internal combustion engine into forward motion: "the car goes on, but my business my ultimate business as an artist was not with where the car goes as it goes but with the movement inside that is of the essence of its going" (*Lectures in America* 194–95).

Stein's interest in modern modes of reproduction and technology—her famous personalization of her Ford car, her excitement over flying in airplanes—helped endear her to a public that, if it did not understand her work, could at least regard her as a supporter of American innovation, an image reinforced by her participation in the war effort of both world wars as a volunteer driver and medical attendant. Yet her endorsement of modern American technology and industry is countered by her lifelong commitment to literary techniques that defy instrumental reason and thwart narrative progress. Even in her later career, when she celebrated series production and cinema in her explanatory essays, her representation of modern technology was ambivalent. Like Henry Adams before her, Stein regards the illumination offered by modern machines as a loss of power from which we will never recover.

We can see this loss allegorized in *Doctor Faustus Lights the Lights* (1938), which rewrites the Faust myth from the standpoint of Thomas Edison. In this play, Edison's invention of the electric light denudes the world of mystery and spiritual potency. The modern Edison-as-Faust sells his soul for the power to "light the lights," but instead of gaining absolute knowledge he receives only superficial illumination. The electric light eliminates the moral component in Faust's fatal pact. In the new, synthetic light, "there is no hope there is no death there is no life there is no breath there just is every day all day" (597–98). Mephistopheles' temptation is meaningless in a world for which heaven and hell, redemption and fall, have been neutralized through the human triumph over nature. Stein had seen her own name broadcast in the lights of the Times Square marquee, and it had suggested both the allure and the dangers of fame.[8] In the play, Faust too is surrounded by a corona of electric lights that seem to take on a life of their own. Such illumination contributes to the phantasmagoria of commodity society that Marx described in *Capital*, a ghostly reality of the commodity removed from labor and removed from a world of human needs. Whatever internal drama the Faust legend may have represented for early modern society, when translated into objective forms of illumination, the agon of temptation and damnation is reduced to the gaudy colors of an advertising display.[9]

## "NEVER TO BE WHAT HE SAID"

Stein's ambivalent response to the productive capacities of modern industry, technology, and commerce helps us understand her seemingly unqualified endorsement of genius and the rational intellect.

The link between both forms of production, mercantile and intellectual, is repetition, whether through Fordist methods on the assembly line or through Cubist faceting. In the former case, repetition leads to the reified product of labor, an object in which relations between individuals are hidden; in the latter case, the constant reiteration of modular units spatializes temporal reality. Fordism eliminates relations between workers and redistributes those relations among products; repetition in art eliminates relations between artifact and phenomenal world and redistributes them among words. In both cases, an unknowable subjectivity realizes itself in what Eagleton, adapting Lacan, calls the "mirror stage of objectification": "When the Kantian subject of taste encounters an object of beauty, it discovers in it a unity and harmony which are in fact the effect of the free play of its own faculties" (87). Kant's "Copernican revolution" involves the conception of the objective world in terms of the subject, but since the subject cannot know itself as a unique entity, it must utilize the objective world as a mirror for its missing substantiality.

When we speak of the bourgeois subject that gains self-knowledge through a world of objects, we speak in universal terms of what, in historical reality, is a gendered concept. Men made the industrial revolution and men developed the aesthetics by which it could be transcended. Hence, it is one thing for a man to escape personality and become the Other since he, as Eliot insisted, presumably "has" a personality to escape. But what does it mean for a woman to objectify herself, to become more objectified than she already is? And in Stein's case, what does it mean for a lesbian, a Jew, a daughter of immigrants, and an avant-gardist to escape being "othered?" Kant's Copernican revolution is carried out in a universe of fixed bodies reflected in the light of a common Sun. But, to extend my metaphor, there are other planetary bodies not accounted for in Kant's epistemology, however much he may have charted their orbits.

I have already spoken of Stein's materialization of herself as plural subject in her various autobiographical writings, but we could see a more complex version of this same tendency in her more abstract texts. Here, Stein's materialization of language coincides with a critique of identity as it is normalized in conventional discourse. It would be tempting to see her experimental work as equivalent to Dada or zaum "transrational" experiments, but as several critics have pointed out, Stein is too much interested in the logical structure of language to be interested in its elimination.[10] Furthermore, the gendered nature of language is often her subject, from her exploration of the contrastive psychologies of Melanchta and Jeff Campbell in *Three Lives* to the pronominal play of her second Picasso portrait: "He he he he and he and he and and he and he and he and and as and as he and as he and he. He is and as he is, and as he is and he is, he is and as he and he and as he is and he and he and and he and he" (*Writings and Lectures* 231). Patriarchy involves not only a hegemonic world of male values but the forms of legitimation by which misogyny is naturalized. Structures of legitimation and verification based on rational proof and logical argument become self-fulfilling prophecies that only repetition can explode: "Let me recite what history teaches. History teaches" (233).

The supreme Western example of a gendered legitimating structure would be Christian incarnation, by which a male generative principle, through its filial reflection in a son, determines the shape of all subsequent creation. Stein, who grew up in a household dominated by men and who for many years lived under the spell of her brother Leo, makes such patriarchal inheritance the subject of many of her works.[11] When she wants an example of the uselessness of living according to human nature, the gendered character of her example should not be lost on us: "What is the use of being a little boy if you are going to grow up to be a man" (*Geographical History* 58). She repeats a variation on this same formula in *The Making of Americans* with an anecdote about a father who convinces his son that it is cruel to kill insects. After putting his son to bed, the father discovers a beautiful moth, which, in contradiction to what he has just said to his son, he kills and pins and then shows to his son: "'see what a good father I am to have caught and killed this one,' the boy was all mixed up inside him and then he said he would go on with his collecting" (*Selected Writings* 310). This little parable of ambivalent reinforcement extends a pervasive theme of oedipal inheritance inaugurated in the novel's opening lines: "Once an angry man dragged his father along the ground through his own orchard. 'Stop!' cried the groaning old man at last, 'Stop! I did not drag my father beyond this tree'" (*Selected Writings* 261).

The phallocentric universe portrayed in these examples is as discursive as it is genetic and familial. Stein explores the priority of male power and succession as a discursive possibility in "Patriarchal Poetry" (1927). In its opening lines, Stein invokes the close proximity of terms for ontological and historical validation: "As long as it took fasten it back to a place where after all he would be carried away" (106). The imperative "fasten it back" suggests the constructed nature of the historical narrative of filiation. The lines that follow blur the boundaries between precession and being:

> For before let it before to be before spell to be before to be before
> to have to be to be for before to be tell to be to having held to be to be
> for before to call to be for to be before to till until to be till before to
> be for before to be until to be for before to for to be for before will for
> before to be shall to be to be.... (106)

Here the terms for temporal priority and spatial proximity ("before") merge with terms for being ("to be," "to be for"), creating a sentence whose grammatical structure embodies the difficulty of establishing a "place" for presence. "There was never a mistake in addition," Stein concludes, and in a world in which existence is based on having gained priority (having been here before), things will always add up to the same thing. In "Patriarchal Poetry," the sum of all equations is patriarchy.

I have spoken of the incarnational structure of Christianity by which an originating voice, or reason, is succeeded by a supplemental logos or word. In "Patriarchal Poetry," this narrative dominates Stein's structure of repetitions and is given explicit emphasis in the work's opening. "To change a boy with a cross from there to there" (107) suggests ways that Christian incarnation ("a boy with a cross") inaugurates history and establishes the terms for repetition:

> Let him have him have him heard let him have him heard him
> third let him have him have him intend let him have him have him
> defend let him have him have him third let him have him have him
> heard let him have him have him occurred let him have him have
> him third. (107)

The sheer monotony of these lines illustrates the rule of succession being invoked. "Let him have him" defines the horizon of progress in terms of male succession. The variation, "let him have him third," neutralizes numerical sequence by the repetitions of male pronouns. The dialectical aporia, the "third" term, can never be anything more than a repetition of the same. The biblical incarnation in John, "In the beginning was the Word," is reconfigured by Stein as a conundrum: if the word is already gendered as male, can it engender anything other than itself again and again? The terms that interrupt the repetitions above—"third," "occurred," "intend," "defend"—

are framed by the phrase "have him" so that all variation is a direct function of a "him" who permits it.

The priority of a patriarchal principle is based in language, specifically in a speech-based linguistics. Stein undermines such phonocentrism by pointing to the pragmatic contexts within which certain linguistic formulations occur. The form that her pointing takes is a satire of male rhetorics of proof and validation. By substituting the term "patriarchal poetry" for other substantives, she indicates the extent to which the proof and the subject-position that establishes proof are connected. In one case, she mocks the way that domestic life—specifically regimens of eating and cooking—is permeated by a patriarchal principle:

> Patriarchal poetry and not meat on Monday patriarchal poetry and meat on Tuesday. Patriarchal poetry and venison on Wednesday Patriarchal poetry and fish on Friday Patriarchal poetry and birds on Sunday Patriarchal poetry and chickens on Tuesday patriarchal poetry and beef on Thursday. (111)

Marianne DeKoven calls the repetition of the title motif "arbitrary," but I find repetitions such as these highly directed, suggesting that along with daily bread, one consumes an ordered logic as well.[12] "Patriarchal poetry" refers both to the gendered basis of daily life *and* its dissemination through poetry.

The criterion upon which DeKoven evaluates Stein's work is its ability to sustain variation and change. Thus, she admires works such as *Tender Buttons* or "Susie Asado" because they constantly vary and reconfigure language in new and interesting ways. Long works such as "Patriarchal Poetry," on the other hand, suffer from redundancy. It is true that the latter makes for difficult reading, but redundancy is very much at issue in its critique of male discourse. By filling her paragraphs with the same words, often subordinated to the phrase "patriarchal poetry," Stein undermines the function of all series—lists, catalogs, and schedules—that appear to structure the quotidian. Far from organizing reality, Stein's lists point back at the rationalizing tendency itself:

> Patriarchal Poetry sentence sent once.
> Patriarchal Poetry is used with a spoon.
> Patriarchal poetry is used with a spoon with a spoon.
> Patriarchal poetry is used with a spoon.

Patriarchal poetry used with a spoon.
Patriarchal poetry in and for the relating of now and ably. (123)

If the function of a list or a schedule is to distinguish and isolate, Stein's lists show the entropic nature of such a will to power. Within the logic of patriarchy all distinctions are moot. The difference between something "used with a spoon" and something "used with a spoon with a spoon" is only the illusion of difference.

I have said that "Patriarchal Poetry" foregrounds pragmatic frames for utterances. Many of the paragraphs create the effect of discourse without any human or social context. If Wordsworth's definition of poetic discourse is a language of men speaking to men, Stein's variation is of systems speaking to systems:

> Patriarchal poetry makes no mistake makes no mistake in estimating the value to be placed upon the best and most arranged of considerations of this in as apt to be not only to be partially and as cautiously considered as in allowance which is one at a time. At a chance at a chance encounter it can be very well as appointed as appointed not only considerately but as it as use. (124)

The humor of such passages lies in their mockery of professional or bureaucratic rhetoric, with all of its minor discriminations, parenthetical qualifications, and unqualified assertions. The glaringly absent term here is any referent for the "value to be placed upon the best." Patriarchal poetry is faultless because, as a structure of legitimation, it has permeated the very logic of value itself.

Where does woman exist within "patriarchal poetry" (the system, not Stein's text)? At one level, she is its object, that about which a male poetry is written. Stein satirizes the goals of traditional love poetry in a sonnet placed at the text's center:

> *A Sonnet*
>
> To the wife of my bosom
> All happiness from everything
> And her husband.
> May he be good and considerate
> Gay and cheerful and restful.
> And make her the best wife
> In the world
> The happiest and most content
> With reason . . .
>         (124)

The poem concludes by hoping that the wife's "charms her qualities her joyous nature" will make her husband "A proud and happy man." The function of the sonnet, as Stein sees it, is not to celebrate the wife but to hope she will continue to satisfy her husband. This is patriarchal poetry with a vengeance, and although Stein was perfectly capable of aping the bourgeois structure of the family herself, with Alice as wife and herself as husband, this sonnet, with its Hallmark Greeting Card sentimentality, suggests how ironically she could treat this ménage.[13] Furthermore, it suggests that what sonnets are "about" is ultimately a system of avowals, the human terms for which are socially determined.

The longest catalog in "Patriarchal Poetry" is one consisting of variations on the phrase "Let her try" ("Let her be," "Let her be shy," "Let her try"), concluding with the appeal

> Never to be what he said.
> Never to be what he said
> Never to be what he said
> Let her to be what he said.
> Let her to be what he said.
> (121)

In terms of Stein's biography, we could see this as representing Stein's attempt to be free of her brother Leo, not to be "what he said" but to "try" to be herself. This may help explain Stein's desire to live outside of patriarchal authority, but it does not address the material form in which this desire is expressed. By focusing on the grammatical and pragmatic contexts of negation ("Never to be"), of commands ("Let her be"), and existence ("to be"), Stein inverts the authority of patriarchal language and points to the discursive nature of subject production itself. That she performs her deconstruction with a great deal of humor and wicked wit makes her task all the more oppositional.

## "THIS IS HER AUTOBIOGRAPHY ONE OF TWO"

Stein's attempt "never to be what he said" was purchased at the cost of a wider readership. All of this changed with *The Autobiography of Alice B. Toklas* in 1932, when Stein became, in the terms developed earlier, an object for public consumption. The American tour that ensued brought her in front of large audiences for the first time and gave her a chance to occupy a stage rather than a salon. She was hounded by the press for her opinions on everything from Roosevelt to American cooking. And for the first time, she was making money for her work. However euphoric Stein may have been over the *Autobiography*'s success, she was depressed about its reception from many of her old friends who found their portraits within the book less than flattering—or accurate. More significant, Stein was concerned that by writing a popular book she had sacrificed entity to identity, aesthetic autonomy to personality. Such worries concern the presumed verisimilitude of the *Autobiography* to Stein's life, but such accuracy was never part of her project.

The public world of the *Autobiography* must be framed by the work that she was writing at the same time, *Stanzas in Meditation*. It is Stein's longest and perhaps most impenetrable book. As Ulla Dydo has pointed out, *Stanzas in Meditation* could be regarded as the "other" autobiography, one in which a distinctly different form of subjectivity is produced from that more mimetic version. It is also an autobiography *of* "otherness" in which Stein details her alienation in a world dependent on what "they" demand from her. Where the *Autobiography* subjects daily life to a linear narrative of meetings, gatherings, gossip, and renewals, *Stanzas in Meditation* reduces that life to a calculus of indexical exchanges. As John Ashbery observes, it is "not events which interests Miss Stein, rather it is their 'way of happening'" (Kostelanetz, ed., 109).

It would be tempting to regard the *Autobiography* and *Stanzas* as the recto and verso of a life, the one public and historical, the other private and hermetic. This assumes, however, that there is a life of which each book is a deformation. Both works problematize the idea of a unitary self, one by adopting the narrative persona of Alice B. Toklas, the other by reducing all human relationships to a skeletal structure of pronominal exchanges. It also assumes that the *Autobiography* is less "composed" than her more abstract work, the "open and public" book in contrast to the closed, hermetic *Stanzas*.[14] Instead, Stein saw both as participants in a common problematic of self-representation, an "autobiography in two instances," as she says at one point in *Stanzas* (389).[15] She could treat herself as something created in public intercourse, utilizing the props of traditional narrative exposition, or she could treat herself as coextensive with the world, part of the landscape itself and not about it. *Stanzas* is an autobiography in which all of the markers that relate one event or person to another (genealogy, chronology, rhetorical subordination) have been erased. One is left only with the linguistic infrastructure—with such functional words as prepositions, articles and conjunctions, and, above all, pronouns.

Those function words are by no means empty. They hint at arguments, misunderstandings, self-doubts, and ardors in Stein's private life that become all the more charged in the absence of proper names. Furthermore, as Ulla Dydo has shown, the notebooks in which Stein wrote *Stanzas* were the sites for a complicated dialogue between Stein, the author, and Toklas, the interlocutor and amanuensis. In many cases, Stein's notebooks included highly coded messages to (and from) Alice, who was transcribing portions of holograph copy into clean typescripts. In a work with as limited a lexicon as *Stanzas*, revisions of single words take on added significance, projecting a formalism based not on superimposed structure but on exigencies of the moment—the size of the notebook, the changes of weather, the psychopathology of everyday life.[16]

The writing of *Stanzas* coincides with Stein's interest in landscape, the theory of which is elaborated in *The Geographical History of America* and summarized in the *Autobiography*: "[Stein] began at this time to describe landscape as if anything she saw was a natural phenomenon, a thing existent in itself" (*Selected Writings* 212). The operative phrase here is "as if." Stein had learned through her studies of Jamesian pragmatism that the phenomenal field includes the one looking at it—that the thing "existent in itself" is the product of the composing process. What we usually expect from landscape poetry—the work of Wordsworth, say, or latter-day romantics such as Gary Snyder—is the use of natural scenery as an objective correlative for nonlinguistic subjective states. But if one searches *Stanzas* for the flora and fauna of the Rhone Valley, where the couple was living during this period, one will be disappointed. Yes, there are references to pansies, mountains, clouds, and dogs, but only as reference points in a more philosophical query:

> It is often that they allow a cloud to be white
> Or not only patently white but also just as green
> Not only theirs in pleasure but theirs in case
> Not only however but not only however
> (374)

The cloud mentioned here is part of a debate over what others permit clouds to be. Once a cloud becomes subject to human characteristics ("I wandered lonely as a cloud"), it might as well be a word like "however," a word that identifies a thing by contrast to something else. Stein mocks the tendency to define a thing by what it is not in her fourth line, "Not only however but not only however," implying that the essence of a cloud (its mutability, its constant alteration of shape) might as well be rendered in words equally unstable. Stein does not meditate "on" the landscape but by means of it:

> What is a landscape
> A landscape is what when they that is I
> See and look
>                            (437)

If Stein's landscape is not filled with trees, rocks, and mountains, it is filled with pronouns, those positional markers by which individuals claim a vantage. One vantage is called "they," and when "I" inhabits it, "I" is another. Stein employs this third-person perspective to refer to that side of herself susceptible of seeing a landscape as a "what," as a field outside of herself. Hence, a landscape is a way of looking, a predisposition to see phenomena as they constellate a series of positions around a viewer. Richard Bridgeman has read the pronominal play of *Stanzas* in terms of Stein's debate with her public or with Alice, and while this may be the immediate locus for individual stanzas there is a larger philosophical argument at stake concerning the construction of identity within language.[17]

Here again, Kant's aesthetics provides a model. For Kant, the task of the aesthetic is to find universal validity for subjective judgments. If matters of taste are, by definition, highly individual and contextual, how can one at the same time assert universal validation for them?

> In a judgment of taste (about the beautiful) the satisfaction in the object is imputed to *everyone*, without being based on a concept (for then it would be the good). Further, this claim to universal validity so essentially belongs to a judgment by which we describe anything as *beautiful* that, if this were not thought in it, it would never come into our thoughts to use the expression at all, but everything which pleases without a concept would be counted as pleasant. (48)

In the pronominal terms already introduced, Kant is asking what role "they" plays in "my" apperception. Do I have a vantage separate from "theirs?" To what extent may I represent reality as an "it," as something that exists independently of a concept? Stein asks similar questions, not to assure herself of the beauty of nature (which is Kant's concern) but to question whether it can be represented at all. Many individual stanzas debate the difficulty of validation and assertion:

> She can think the thought that they will wish
> And they will hold that they will spell anguish
> And they will not be thought perverse
> (352)

> I do not wish to say what I think
> I concluded I would not name those.
> (375)

> This that I think is this.
> (387)

> How I wish I were able to say what I think
> In the meantime I can not doubt
> round about because I have found out
> (392)

If we read these lines in the context of the *Autobiography*, we may hear echoes of Stein's argument with her skeptical public, but the unrelenting abstraction of such language renders such allegorization irrelevant. When Stein says, "This that I think is this," she dissolves the sentence's constative function, placing all the emphasis on the speech act itself. The repetitions of "th" sounds and the use of monosyllables focus attention not on the object of thought but on the act of saying itself. And this act, because it does not depend on logical proof, has the effect of collapsing thinker and thought, speaker and interlocutor, into one.

The emphasis in the above examples on what "they will wish" is a dominant motif, as I have said. The authority of "they" and the identity of "I," "she," and "he" create the effect of a private argument in which the players' identities have been removed:

> It is useless to introduce two words between one
> And so they must conceal where they run
> For they can claim nothing
> Nor are they willing to change which they have
> Oh yes I organise this. But not a victory

> They will spend or spell space
> For which they have no share
> And so to succeed following.
> This is what there is to say.
>                    (342)

Stein plays on the ambiguous nature of "one" to refer both to words and to persons. On one level, this is a meditation on language and its ability to claim permanence when based on a series of arbitrary relationships. Despite our best attempts to organize words toward greater clarity, they will ultimately "conceal where they run." On another level, the passage contains a covert description of some kind of personal deception for which adding more words becomes "useless." If we lack adequate information about the source of this deception, we at least retain the rhythms of argument. The fact that "They will spend or spell space / For which they have no share" can apply both to words and persons, the former insofar as words are differentiated by (do not share) phonemes and the latter insofar as spending and spelling involve the expense of information (letters, money) within a system of exchange. When Stein asserts, "Oh yes I organise this. But not a victory," she defends her own highly idiosyncratic construction, even while recognizing that in the larger scheme of things, others "will spend or spell space" according to their own whims.

The subtle distinctions between words such as "spend" or "spell" and the mathematical possibilities of integers ("two words between one") bespeak an interest in certain irreducible particles that form the basis for meditation. If Stein has any affinities with her Jewish heritage, it is here, in the twisting and turning of elementary particles to reveal the name of that which cannot be named:[18]

> I come back to think everything of one
> One and one
> Or not which they were won
> I won.
> They will be called I win I won
> Nor which they call not which one or one
> I won.
> I will be winning I won.
> Nor not which one won for this is one.
> I will not think one and one remember not.
> Not I won I won to win win I one won

> And so they declare or they declare
> To declare I declare I win I won one
>
> (381)

It would appear that Stein thinks of her writing in strategic terms as a matter of winning or losing. Only through this struggle could she become "one," someone unlike others. To debate *who* won is to become vulnerable to "their" logic; better to declare "I will be winning I won" and claim unity ("one") and victory ("won") at the same time. This is why Stein may assert with some confidence that she is one of the three geniuses of the modern era—an assertion that cannot be verified, only insisted upon.

Identity is additive; one and one makes more than one, and what is unique and singular quickly becomes a sum. Stein tries not to think of adding one to one in order to gain two but rather to name one over and over again. In "An Instant Answer or a Hundred Prominent Men," she counts to one hundred by repeating the word "one" one hundred times (*Useful Knowledge* 150–51). It is Stein's way of adding while not losing sight of the basic elements of which addition is made. *Stanzas* does something of the same thing for the question of identity, asking over and over again how many ways "one" becomes more than itself. The result is a sustained attempt to make distinctions and find points of fracture. Word play ceases to be playful, revealing instead contingencies between things such as power (win) and identity (one).

This quality of struggle informs Stein's version of meditation. Hers is not Kant's disinterested reflection on the sources of pleasure but a kind of active interrogation of the nature of legitimation. Like other meditative poems before *Stanzas* (one thinks of Thomas Traherne's *Centuries of Meditations* or Edward Taylor's *Preparatory Meditations*), the ineffable object of reflection implicates the process of meditating itself. Stein's are not stanzas *of* meditation but stanzas *in the form of* meditation and as such do not admit of structural boundaries, a fact embodied in extensive repetition and punning. Her stanza breaks often provide a false pause in what is, in reality, a continuing reflection:

> Now there is an interference in this.
> I interfere in I interfere in which this.
> They do not count alike.
> One two three.

> *Stanza XL*
>
> I wish simply to say that I remember now.
>
> *Stanza XLI*
>
> I am trying to say something but I have not said it.
> Why.
> Because I add my my I.
>
> (439)

Interruption here is an operative feature of meditation, just as sustained attention to a landscape consists of a series of relatively discrete perceptions over time. Whatever the landscape is, it is something composed, something in a state of composition. Stein has little faith in the unitary consciousness of romanticism, despite her claims for genius. Rather, as her omnipresent participials testify, consciousness occurs in real time, and composition must reflect its unclosed, processual nature.

Stein made it clear that writing according to memory sounds the death knell for masterpieces. The masterpiece, like the composition, "is the thing seen by every one living in the living they are doing, they are the composing of the composition that at the time they are living is the composition of the time in which they are living" (*Selected Writings* 516). This famous formulation, written only two years after *Stanzas*, expresses the ineradicable bond between consumer and producer, between something made and its residual effects on the maker. *Stanzas in Meditation* insists on this interplay between subject and object, between observer and landscape, in which the one is constituted by the other. And the form of this interplay is meditation, a form of reflection in which sustained response to nature reintegrates the isolated ego with a social realm it does not need to convince.

## THE GOLDEN BOWL

In his 1957 review of the Yale edition of *Stanzas,* John Ashbery compares the work to the late novels of Henry James, "which seem to strain with a superhuman force toward 'the condition of music,' of poetry" (105).[19] Ashbery's equation of James with Symbolism is perhaps inevitable if one thinks of the desultory prose of late works such as *Wings of the Dove* or *The Golden Bowl*.[20] There, characters are developed through a language of innuendo and indirection that provide a narrative equivalent to the "music-envy" (as David Antin calls it) of Symbolism ("Some Questions" 11). The complexity of deixis, interplay of pronouns, and use of indirect address, offer close analogs to Stein's practice in *Stanzas*. One could say that both James and Stein, by focusing their attention on the rhythms of speech rather than the content of any utterance, achieve that temporal stillness of the well-wrought urn.

But the golden bowl of aestheticism has, as we know, a flaw:

> "It isn't gold." With which, somewhat strangely, Maggie smiled.
> "That's the point."
> "What is it then?"
> "It's glass—and cracked, under the gilt, as I say, at that." (420)

Whether or not the golden bowl in James's last novel is actually flawed, as Maggie Verver asserts, is less important than the ways this object frames each character's relationship to it. What begins as an object of aesthetic beauty for Charlotte Stant becomes, for Maggie Verver, a mockery of her own marriage to the Prince. Extending this metaphor to Stein, we might say that although she inherited a Symbolist desire for a totality outside the realm of human interests, she recognized the human and social costs of such totalization. In place of the autotelic object, Stein substituted a writing conscious of its status as social discourse.

For Stein, the flaw in the golden bowl involves that paradox encountered in my opening pages: the difficulty of the aesthetic object in capitalist society of escaping its commodity status. For Adorno, it is enough that the autonomous object stands as the dialectical other to the culture industry. Stein goes another step by writing in the space between the two realms, much as she wrote notes to Alice in the pages of her notebooks. In this sense, she seems closer to postmodern theories of intransitive writing for whom Kant, in a retrofitted version, plays an important role.[21] In Kant's analytic of the sublime, Jean-François Lyotard finds a paradigm for the nontotalizable and nonmimetic. Abstract art is that presentation of "the fact that the unpresentable exists. To make visible that there is something which can be conceived and which can neither be seen nor made visible" (*Postmodern Condition* 78). As I have argued, Stein's abstraction is not an "index to the unrepresentable" but a critique of those judgments that depend on totality as their starting point. Lyotard's use of Kant, in this respect, becomes the latest in a series of attempts beginning with Clement Greenberg and John Crowe Ransom to utilize Kantian aesthetics to deny modernism any reflective or critical potential.

When readers first saw Stein's writing, often in degraded versions in the public media, they recognized it for what it was—a reflection of their own objectified reality. This reflection was the flawed mirror that Stein inherited from James and held up to a new generation. Stein was ahead of her time not because she created new forms or wrote angry manifestos but because she diagnosed the limits of nineteenth-century thought in the terms it bequeathed to the twentieth. Those terms included a separation of identity from entity, sentient subjects from the objects they apprehended, private from public sphere. Rather than reinscribe such a dualism by fetishizing one term over the other, Stein rewrote Kantian aesthetics by focusing on its critical function, its ability to make judgments in a world increasingly dependent on the market as guarantor of value. Buttons could become tender not by making them ever more subject to human uses but by making them more like words. By practicing the sign rather than using it to achieve cultural ends, Stein made language hard to consume. Perhaps W. C. Fields was right—her writing *was* about apples after all. Perhaps Fields's wife was right as well—her writing was beautiful because there was no punctuation.

# 2

# Palimtexts
*George Oppen, Susan Howe, and the Material Text*

Piling up pieces of paper to find the words
George Oppen

In the previous chapter, I described how Gertrude Stein's most recalcitrant work reveals a social narrative in textual practices that would seem to serve entirely aesthetic ends. Those practices include her use of repetition, her deployment of social idiolects, her puns and pronominal play, her satirical use of canonical genres (play, sonnet, Bildungsroman), her flattened diction. What I have called "textual practices" Stein called "composition" to invoke both the evolving character of writing in time and the overall shape of the text. But perhaps we can see this social narrative in the physical page itself—not the published version of a text but the handwritten or typed manuscript on which the author first begins to compose. How does the materiality of the page interact with the materiality of social forms beyond the archive? What happens when the writer foregrounds manuscript and archive in the final published version? What is on the surface of the page?

To answer these questions we might turn to a page from the papers of George Oppen (Fig. 4). It is relatively free of penciled marks or emendations. Brief prose remarks are spaced at intervals, sometimes separated by typed underlining. At the top of the page is a short lyric entitled "Rembrandt's Old Woman Cutting Her Nails":

> An old woman
> As if I saw her now
> For the first time, cutting her nails
> In the slant light

It is a poem whose brevity and economy embody many of the values one associates with Imagism and Objectivism. The only concession to a larger theme is the phrase beginning "As if," which introduces

```
Rembrandts's Old Woman Utting Her Nails


An old woman
As if I saw her now
For the first time, cutting her nails
In the slant light



WE HAVE A LONG TRADITION OF CONTEMPT FOR MATTER, AND HAVE
CEASED TO NOTICE THAT ITS EXISTENCE __ AND ONLY ITS EXISTENCE __
REMAINS ABSOLUTELY UNEXPLAINED


   No raod now ends   : a network of roads.
   ─────────────────────────────────

Wespeak of people's death, except the deaths of the extremely
old, as if they might have lived forever   Of course they could
not have, and therefore the difference bewteen thirty years of
life and seventy years does not in itself define thexdifference
tragedy
         But the wives or husbands and parents and children!!
That is, when the young die, there are the bereaved   By the time
the old man or woman dies, no on e is bereaved?   Dare we say that?

By the time a man or woman is very old, the tragedy has already
happened
   ─────────────────────────────────

   'Mankind' is a conversation

       ─────────

It would be hard for human nature to find a better ally in this
enterprise than love'      Symposium

One knows what he thinks    but not what he will find

the classic love of the finite has no relevance to our knowledge
```

Figure 4. George Oppen, "Rembrandt's Old Woman Cutting Her Nails."

the absent poet, a third participant in the conversation between painter (Rembrandt) and old woman. This "As if" finds its visual correlative in the reference to "slant light," which hints at the indirect source of sight, mediated through a painter, a historical period, an aesthetic frame, a rhetorical displacement: "As if I saw her now."

Below the poem, perhaps serving as a commentary on it, is a prose remark, typed in caps:

WE HAVE A LONG TRADITION OF CONTEMPT FOR MATTER, AND HAVE CEASED TO NOTICE THAT ITS EXISTENCE—AND ONLY <u>ITS</u> EXISTENCE—REMAINS ABSOLUTELY UNEXPLAINED

To some extent this prose extends the poet's meditation on Rembrandt's design but shifts the emphasis from the painting's subject—the old woman—to its materiality, a shift that, as subsequent lines make clear, has distinctly existential implications:

We speak of people's death, except the deaths of the extremely old, as if they might have lived forever Of course they could not have, and therefore the difference between thirty years of life and seventy years does not in itself define tragedy

But the wives or husbands and parents and children!! That is, when the young die, there are the bereaved By the time the old man or woman dies, no one is bereaved? Dare we say that?

What began as a depiction of an old woman has now become an interrogation of the life beyond her. The author seems anxious to interpret the painting by understanding the world he shares with it, a world in which matter "matters." And to the degree that both painter and poet engage the problem of mortality, they share the same world. What links poet and painter, youth and age, painting and subject is care: "It would be hard for human nature to find a better ally in this enterprise than love," the poet quotes from *The Symposium*. But care alone is not enough; the material expression of that care, as presented in painting, poem, and prose, is the form that love takes. "Mankind is a conversation," and one might add that the page itself, in its wandering and questioning, is the material analog of that conversation.

This page by George Oppen, one of thousands like it among his papers housed at the Archive for New Poetry at the University of California, San Diego, represents a crucial problem for any consideration of literary genre: that of the poem's materiality, its existence as writing.[1] Once we have seen the poem in this context, it becomes difficult to isolate it from its written environment. Indeed, can we speak of "poetry" at all when so much of it is embedded in other quotations, prose remarks, and observations? Does Oppen's oeuvre end in the work we know as *The Collected Poems*, or does it end on the page where it began? I would like to take up some of these questions by thinking about the status of the manuscript page, not out of some antiquarian interest in early drafts but out of a concern for epistemological and social questions that lie at the heart of genre theory. For if genre implies a way of organizing knowledge, then to "think genericity" is to think thinking.

The question of genre in recent literary theory has most often taken the form of a debate over "new" genres (various forms of nonnarrative prose, sound poetry, procedurally derived forms) or the rediscovery of previously marginalized genres (the manifesto, the fragment, the epistle). And while this discussion has had a useful taxonomic function, it has not addressed the issue of genericity itself, the degree to which modern and postmodern texts challenge notions of categorization altogether. It could be said that the current debate extends a more pervasive romantic skepticism over formal categories, manifesting itself on the one hand by a pursuit of some idealized, Mallarméan *livre* or on the other by a ruthless exhaustion of types through forms of appropriation, quotation, and parody.[2] It could equally be said that both positions rest on an opposition between literary and ordinary language that can be transcended only by exploiting the possibilities of the former to accommodate selective aspects of the latter.

The most significant critique of genericity has occurred within the context of poststructuralism with its emphasis on *écriture* as the recognition of difference (*différance*) within the linguistic sign. Literature ceases to be defined by its "signs of literariness" but rather by its intransitivity, its refusal of rhetorical and generic markers. And as we will see in the second half of this chapter, this refusal is a deterritorializing gesture that displaces the authority of official print culture in favor of what Deleuze and Guattari (1991) have called a "minor literature." I would like to retain poststructuralism's emphasis on writing as trace, as inscription of an absence, but emphasize the material fact of that trace, an inscribing and reinscribing that, for lack of a better term, I have called a "palimtext." By this word I mean to emphasize the intertextual—and interdiscursive—quality of modern writing as well as its materiality. The palimtext is neither genre nor object but a writing-in-process. As its name implies, the palimtext retains vestiges of prior inscriptions out of which it emerges. Or, more accurately, it is the still-visible record of its responses to those earlier writings.

The palimtext is a kind of ruin that emerges in an era when ruins no longer signify lost plenitude. The modern ruin, as Walter Benjamin points out, is immanent in mass-produced commodities, an allegory of modern materiality's impermanence and ephemerality. Like the electric lights in Stein's Faust play, the modern commodity-as-ruin transforms the idea of illumination to a gaudy display, invented for maximum exposure and salability, not for the subtleties of chiaroscuro. Textual self-referentiality—the modern equivalent of the baroque allegorist's memento mori—becomes a recognition of transitoriness and ephemerality in a world committed to the illusion of progress and permanence. Baudelaire is Benjamin's example of the modern allegorical poet precisely because he first diagnoses the shock features of modern urban life—the juxtapositions of dissimilar phenomena encountered among crowds in the city. The Paris of Baudelaire's poems "is a submerged city, more submarine than subterranean," and like the city the poet's lyrics are an archaeology of historical transformations and ruptures; they provide a "pictorial image of dialectics, the law of dialectics seen at a standstill" (*Reflections* 157).

It is this image of dialectics at a standstill that best describes the manuscripts of George Oppen, a poet whose lyricism has often been treated as the replacement or repression of his own political involvement. By looking at his manuscript page, we can test his avowed interest in separating art and politics by showing his poetry as a form of daily practice. Because Oppen's work so little challenges generic boundaries, his material text becomes important for reconsidering the authority of those boundaries. The image of historical rupture in the lyric also animates my understanding of more recent writers such as Susan Howe, whose self-conscious manipulation of the material features of the page attempts to animate voices that speak from the margins of American frontier ideology. In both poets, the material nature of the sign and its specifically social and discursive contexts become part of what Oppen called a "lyric reaction to the world."

## "A LYRIC REACTION TO THE WORLD"

Poetry, according to Louis Zukofsky, "is precise information on existence out of which it grows" (*Prepositions* 28). It is seldom observed, however, that this growth begins and ends on a page. Traditional textual research has provided us with a methodology for investigating such materiality, but always with an eye toward some definitive version out of which to establish a copy text. As Jerome McGann points out, textual criticism has had until recently one end: "to establish a text which . . . most nearly represents the author's original (or final) intentions" (*Critique of Modern Textual Criticism* 15). That desire to recover the author in the work is part of a "paradigm which sees all human products in processive and diachronic terms" (119). Those intentions can be discovered by locating the last text upon which the author had a primary hand before it came under the influence of copy editors, compositors, and house style. The textual editor must master the corrupt text and delete any superfluous or extraneous material not directly related to the work in question. Genre becomes an ally in such mastery insofar as it provides a codified set of rhetorical and textual markers to which the text must ultimately conform. The editor's service to the author therefore is mediated by generic expectations.

Modern poets, in this context, are no different from previous generations in the way that they keep notebooks, use paper, and revise their work. But poets since Pound have incorporated the material fact of their writing into the poem in ways that challenge the intentionalist criteria of traditional textual criticism. At the same time that poets have foregrounded the page as a compositional field, they have tended to "think genericity" to an unprecedented degree, making the issue of formal boundaries a central fact of their poetics. Indeed, for many poets today it has become meaningless to speak of "the poem" but rather of "the work," both in the sense of oeuvre and of praxis. We can see the evolution of such a poetics not just in the writings of poets but in their papers and manuscripts that, in increasing numbers, have been deposited in academic libraries. What we see in such collections is the degree to which writing is archaeological, the gradual accretion and sedimentation of textual materials, no layer of which can ever be isolated from any other. George Oppen's page, to return to my initial example, is only one slice through a vast, sedimented mass that quite literally rises off the page, carrying with it the traces of prior writings. That page is part of a much larger conversation for which the published poem is a scant record.

One of the most important implications to be derived from studying the material text is the way that the page reinforces certain epistemological concerns, notably the idea that writing is a form of knowing. Robert Creeley's remark, "One knows in writing," Charles Olson's equation of logos and mythos (thought and saying), and Allen Ginsberg's poetics of spontaneity are but three examples of a pervasive attempt to ground thought not in reflection but in action (Creeley, "An Interview," 279; Olson, *The Special View of History* 20). George Oppen is no exception. In a letter to Rachel Blau DuPlessis, he speaks of the poem as a "process of thought" and then goes on to qualify this remark:

> but it is what I think. A poem which begins with an idea—a "conceit" in the old use of the term—doesn't learn from its own vividness and go on from there unless both terms of the conceit or one at least is actually *there*. I mean, had it begun from the parade, the experience of the parade and stuck to it long enough for the thing to happen it could have got one into the experience of being among humans—and aircraft and delivery trucks—? ("Letters to Rachel Blau DuPlessis" 121)

For Oppen the poem does not represent the mind thinking; it *is* the thinking itself, including its marginal references, afterthoughts, and postscripts. One may begin with a "conceit," but, if one attends to the "parade" of passing things, one will find oneself "among humans—and aircraft and delivery trucks." Like one of his favorite philosophers, Heidegger, Oppen understands that knowledge is gained not by bracketing experience but by finding oneself already in the world, engaged in human intercourse. The poet strives to reduce words to their barest signification, prior to their subordination to cognitive or rhetorical schemes.

The ideal of a poetry that no longer represents but participates in the process of thought is hardly new. It is part of the romantic movement's desire to escape forms of associationism and empiricism by a belief in the poem's creative nature. George Oppen is seldom mentioned in such contexts, but this is because we have tended to read his poetry through modernist spectacles. Critics have seen his work as the logical extension of certain Imagist principles involving "direct treatment of the thing" and economy of language. It is as though we have focused only on the first word in the title to his first book, *Discrete Series*, to the exclusion of the second. By doing so, we have reified the processual—and I would argue dialogical—nature of his thought in an ethos of the hard, objective artifact.[3] Such a reading is not surprising; many of Oppen's own comments speak of the poem as a discrete object among others, "a girder among the rubble," as he liked to quote from Reznikoff. This emphasis on the single poem is supported by his oft-stated desire to find the final real and indestructible things of the world, "That particle of matter, [which] when you get to it, is absolutely impenetrable, absolutely inexplicable" ("Interview" 163).

My contention is that, rather than being regarded as a series of single lyric moments, George Oppen's poetry should be seen as "a lyric reaction to the world," a fact that becomes dramatically evident once one looks at a page like the one described earlier ("Interview" 164). His poems represent the outer surfaces of a larger debate that appears fragmentarily in broken phrases, ellipses, quotations, and italics. We know, for example, that *Of Being Numerous* is constructed largely around quotations from Meister Eckhart, Kierkegaard, Whitehead, Plato, Whitman, as well as friends such as Rachel Blau DuPlessis, Armand Schwerner, and John Crawford, all of whom enter the poem silently in the form of inverted commas. And even where such obvious quotation does not occur, as in the poems from *Discrete Series*, Oppen's paratactic logic, truncated syntax, and ambiguous use of antecedents embody the shifting attentions of a mind dissatisfied with all claims to closure. Like the "Party on Shipboard" in that volume, Oppen's narrative movement is "Freely tumultuous" (*Collected Poems* 8).

This idea of poetry as a "lyric reaction" can be understood best by comparing a poem from *Of Being Numerous* with a page from which it emerged. In the fourth section of "Route," we encounter the image of a sea anemone, which launches a series of observations on language:

Words cannot be wholly transparent. And that is the
"heartlessness" of words.

Neither friends nor lovers are coeval . . .
  as for a long time we have abandoned those in

> extremity and we find it unbearable that we should
> do so . . .
>
> The sea anemone dreamed of something, filtering the sea
> water thru its body,
>
> Nothing more real than boredom—dreamlessness, the
> experience of time, never felt by the new arrival
> never at the doors, the thresholds, it is the native
>
> Native in native time . . .
>
> The purity of the materials, not theology, but to present
> the circumstances
> (*Collected Poems* 186)

"Route" deals with the difficulties of achieving clarity, the lure of the finite and indestructible in a world of fluid boundaries. The section quoted here appears to be a qualification of that clarity, an attempt to express the "heartlessness" of words when they refuse transparency.[4] This qualification takes the form of a meditation on boredom, a state in which the world is reduced, as Oppen says, to "dreamlessness." The reality of boredom is, as he says elsewhere, "the knowledge of what *is*," a state in which things have been divested of instrumental reason and may be encountered spontaneously, without reflection ("Interview" 169). It is a state in which one is naturalized in one's environment, "Native in native time." Things have lost their novelty and may now be encountered ready-to-hand. This is a far cry from modernist despair over *ennui* as expressed in writers from Baudelaire to Eliot. In Oppen's version, boredom is the condition within which the "purity of the materials" may be experienced.[5]

The most confusing lines of this passage are those concerning the sea anemone. It is the only concrete image of the section and so becomes all the more important in establishing exactly how Oppen understands boredom. On the one hand, the sea anemone could represent a kind of ultimate passivity in which the organism's whole existence is conceived around "filtering the sea / water thru its body." This interpretation would seem to be borne out by a brief prose remark included among Oppen's papers:

> Boredom, the sense of lack of meaning—In the cities from the sense of being submerged in the flood of people, of not being able to see out, of being a passenger—In the small cities from the sense of shal-

lowness, the shallowness of affairs———Actually, of nothing happening

Here boredom is compared to "being submerged in the flood of people," a sort of urban analog to the anemone's condition. On the other hand, because it is capable of dreaming (at least in Oppen's version), the sea anemone might represent the endurance of concern and novelty against the deadening effects of routine. However the "conceit" is being used, Oppen is clearly trying to find an image of reduced nature, a biological reality that challenges the theological and metaphysical. In its published version, the image of the sea anemone cannot be interpreted symbolically; it is one of those "heartless" words that must be interrogated over time and through the poem.

This refusal of the anemone to become symbol is all the more evident when we look at a page upon which it makes an earlier appearance. Unlike the final published version in which all lines are relatively long, the typescript page contains a variety of prose and lined verse forms (Fig. 5). The image of the sea anemone is contained in considerably shorter lines and seems to respond to a previous prose remark:

> Impossible to use a word without finally wondering what one means by it. I would find that I mean nothing, that everything remained precisely as it was without the word, or else that I am naming absolute implausibilities, which are moreover the worst of all nightmares

The attempt to name, to "use a word without finally wondering what one means by it," leads to a cycle of repetition in which the only thing to say is that "we die":

> We die we die we die
>
> All there is to say
> The sea-anemeone dreamed of somethong
> No reason he shoul d not
> Or each one does
> Filtering the sea water thru his body

I have retained Oppen's typos and misspellings to indicate how, at least in his early writing of it, the sea anemone was closely identified

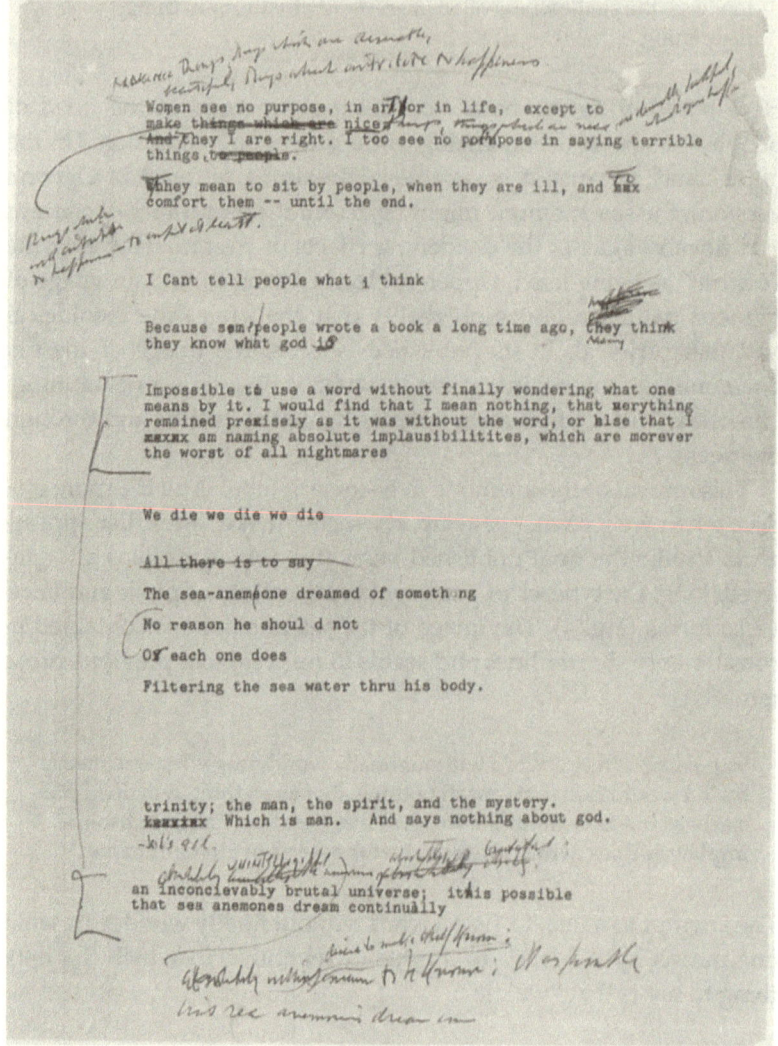

Figure 5. George Oppen, "Women see no purpose..."—manuscript page.

with the individual. The pronoun "one" is hidden in the misspelled word "anemeone," and "somethong" is explicitly developed in the penultimate two lines (deleted from the published version). These two lines also provide an alternate antecedent for "his" in the final line, uniting anemone and human subject. Oppen wants to link human mortality with that of other creatures—as if to say "each one of us is like the sea anemone, living in a perpetual state of boredom, filtering the world rather than reflecting upon it. In this state all we can say of existence is that 'we die.'"

This existential fact is not alleviated by theological alternatives. In the published version, Oppen stresses "The purity of the materials, *not theology*, but to present the circumstances" (emphasis added), but in the typescript version an attack on theology becomes the central feature, directly linked to Oppen's concern with language: "Because some people wrote a book a long time ago, they think they know what god is." This remark on the limitations of an authorizing logos is extended later in a definition of the trinity as "the man, the spirit, and the mystery. / Which is man. And says nothing about god." In pencil, Oppen has added "Job's God," a remark that may very well have inspired the final remark: "an inconceivably brutal universe; it is possible that sea anemones dream continually." Clearly a logocentric world view is inadequate to the brutality of the universe, a disparity given secular force by the image of the anemone and salvific force by the story of Job.

What we see in the typescript page but not in the published poem is the dialogue between individual sections, each responding to and qualifying the previous. The sections are linked, one to the next, in a debate or argument over the efficacy of language in a "brutal universe." Language is both the vehicle and the object of Oppen's speculations as he oscillates between competing propositions. Such dialectical progress can be seen in the published version to be sure, but the page—with its spelling mistakes, holograph emendations, and variable lineation—provides a "graphic" indication of how immediate and personal that progress is. Where the published page provides us with a series of more or less balanced (if truncated) prose statements on the theme of language, the typescript page provides us with the "graphic voice" out of which that theme emerges. The page shows Oppen grousing about difficulties of self-expression, the image of the sea-anemone serving as a satiric version of the poet himself dreaming in his watery environment. The sea anemone, rather than serving as an icon of either boredom or conscious reflection, is a term around which all other sections constellate. It does not "serve" the poet's purpose but gets in his way, forces him to ask each question anew.

## THE ARCHIVE

The varieties of intentions I have described on one page are repeated throughout Oppen's archive. Like the individual page, the archive returns a quality of voice and physicality to work that may seem, in its published version, hermetic and isolated. In terms that I have already employed, the archive revises generic expectations, turning lines of poetry into quotations, queries, and speculations. As this chapter's epigraph suggests, Oppen was engaged in "Piling up pieces of paper to find the words" that would ultimately become poems. The archive is the physical remains of that piling up and deserves to be described as a text in its own right.

As the onetime curator of the Archive for New Poetry, I had a unique chance to view Oppen's papers in their pristine state, before they were divided up into separate categories according to genre (manuscripts, notes, correspondence, daybooks, etc.). When I first opened the boxes in which the papers were sent, I was not prepared for the chaos that appeared. Where some archives come in folders or envelopes with dates or other identifying marks on them, Oppen's papers appeared as a great midden with shards of writing in every conceivable form, no one page related to the next. A page containing a verse from the early 1960s would be followed by a page with scribbles from his last days. Prose and poetry were interspersed with grocery lists, phone numbers, quotations from philosophers, observations on films, tables of contents from books (his own and others). Every conceivable type of paper had been used, from cheap, high-acid newsprint (seriously decaying and flaking) to letterhead bond. Writing had been performed equally by typewriter and pen, the former often heavily annotated by the latter. Occasionally, passages of particular importance had been circled by crayons or felt-tipped pencil. Each manuscript page was like the collection as a whole: a marvelously scribbled, jumbled, and chaotic written field.

Although the bulk of the collection consists of individual pages like those already discussed, there are numerous larger manuscripts made up of anything from two to several hundred pages. In some cases, these manuscripts consist of a final typed draft of poems for a book, but in most cases the gathering is simply a heterogeneous scatter of poems, jottings, and typings. The methods by which these groupings are held together deserve some comment. Oppen used a variety of fasteners—from safety pins, pieces of wire, and pipe cleaners to ring binders. The manuscript for the poem "The Little Pin" is held together, appropriately enough, by a little pin. Another batch of pages is held together by a nail driven through the upper left-hand corner into a piece of plywood. A better definition of Objectivism cannot be imagined.

Oppen's method of composition can be best glimpsed by considering what I will call his "palimpsestic" manuscripts: pages of individual poems onto which new lines or stanzas have been glued so that the revised draft seems to rise vertically off the page in a kind of thick, textual impasto. Rather than add new lines on fresh sheets of paper, he would build his poem on top of itself, adding new lines, in many cases ten or twelve pages thick. One such palimpsest, containing work from *The Materials*, appropriately enough given the title, is "built" out of a ring binder. On the front and back inside covers, Oppen glued the entire script for a reading given at the Guggenheim Museum, including his own interlinear commentary.[6] The binder's metal clasps hold part of a manila envelope (addressed to the Oppens in Brooklyn) to which other drafts and fragments are glued. The whole pile of pages is held together by pipe cleaners that are wrapped, at the top, around a number 2 pencil and a one-inch roundhead screw.[7]

My purpose in describing the material component of Oppen's work is to suggest the degree to which writing was first and foremost a matter of something ready-to-hand—as immediate as a coat hanger or piece of wire. The pipe cleaners, metal clasps, and glue are visible representations of those "little words" that Oppen liked so well, the basic materials of a daily intercourse. "Gone for Breakfast in Z coffee shop across the street," reads the back of one heavily scribbled folder, indicating that the recto of poetry easily became the verso of daily living. And just as he used whatever writing surface was nearby, so he drew upon the "signage" that surrounded him: newspapers, books, magazines, and, of course, conversations, parts of which can be found recorded through the collection. Oppen did not keep a separate notebook for poems and another for quotations and another for prose but, rather, joined all of them together in a continuing daybook.[8] One finds drafts of letters to friends on pages that contain the beginnings of poems. In many cases, a quotation from a newspaper would become the genesis of a poem, a poem the genesis for a prose commentary on an article in the newspaper.

This daily, unbound diary covers an extraordinary range of subjects: the youth culture of the 1960s, the civil rights movement, rock and roll, the poetics of Imagism, the work of John Berryman ("shameless but seductive"), Jung, the Vietnam War, the Altamont concert, Elizabeth Bishop's "The Fish" ("I had always thought 'o to be like the Chinook' was the silliest line ever written, but I see that it is not"), Charles Olson on PBS ("giving birth to the continent out of his head like Jove"), Plato, Hegel, and Marx. His comments on Robert Lowell's "Skunk Hour" are worth quoting in full:

> perhaps I simply do not understand the Christian sense of "sin." I do not understand a sin by which no one was injured. If the people in the love cars were embarrassed by his peeking, then it was a sin. If not, it was merely undignified.

Or his remarks on Pound:

> —and if Pound had walked into a factory a few times the absurdity of Douglas' theory of value, which Pound truculently repeats in the *Cantos* would have dawned on him—it sometimes pays to have a look And to keep still till one has seen.

Treated palimtextually, such remarks elucidate that trinity of concerns that informs Oppen's entire life: politics, epistemology, and poetics. The archive suggests that all three are inextricably united like those jerry-rigged manuscripts held together with pipe cleaners. As he meditated on contradictions in American politics, so he drafted poems; as he drafted poems, so he thought about the relationship of old age to love. The manuscripts do not suggest someone working toward the perfect lyric but one struggling for a vision of society in which the poem plays an instrumental role. To adapt a remark on the page mentioned earlier, Oppen "knows what he thinks but not what he will find."

## RECALCITRANT SILENCES: SUSAN HOWE'S SALVAGE HISTORICISM

John Taggart records a conversation in which Oppen claimed that "he did not think of his books as collections of individual poems but as developments of a thought" (259). The study of Oppen's manuscript certainly verifies this developmental aspect of his writing and suggests the need for an alternate mode of analysis that takes the entire archive—including its material form—into account. As I have pointed out in my introduction, much modernist criticism has defined "materiality" in rhetorical terms—the foregrounding of poetic devices and defamiliarizing of language—thus validating artisanal aspects of the poem to the exclusion of the social world in which it is produced. For Oppen, materiality implies "objects" and the realms of value that objects constellate:

> There are things
> We live among "and to see them
> Is to know ourselves".
>         (*Collected Poems* 147)

Oppen's use of the inclusive pronoun "ourselves" marks the limits of his humanism, his participation in a modernist epistemological project. But, for a woman poet, what does it mean to "know ourselves" when "she" is often the object known, the materiality formed (or observed) by the male author. What does it mean to gain self-knowledge when interiority has been appropriated into the masculine gaze? Emily Dickinson frames this conundrum as a form of gothic horror:

> Oneself behind ourself, concealed—
> Should startle most—
> Assassin hid in our Apartment
> Be Horror's least.
>         (*Collected Poems* 333)

Dickinson's "Oneself behind ourself" unsettles not because of her medusan strangeness but because she is nearer-to-hand, "hid in our Apartment." These are questions that Susan Howe often asks in her work, but she asks them through textual practices that foreground the difficulty of reading. Since many of her lines physically overlap, leaving little room to read them, she calls attention to the physicality of the print medium and its presumed transparency to something more "real" beyond the page. She shares Oppen's poetics of the fragmentary, metonymic text, yet where Oppen's palimtext is immanent—a residue of sources from which the lyric emerges—Howe's page raises such sources as the textual field, the archive, in which the lyric voice is produced. Moreover, whereas Oppen's epistemological horizon is marked by a universal (male) subject, Howe's field is composed of specific historical speakers (women, native Americans, sexual others) who have been refused a voice altogether.

As Peter Quartermain observes, there is a "deceptively literary or bookish" quality to Susan Howe's work (182). References to editors, editions, dictionaries, textual variants, and corrupt texts abound in her interviews and essays, and most of her poems involve readings of passages from historical and literary authors. Many poems collage quotations taken from other sources, often superimposed upon each other to complicate their decipherment. She is, to adapt one of Howe's favorite quotations from Coleridge, a "library cormorant" who dives into the sea of books in search of lost or erased voices. Like Robert Duncan, her scholarly curiosity is that of an especially adept listener who struggles with recalcitrant silences. Howe's task of listening is complicated by the fact that persons who are speechless leave few records, and when they do their words become the province of official clerics, publishers, and editors who mediate and distort access to them.

This distortion forms the basis of an argument that Howe has with Thomas Johnson and the Belknap Press of Harvard University, whose 1955 edition of Emily Dickinson's poems normalized that most idiosyncratic and experimental of New England writers. When Howe titles her book on the poet *My Emily Dickinson,* her possessive pronoun announces its proprietary claim. No disinterested perspective here; this will be *her* Emily Dickinson, much as that author appropriated George Eliot upon reading of the British novelist's death in 1880:

> The look of the words as they lay in the print I shall never forget. Not their face in the casket could have had the eternity to me. Now, *my* George Eliot. The gift of belief which her greatness denied her, I trust she receives in the childhood of the kingdom of heaven. (*Letters* 3:700)

Dickinson's contrast of the textual body—Eliot's obituary lying in print like a corpse in a coffin—to the redeemed body resurrected in the poet's appropriation speaks to Howe's efforts at reviving the "kingdom of heaven" in New England's green and pleasant land. Howe's act of redemption begins with that textual body as materialized flesh from which "the gift of belief" begins.

*My Emily Dickinson* reveals the Amherst poet as an experimentalist whose daring is manifest in her holograph page—its use of spacing, orthography, lineation, and the inclusion of variant words at the end of the poem. It is also evident in the way Dickinson constructed her poems in fascicles or poetic series, a method that challenges the integrity of the single, metaphysical lyric upon which her reputation has been based. But Howe is not interested simply in rescuing the "real" Emily Dickinson from a faulty edition; she wants to materialize the complexity and contradictoriness of American frontier ideology as it is embodied in a woman who lived on the intellectual and geographic margins of the modern era. In Dickinson, Howe sees evidence of a kind of antinomian resistance that has threatened the American errand historically and that continues to challenge latter-day versions of manifest destiny. Attempts to marginalize Dickinson as the "myth of Amherst" or to regularize her poems in standard editions are symptomatic of a larger intolerance of female creativity and social otherness in American society. Howe's own experimentalism is similarly implicated.

What we might call Howe's "salvage historicism" begins, as I said above, in silence—in a not-said that is both textual (the page as inscription or trace of an absence) and historical (the word of God as hieroglyph in nature).[9] In Alice Jardine's terms, the gendered form of this not-said is "gynesis"—the "putting into discourse of 'woman'"—within a male sexual economy on which western patriarchal thought has erected a subject (25). Howe's poetry attempts to reveal a hermeneutic of power in the nation's early exploration and colonization that continues well into the modern era. This hermeneutic attempts to inscribe a divine intent (and, later, a market imperative) upon a "virgin" wilderness, figured as female.[10] Building upon American literary historians such as Perry Miller and Sacvan Bercovich, Howe retells the story of Puritan origins with an eye to excessive or nonconforming interpretations that defy biblical exegesis. Building on French feminist theorists such as Luce Irigaray and Julia Kristeva, she retells the story of gendered origins with an eye to female subjectivities marginalized within patriarchal culture. Marginal spaces in both historical and physical texts become privileged sites of recuperation and agency.[11]

American authors have often regarded themselves as privileged readers, but certain "isolatos" from Anne Hutchinson and Mary Rowlandson through Melville and Dickinson to Gertrude Stein and Hart Crane have "spoken" in the margins of their texts of a New

Jerusalem preempted, as Howe says, "by our predatory founding fathers" ("Women and Their Effect" 90). Escaping such predation means telling the truth but telling it slant, creating a text that acknowledges its inscription in the father's text. Mary Rowlandson's narrative of captivity, to take one example, speaks in the rhetoric of Calvinism ("Thus the Lord carried me along from one time to another") at the same time that it expresses anxiety about the violence forced upon native populations by early settlement. Rowlandson is not simply a dissenting Puritan; in her attempt to reconcile the violence of her captivity with the violence perpetrated upon her captors, she "saw what she did not see said what she did not say," a remark that could describe the curious angle of vision that animates Howe's work (*Birth-mark* 12).

## IN MELVILLE'S MARGINS

> History may be a record written by winners, but don't forget Nixon taped himself for posterity. If you are a woman, archives hold perpetual ironies. Because the gaps and silences are where you find yourself.
> (Howe, *Birth-mark*, 158)

In many of her poems, Susan Howe finds herself in a library, staring at a page in a little-used book. That page might be from Shelley's manuscript book, held at the Bodleian Library at Oxford (Fig. 6). The editors of Shelley's manuscript books, Donald H. Reiman and Hélène Dworzan Reiman, have patiently rendered the poet's holograph—his excisions, deletions, and doodling—and have provided a typewritten transcription on facing pages (Fig. 7). One such page that Howe reprints in *The Birth-mark* is drawn from a notebook recovered from the boat in which Shelley drowned off Leghorn in 1822, "pulled from the bottom of the sea . . . heavily damaged by water, mildew and restoration" (20). The page has suffered physical damage, yet it forms a fascinating ideogram for a poet whose life was taken prematurely in death by water. Milton's and Shakespeare's names, superimposed upside down, hover over Shelley's page like spirit guides, emblems perhaps "of love & health." Writing on the verso bleeds through the paper, giving depth to the two-dimensional surface, much as Milton and Shakespeare's names gesture beyond the poem being composed. Howe is fascinated by Shelley's page as a

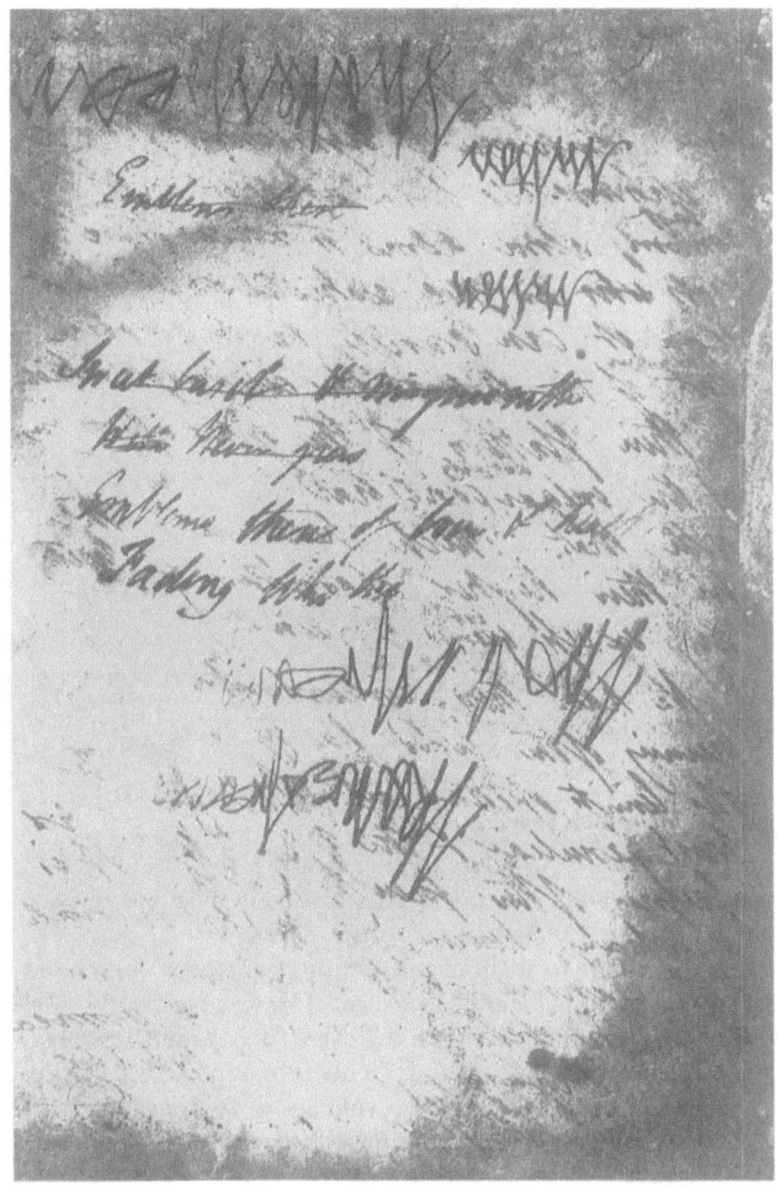

Figure 6. Percy Bysshe Shelley, page from Shelley's Manuscript Book (Bodleian MS. Shelley adds. e. 20: Quire II Folio 2 Recto = 2 Recto).

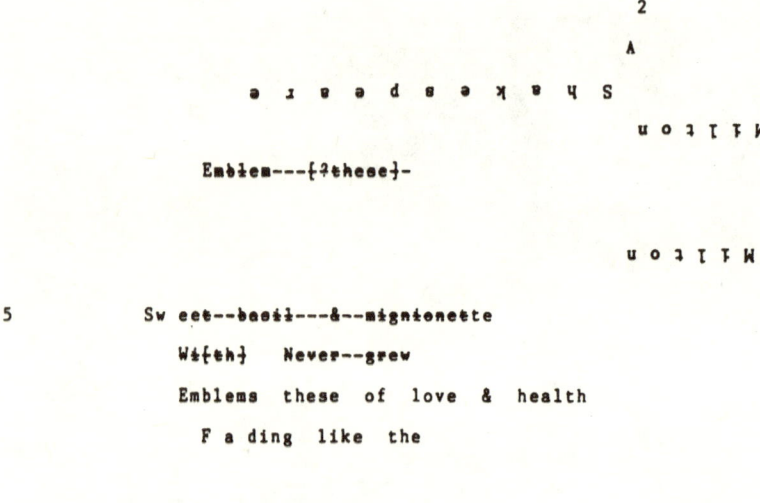

Figure 7. Transcription of Shelley manuscript page by Donald H. Reiman and Hélène Dworzan Reiman.

visual field in which the poet's processes of writing and revision, sketching and speculating, are returned to view.[12]

The sea change wrought by poet musing upon poet, verso bleeding through recto, is the explicit subject of Howe's 1991 work, "Melville's Marginalia," in which she discovers Shelley quite literally in the margins of Melville's reading. In her introduction to the series, she describes uncovering the two volumes of *Melville's Marginalia* in a library while doing research for a course that she was giving on the novelist (*Nonconformist's Memorial* 89). These volumes contain all of the annotations Melville made in the books of his library—including works by Shelley. The editor of the volume, Wilson Walker Cowen, notes that some of the annotations—particularly those concerning women—have been erased. "The misogynous nature of the markings suggests that he was too much bothered by the subject to trust himself to write about it" (Cowen, xix). The erasure of women in Melville, either by himself or by his wife, provides a subtext for Howe's larger interest in the marginalization of others in mid-century anglophone culture.

It is not only the feminine that has been erased from Melville; Howe feels that aspects of his political views have been excluded from critical consideration, especially his refusal, best represented by Bartleby, of mercantile America and of the emergent capitalist machine in mid-century America. Through her reading of Melville's marginalia, Howe surmises that Bartleby is based on the figure of an Irish poet and Catholic rebel, James Clarence Mangan.[13] Melville knew of Mangan's life and works and made copious annotations in John Mitchel's biographical introduction to Mangan's 1859 edition of poems. Mangan worked as a scrivener during his early career and like Bartleby registered, as David Lloyd says, "a chronic sense of psychic wretchedness throughout his life" (29). Although "Bartleby the Scrivener" was written in 1853 and Mitchel's edition was published in 1859, Howe insists that Mangan was well known in America by 1850 (some accounts comparing him with Edgar Allan Poe), and thus the creation of Melville's scrivener out of the Irish poet, translator, and reformer was not altogether impossible. Such speculative joining of historical author and literary character reinforces the collective implications of Bartleby's "I would prefer not to," taking it out of the psychological realm where it is usually found and placing it in the historical circumstances of antebellum urban life. Bartleby's refusal to participate in corporate America (Melville's subtitle is "A Story of Wall Street") and Mangan's refusal to participate in British cultural institutions suggest a common strain between the two figures.

Howe states that she began to write the work "by pulling a phrase, sometimes just a word or a name, at random from Cowen's alphabetically arranged *Melville's Marginalia*, and letting that lead [her] by free association to each separate poem in the series" (105). But she adds a caveat that "free association isn't free" and that the lines linking marginal text to her own speculations are informed by more than propinquity. To take one example, the fact that Mangan lived on Fishamble Street during his childhood resonates with the fact that Shelley gave his "Address to the Irish People" on that same street when Mangan was nine years old.[14] Thus, we are provided with circumstantial evidence for an otherwise undocumented meeting between the two supporters of Irish nationalism.

What drives these associations are tenuous links among widely disparate anglophone authors—from Melville and Mangan to Shelley, Massinger, and Joyce—who represent political resistance and mass appeal that stand in opposition to British cultural elitism, embodied by someone such as Matthew Arnold. These authors form what Deleuze and Guattari call a "minor literature," a literary culture that exists in the interstices of the dominant. A minor literature is defined by its linguistic deterritorialization (Irish or American writers writing in English), its political immediacy, and its "collective assemblage of enunciation" (18). A major literature, in David Lloyd's terms, involves the production of "an autonomous ethical identity for the subject" buttressed by an aesthetics of disinterestedness and a canon of self-evident classics (19). Mangan's refusal to publish in British journals, his writing in "low" genres such as the ballad, and his translation of non-European languages (Welsh, Turkish, Persian) place him well outside the major (e.g., British) national tradition. When Howe free associates on a "word or name" chosen at random from Melville's marginal jottings, she does so through the optic provided by Mangan, Shelley, and Joyce in their search for alternate national identities. Her text coalesces these identities into a conversation that never took place but that *could* have taken place in the margins of Melville's reading.[15]

If a minor literature is occluded by an ideology of disinterested aesthetics and national consensus, how is it to be seen? Howe's answer is to provide us, at least in part 1 of the series, with a text that is almost unreadable, in which deciphering the page implicates the reader in the tasks of archival recovery, interpretation, and revision that preoccupy the author. Lines are juxtaposed at odd angles, occasionally violating normal typographic spacing and overlapping one another (Fig. 8). Peter Quartermain notes that such jumbling ("skumbling" is Howe's phrase) of textual materials calls attention to itself as "text, as written rather than spoken language" (184).[16] We could extend this remark to say that by subverting the voice, the text as mark of absence begins to "speak" on its own terms. Since Howe's ostensible subject, Melville, never "speaks" except through the words of others, he is therefore "spoken through" his reading.

While such typographic display might suggest a kind of absolut-

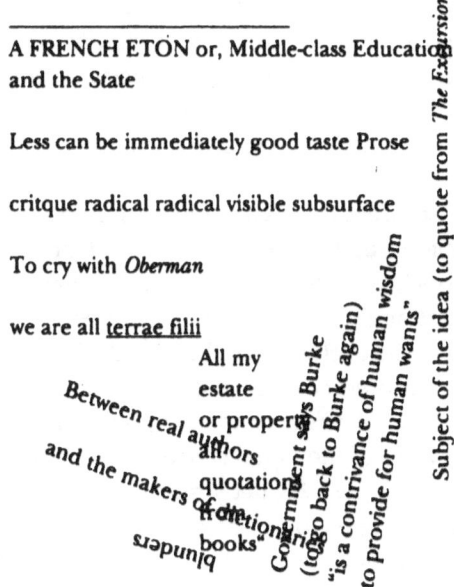

Figure 8. Susan Howe, from "Melville's Marginalia" in *The Nonconformist's Memorial*.

ism of the word, its function is to reveal language as productive agent in social speech.[17] Arnold's "The Function of Criticism," from which the lines in Figure 8 are taken, worries over threats to bourgeois normalcy by collectivism and mass culture, vaunting instead a disinterested criticism based on "the best that is known and thought." Melville quotes at length from Arnold's satire of the new middle-class morality:

> We are all *terrae filii* . . . all Philistines together. . . . Let us have no nonsense about independent criticism and intellectual delicacy, and the few and the many; don't let us trouble ourselves over foreign thought; we shall invent the whole thing for ourselves as we go along; . . . we are all in the mass movement, we are all liberals, we are all in pursuit of truth. (Cowen 23)

The critic's duty, Arnold concludes, is to refuse mass movements and liberal thought, "or if resistance is vain, at least to cry, with Oberman, *Perissons en resistant* [Let us perish resisting]" (23). Howe's textual collage destroys the force of Arnold's condescending rhetoric and reveals its class biases. Oberman, the hero of Étienne Pivert de Senancour's psychological novel, is not permitted to utter his defiant appeal. The line immediately following "to cry, with Oberman" is that of the Philistine—"We are all *terrae filii*"—sons of the earth. Howe seems to be saying that Oberman's admirable appeal to resistance is neutralized when it depends on the exclusion of others, when political resistance is invoked to justify aesthetic distance. And by quoting fragments of lines that foreground notions of "good taste," "real authors," and Eton, Howe suggests that Arnold's "best that is known and thought" is an ideological category, promulgated by a cultural elite to the exclusion of those—like Mangan and Shelley—who yoked their literary careers to mass movements. By taking Arnold's comments out of context and by typographically enjambing them, we hear the voice of the moral censor whom Melville internalized as his British antagonist. Bartleby may lapse into silence, but he continues to speak through Howe's page.

Such considerations of literary authority form a consistent theme in *Melville's Marginalia*. Howe interrogates the division between an emerging aesthetic culture and mass society during the Victorian period. For an American author such as Melville, who had gained early popularity through the adventure novels *Typee* and *Omoo* and whose later novels continued to draw on urban sensationalists such as Edgar Allan Poe and George Lippard, the accusation of provinciality rankled, especially in light of the dismal reception of *Moby Dick* and *Pierre*. Many of Howe's lyrics in part 1 are based on Melville's annotations to Matthew Arnold's *Essays in Criticism*, particularly those portions that deal with threats to middle-class society by popular genres and expressive styles. Melville's feelings of inferiority in the face of Arnold's francophilic, classist rhetoric can be felt in Howe's montage of passages:

> So baneful
>     He could not storm the alphabet of art
>       bête      x[Bestial?]
>     and social weakness
> A style so bent on effect and the expense of soul
> so far from classic truth and grace
> must surely be said to have the note of
>           PROVINCIALITY
>
> (96)

In this passage, accusations of provinciality are leveled by Arnold at the historian A. W. Kinglake, author of *The Invasion of the Crimea* (1863), whose style is dismissed as journalistic ("it has glitter without warmth, rapidity without ease, effectiveness without charm" [Cowen 26]). The passages are taken from Arnold's "The Literary Influence of Academies," which deals with the humanizing force of the French Academy and the corresponding absence of same in Britain, a loss that occasions Arnold's remarks on the disadvantages of a literary style "so bent on effect and the expense of soul."

Although Howe draws seemingly at random from Arnold's essay, her arrangement of lines exploits alliterative possibilities of certain words associated with the French word *bête* (beast). Arnold uses it to describe a "blank defect of intelligence" in Kinglake's writing. Melville's translation in brackets, "Bestial," is one of the few moments in his marginalia when he speaks in propria persona, yet it offers a brief intervention into Arnold's celebration of French culture and language. "Bête" picks up the third syllable of "alphabet" in the previous line, thus turning an accusation ("He could not storm the alphabet of art") into an actual "storming" of the alphabet to yield new meanings. The alliteration of "b" sounds continues in the word "baneful," which in the original passage reads as follows: "So baneful to the style of even the cleverest man may be the total want of checks" (27). However "baneful" Arnold may have found the excessive style of this "cleverest man," Howe's alliteration ("bête," "bestial," "baneful," and "bent") turns reasoned polemic into excessive music. Thus, Melville's anxiety about provinciality becomes an indictment of Arnold's elitist rhetoric.

### STRUCK AGAINST PARENTHESIS

"In Billy Budd 'the stutter is the plot.'"
Charles Olson, quoted in *The Birth-mark*

One might say of Susan Howe that in *Melville's Marginalia* she is attempting to render the stutter of American national rhetoric. Shelley becomes a key ingredient in this project not because he necessarily influenced Melville or Mangan but because his own minoritized status—as radical, as rhetorically excessive, as supporter of Irish nationalism—becomes a model for the engaged (in Arnold's terms, "bestial") writer. Shelley's notebooks, which dominate part 2 of *Melville's Marginalia*, display this stammer graphically:

Narcis if I h
"Forct" in copy
"h" from bough
Thissby this
hishis spirit
I th For th

If I am the N
This is an error
Fy
       (118)

What appear to be random copy-editing notes, taken from Shelley's notebooks, contain a playful narrative of sexual doubling and repetition. The figure of Narcissus that opens the passage is a copy or is "in copy" of himself; "hishis spirit" represents the duplication of identity embodied in his watery mirror. As an allegory of homosexual desire, Narcissus yearns for the same, a desire that within compulsory heterosexuality is regarded as error, a denial of difference. Sexual mistakes and textual errors collide in such passages to suggest forms of expression broken or closeted. "Fy" or "fye" on men who love men, the moral censor seems to say, but Howe makes of error a new text.

The theme of error is broached in the next poem, in which Howe consults Shelley's manuscript page during his last year:

> Shelley's pen slipped
> referring to the Sun
> Isle Continent Ocean
> The date July 1st 1822
> across "?fury" may be
> "day" or "fiery"
> by mischief superimposed on *wild*
> tercet mask tercet
> (119)

Here, Howe discovers slips of the pen that provide a haunting anticipation of Shelley's drowning. From "Sun" we are led through "Isle Continent Ocean" and from "fury" to "wild." Howe does not attempt to link these words rhetorically but allows them to remain incomplete, not unlike marginal comments themselves. The last line, "tercet mask tercet" would seem to refer to the terza rima of *The Triumph of Life* and to the masks within masks that make up its narrative. The reference also looks further back to *Prometheus Unbound*, a masque whose central character embodies all of the miswritten terms: "fury," "day," "fiery," and "wild."

In the next poem of the sequence, Howe develops the Promethean reference further:

> Travelling in the direction
> of an imagination of morning
> he was brought back mortal
> Struck against parenthesis
> across an anarchy of light
> Dare I uncreate Prometheus
> Chorus Semichorus Semichorus
> flame in greek by a copyist
> (120)

Here the references to Mediterranean landscape in the previous poem are linked to the poet's death. By confusing nautical journey with writing ("Struck against parenthesis"), Howe suggests the inextricable relationship between oppositions (poetry/history, history/text, text/practice) that for a deconstructive critic such as Paul de Man signify poetic language's irreconcilability.[18] This poem seems to ask whether or not Shelley's fatal journey was not always anticipated in his poetry—as though the "anarchy of light" that brings forth ruin to Prometheus is also the fire of social reform that Shelley hoped to bring to a benighted Europe. That these realms were confused in his work can be seen on the notebook page, recovered from its marginal status in the poet's oeuvre through Howe's poem. The fact that these speculations derive from reading in the margins of another Promethean questor doublet (Melville/Ahab) makes them all the more provocative.

One might say that *Melville's Marginalia* contains its own marginality insofar as it refuses closure, either by reference to Shelley's informing spirit or by some totalizing theory of textuality that will liberate all signifiers. It demands that we consider the page not as the background upon which questions are asked but as the questioning itself, an interchange between authors and characters, words and variants, texts and margins. Howe acknowledges Shelley's Promethean goals for social amelioration, even as she calls attention to their constructed and discursive character. Moreover, the poem is fully conscious of its own marginal status within a tradition of avant-garde textual practices for which Shelley and Melville are antecedents. Hers is, as she says, an "author-evacuated text" in which the absence of a central voice carves out a space where other identities may speak (*Nonconformist's Memorial* 113).

### "I WILL DISMEMBER MARGINALIA"

In this chapter, I have attempted to expand genre theory by looking at two examples of a writing for which there is no name. Attempts to classify Oppen's poems under Objectivist principles of direct presentation or Howe's under various theories of Language-writing do not account for the material character of their work or for the social implications of such materialization. A palimtextual study of poetry would look not only at the poem in relation to similar poems (the traditional task of genre study) but to the writing each poem displaces, a displacement "represented" in the manuscript as a kind of overwriting. When that displacement is seen as a "dismembering" of marginal comments to reveal cultural hierarchies, the poem as palimtext becomes a window onto forces of stabilization in the culture at large. Both Oppen and Howe distrust the instrumental character of much engaged verse; for them, poetry retains its function as aesthetic alternative to rationalized society. At the same time, both poets see their work as fatally complicit with that society, as physical and contingent as the paper on which it is written.

Oddly enough, we can see their relationship to a social nexus best in those areas where an audience is least invited: in the poet's papers and manuscripts, in overlapping lines of typed print. What we learn from the material fact of archive and page is the degree to which poems are a temporal process of marking and remarking, of response and contention. The terms of intertextuality, as developed by Barthes and Kristeva, describe only the transposition of signifying systems, not the forms of that transposition, the layering of physical documents and their institutional origins. "Poems should echo and reecho against each other," Jack Spicer says; "They should create resonances. They cannot live alone any more than we can" (61). More self-consciously antigeneric texts, like those of Susan Howe, far from distinguishing themselves from the past, force us to look at traditional forms from new perspectives. Shakespeare's heavily annotated acting folios, Blake's illustrated books, Emily Dickinson's fascicles, and Pound's ideogram-encrusted late cantos are examples of a materializing tendency in every writer, a tendency that gets lost in the attempt to establish copy text. So long as we search for "new" genres in the interstices of the old, we will be searching within the terms of normative criticism that seeks consensus among dissimilar elements. We will fail to see processes that occur at (or *in*) the margins of the material artifact, an object that can never be recovered strictly within textual terms. If that object fails to stay in one place, perhaps it is because it is the trajectory rather than the fulfillment of writing.

# 3

## "From the Latin *Speculum*"
### Ezra Pound, Charles Olson, and Philology

### THE LEXICAL INSERT

One of the more unusual gestures to be found in recent poems is what could be called the "lexical insert." The poet turns to the dictionary in order to provide a gloss on a word or phrase, the etymology being included as part of the poem itself. In Robert Duncan's "At the Loom," for example, the words "warp" and "shuttle" are subjected to such an etymological gloss as the poet seeks to find in their roots something of the sensuous richness they once exhibited:

> warp, **wearp, varp:** "cast of a net, a laying of eggs"
> from *\*warp-* "to throw"
>
>> the threads twisted for strength
>>> that can be a warp of the will.
>
> **"O weaver, weaver, work no more,"**
>> Gascoyne is quoted:
> **"thy warp hath done me wrong."**
>
> And the shuttle carrying the woof I find
>> was **skutill** "harpoon" —a dart, an arrow,
>> or a little ship,
>
>> **navicula      weberschiff,**
>
> crossing and recrossing from shore to shore—
>
> prehistoric   *\*skutil   *\*skut-*
>> "a bolt, a bar, as of a door"
>> "a flood-gate"
>
>> (*Bending the Bow* 12)

Duncan's gloss, taken from the *Oxford English Dictionary*, follows the words back through their Anglo-Saxon roots, imitating in the twisted threads of etymology and citation the "forward and back movement" of the shuttle. The poem's lineation, with its variable indentations and spacings, assists the image of the shuttle moving back and forth across the page, "crossing and recrossing from shore to shore." The lexical insert serves both to return a certain materiality to the word (the warp as a dart or arrow, the shuttle as a door or floodgate) and to illustrate the "loom of language" that is the poem's subject. But it does something more; it foregrounds etymological research as an act in itself, a dimension of the poem's composition. Instead of simply verifying a word's origins, the lexical insert testifies to the word's life in the present.

We could see Duncan's use of the dictionary as part of a larger modernist concern with philology that originates with such nineteenth-century figures as Bopp, Schlegel, Renan, Von Humboldt, and Herder. As Edward Said points out, philology is synonymous with modernism, "a way of historically setting oneself off, as great artists do, from one's time and an immediate past even as, paradoxically and antinomically, one actually characterizes one's modernity by so doing" (*Orientalism* 132). The "new philology" (as opposed to the theological hermeneutics of the preclassical era) involves the classification of languages into families and the identification of specific properties within each one. Language becomes an object of speculation in itself, a living organism with its own internal laws and powers of generation not unlike those that the natural sciences were discovering in nature. When Emerson claimed that "language is fossil poetry," he was reflecting a pervasive attitude among nineteenth-century thinkers who saw in the structure of language analogies with the organic world. Emerson's phrase offers more than a figure of speech; it reflects a distinctly modern tendency to see language as the trace of an earlier, living organism:

> As the limestone of the continent consists of infinite masses of the shells of animalcules, so language is made up of images or tropes, which now, in their secondary use, have long ceased to remind us of their poetic origins. (231)

According to Emerson, the poet is one who not only names the world but, through the new positive sciences ("astronomy, chemistry, vegetation and animation" are advocated), digs back to a word's material manifestation in nature.

Emerson may have been the first to think of the poet as philological archaeologist, but he was certainly not the last. For the modernist generation of writers, philology provided a secular guide to lost cultural plenitude by means of scientific procedures of comparison and analysis. *Ulysses,* the *Cantos,* "The Waste Land," and *Helen in Egypt* are archaeological digs through Western (and occasionally Eastern) culture, impelled by discoveries in comparative philology, archaeology, anthropology, and other fields that emerged during the second half of the nineteenth century. Philology can be felt most forcefully in those literary works just mentioned where the desire to shore cultural fragments against spiritual ruin is expressed by dense layering of texts in many languages. These works search not for an original language bequeathed by God but for a proto-language (Indo-European, Hittite, Semitic), the diaspora of which may be regathered by the polylingual text. "The province of these works," as Hugh Kenner says, "is the entire human race speaking, and in time as well as space" (*Pound Era* 95). The voice of God that speaks out of the thunder in "The Waste Land" compels the quester to "Give, Sympathize, and Control," not because it speaks ex cathedra but because it speaks Sanskrit. If its injunction goes unheeded, it is because we lack a sufficient philological education. Many early modernist poems remain elegies for this particular failure.

The philological imperative in modernism takes many forms. It can be felt in Nietzsche's genealogical critique of morality and in Heidegger's etymological reading of Western metaphysics; it animates the growth of semiotics from Peirce to Saussure and accounts for the various forms of cultural criticism (*Geisteswissenschaften*) that lead to modern sociology and anthropology. Perhaps most significant for our purposes in identifying the links between social and textual materiality, philology emerges simultaneously with the expansion of colonialism. Contact between missionaries, military personnel, capitalist entrepreneurs, foreign office bureaucrats, and indigenous populations necessitated the creation of language guides, dictionaries, and grammars that would assist the colonizing process. Johannes Fabian notes that such guides were "mirrors of ethnic and cultural diversity; they could become instruments of government inasmuch as they imposed a semblance of order on a bewildering multitude of languages and helped to create a frame for language policies" (2).

On one level, philological research provided access to "foreign" languages for purposes of commerce and trade, but it served a more insidious function by legitimizing racism and ethnocentrism. Modern nation-states were formed around certain narratives of origin and conquest, buttressed by linguistic theories that would support the myth of a national language and common root system. Edward Said notes that Renan's *Histoire générale et système comparé des langues sémitiques* presents examples of Arabic, Hebrew, and Aramaic languages accompanied by editorial remarks on "defects, virtues, barbarisms and shortcomings in the language, the people, and the civilization" (*Orientalism* 143). The "disinterested character" of oriental philology could thus legitimate colonial power by defining other languages as "inorganic," "underdeveloped," or "immature." Given these parallels between comparative methods in language and eugenically related theories of racial identity, it is not surprising that Pound could develop his anti-Semitism in concert with (not despite) his interests in romance philology, translation, and print culture.

Much has been written about the specific philological interests of modern poets, but less has been said about what is at stake in their use of citations, quotations, translations, and lexicology.[1] Such gestures represent a desire to authenticate the present moment by an appeal to the past—a past preserved in a language still very much alive. The use of citation—the direct quotation from other documents and nonliterary materials—permits the two temporal spheres to exist conjointly, the inserted quotation providing "authentic" evidence that such-and-such happened, and, moreover, that this *present* poet read the original document.[2] Citationality is hardly new.[3] The practice of quoting from previous tales and texts is at least as old as Homer. What is unique about modernist uses of citation—and particularly the use of quotations from philological works—is its historicizing role at a moment when language is under siege from mass cultural phenomena—journalism, dime novels, and new electronic media. As a poetic strategy, the lexical citation foregrounds the institutional authority of philology and its commitment to accuracy and rigor. In a paradox that haunts many modernist poems, the text's novelty is established by its ability to bracket the past *as past*. At the same time, the act of showing one's lexical research—the display of the dictionary—emphasizes the current status of language by showing its contingency within the life of the poet.

Leonard Diepeveen has discussed the implications of such display in his important book, *Changing Voices*. He distinguishes between "allusion," the use of source texts that have been manipulated or altered by the poet, and "quotation," in which a source text is reproduced without mediation. Allusion in a poet such as T. S. Eliot signals the author's control over the source text, his ability to assimilate borrowings (Dante, Spenser, Baudelaire) into the new work. Quotation, on the other hand, brings with it the "texture of a previously existing text," discursive features of which are important to creating a new, contrasting register (2). What Diepeveen calls the quoting poem is similar to what I am calling the lexical insert in its insistence on the historicity of the source text, its origins in a fundamentally different time and textual space. The strangeness that the lexical insert introduces into the current text is both a rhetorical shift in register and an alienating effect that alters the reading experience. Although Diepeveen sees the quoting poem in service to a distancing tendency in modernism, I see it more as a critical practice whereby the poet establishes the historicity of the present with respect to a past about which he or she has an opinion.

These historicizing tendencies are most thoroughly displayed in the work of Ezra Pound, whose task initially was to efface the seams between languages in an effort to establish continuities between texts in different historical periods, although in the later cantos, as I will point out, he began to expose the seams. Among poets who followed in Pound's footsteps, the lexical insert became increasingly important as a way of validating speculative acts for which no historical precedent could be claimed. Lexical archaeology, then, begins as a way of historicizing value and becomes a way of validating history. The differences between these two tendencies suggest some of the tensions between modern and postmodern poetics in general.

## "DERIVATION UNCERTAIN"

The passage by Robert Duncan that begins this chapter deals with more than etymology; it is a tribute to the originator of certain philologizing tendencies that made a powerful impact on postwar poets:

>     A cat's purr
> in the hwirr thkk   **"thgk, thkk"**
>   of Kirke's loom on Pound's Cantos
>         **"I heard a song of that kind..."**
>             (*Bending the Bow* 11)

Duncan's use of phrases from Canto 39 indicates that the whirring of Pound's linguistic shuttle continues to sound on the later poet's loom. Duncan's permission to quote from the *OED* has been granted by a poet who, in his very first canto, finds it necessary to establish continuity not only with Homer but with Homer's translator: "Andreas Divus, / In officina Wecheli, 1538, out of Homer" (Pound, *Cantos*, 5). An antiquarian's fussiness, perhaps, but to Pound such dates and apprenticeships are part of the fabric that we know as Homer. They inscribe Homer into the cultural nexus by which he may be known at all.

Pound's interest in philology begins with his early work in Romance languages while at the University of Pennsylvania, but from the outset he makes distinctions between philological method and what he, somewhat pompously, calls the "history of masterwork." In *The Spirit of Romance* (1910), Pound distances himself from traditional studies of language, claiming that he has "floundered somewhat ineffectually through the slough of philology" and that he looks forward to a time "when it will be possible for the lover of poetry to study poetry . . . without burdening himself with the rags of morphology, epigraphy, *privatleben* and the kindred delights of the archaeological or 'scholarly' mind" (7). What he has in mind is another kind of comparative method, one that will "weigh Theocritus and Yeats with one balance" and will isolate a particular *virtu* among writers in different historical periods (8). While this may sound like a form of belletristic connoisseurship, Pound's practice is to stress original materials and archival research, to insist that the adept know several national literatures in the original language. Paradoxically, Pound's critique of academic philology proceeds by means of the very methods it stresses—as though by quoting chapter and verse he may assign value to Theocritus and Yeats while indicting those professional, academic structures that remove them from art. Lawrence Rainey points out that in his early cantos Pound "invokes the standards of philological accuracy only to savage the institutional apparatus that sustains them" (68).[4] Thus, Pound's use of citation in the Malatesta cantos makes a double claim: "that his citation follows the rules of his antiphilology, and that only an instrument of this sort enables one to perceive, rescue, and represent the lost vitality of a culture where courtly 'refinement' and colloquial 'levity' had been one" (69).

What sustains Pound's antiphilological sentiment in his studies of medieval romance is the idea of a Mediterranean virtu that links dissimilar times and authors. If all ages are contemporaneous, they are held together by more than their common origins in Latin. They are the product of a "cult of Amor," a psychological *phantastikon* based on the idea of a vitalist universe. A dramatic change in Pound's quasi-Hegelian approach to languages came in 1913 with the discovery of Ernest Fenollosa's papers on the Chinese character, which initiated his interest not only in the ideogram as a method for composition but in Confucian thought as well. The two areas are inextricably intertwined. The Chinese ideogram, as described by Fenollosa, represents the perfect balance between natural image and human construct, action, and sign. In language reminiscent of Emerson, Fenollosa extols the Chinese character's ability to create a "vivid shorthand picture of the operations of nature" (*Chinese Written Character* 8). Pound, while certainly no Emersonian, saw the possibilities offered by the ideogram as means of juxtaposing images in poetry without subordinating them to a discursive frame. At the same time, what he called the "ideogrammic method" allowed him to juxtapose languages from various cultures and historical periods in a single, cultural hieroglyph (*ABC* 17–27). More important, Pound could justify his practice according to supposed "natural" principles; his method would resemble that of the biologist and philologist, who proceed by comparison and observation, not by deductive reasoning.

Beginning with Canto 51, Pound used individual ideograms to focus and articulate the constellating principles of his epic. Lacking a proper sinological education, he relied on dictionaries as well as bilingual translations of Chinese classics such as those by Legge, Pauthier, and Karlgren. In these texts, Pound saw philological speculation at work, words being compared and sources being adduced, and this kind of comparative scholarship provided him with a model for combining research and poetry. He could pursue the eternal truths of Confucianism or Neoplatonic philosophy through histories of dynasties, philosophical works, and chronicles at the same time that he could expose his research *in history* and thus give contemporary validity to those truths.

In the early cantos, lexicology and philology appear via the superposition of texts, one upon the other, to create a relatively seamless, polylinguistic surface. But as the cantos progress, and as Pound

"From the Latin Speculum"   101

delves deeper into chronicle and narrative, his lexical research comes more and more to the surface. In Canto 23, for example, tracing out the Neoplatonic light philosophy of Porphyry, Gemisto, and Psellos, Pound uncovers a fragment of Steisichorus that describes Herakles' tenth labor. Pound quotes the Greek, accompanied by a Latin version:

> With the sun in a golden cup
>     and going toward the low fords of ocean
> "Αλιος δ' 'Υπεριονίδας δέπας ἐσχατέβαινε χρθσεον
> "Οφρα δἰ ὠχεανοίο περάσας
>     ima vada noctis obscurae
> Seeking doubtless the sex in bread-moulds
> "ηλιος, ἅλιος, ἅλιος = μάταιος
> ("Derivation uncertain." The idiot
> Odysseus furrowed the sand.)
>                           (*Cantos* 107)

Coming upon Αλιος ("With the sun in a golden cup"), Pound goes to his *Abridged Greek-English Lexicon* and looks up the word. He discovers that, in addition to meaning "sun," the word could also mean "of the sea" and "fruitless, unprofitable or idle." The latter definition Liddell and Scott qualify as "derivation uncertain." Pound includes not only the Greek words but the editor's remark as well. He then supplies his own "derivation," equally uncertain, by seeing in the word ἅλιος ("fruitless") and μάταιος ("vain," "empty," or "idle") a hidden reference to Odysseus, whose feigned madness kept him, initially, from the journey to Troy. Hence, by exploiting the plural meanings of the word "sun" in Steisichorus, Pound is able to link Herakles' solar journey with Odysseus' marine journey. Pound becomes a third voyager through his philological intervention, turning an editor's remark on the ambiguity of one derivation into a positive association between two mythical travelers.[5]

Such moments of lexical commentary are rare until the late cantos, where Pound begins to show his researches as a prominent element of the poem. As Hugh Kenner points out, the "science" of *Rock-Drill* and *Thrones* is philology, and the two books are replete with textual asides, footnotes, and queries ("*Drafts*" 15). The reasons for this increased use of the lexical insert are several. They could reflect the experience at Pisa, where his reading matter included only Legge's translations of Confucius and a Chinese dictionary. Lacking his usual resources, he was thrown back on himself as subject, a "lone ant" on the broken anthill of contemporary history. Another, more probable, source is Pound's increased interest in Chinese during the St. Elizabeth's period, now not as a method of composition but as a language whose structure and origins were "foreign" to Pound in ways that Western languages were not. In a sense, then, Chinese was Pound's first "foreign" language, and its otherness became part of the poem's concern.

Chinese makes its first major appearance in Cantos 52–71, the "Chinese History Cantos," which remain relatively readable, especially if one has a copy of Mailla's *Histoire générale de la Chine* handy. In a prefatory remark to the sequence, Pound assures us that "foreign words and ideograms . . . enforce the text but seldom if ever add anything not stated in the english" (*Cantos* 257). With *Rock-Drill* and *Thrones*, however, this ancillary quality of Chinese gives way to extensive presentation of characters in bold relief on almost every page. Many of these later cantos are derived from Couvreur's translation of the classic Chinese history, *Chou King*, Pound supplying his own versions, transliterations, and hypotheses from a variety of sources. Translations are often derived from R. H. Mathews's *Chinese-English Dictionary*, complete with page numbers and marginal glosses. The ostensible purpose of his lexical researches is to verify certain Confucian principles about right government, but it is clear that such principles are linked to philology itself. That is, the authority of Confucian ethics is directly tied to the processes of mind engaged in discovering that authority; hence Pound's desire to present not only the translation of a given character but the lexical accoutrements of his research.

John Peck sees this increased use of what he calls "lexical archaeology" as a sign of Pound's mythopoeic intent—an opportunity to turn "translation into recovery" of vital cultural materials (6–7). I would add that at the same time it is a way of subverting a text's authoritative rhetoric by returning it to an ongoing intellectual practice, a daily activity of research and speculation. Thus, the very object that would sediment a word's origins—the dictionary—serves as a sign of a word's ultimate contingency. Just as important, these philological excursions assert a pedagogical imperative as Pound urges the reader to learn by example. Lexical inserts, footnotes, and marginalia are all gestures outward, to a world of texts, editions, and monographs, in which history is an active process of transformation and change. The Poundian paideuma offers more than a series of Confucian principles; it shows the means and materials by which it may be realized.[6]

Pound appears to be speaking directly to this pedagogical point in Canto 96:

> If we never write anything save what is already understood, the field of understanding will never be extended. One demands the right, now and again, to write for a few people with special interests and whose curiosity reaches into greater detail. (*Cantos* 659)

This passage has particular relevance for the later cantos, dominated as they are by obscure historical chronicles, Chinese ideograms, and economic theory. The reader who has at last come to appreciate Pound via the more accessible Pisan sequence may well give up in dismay at the daunting body of arcane material in subsequent cantos. Adding to the difficulty is Pound's increasing tendency to comment on his sources: "in fact this item, with that bit from the Eparch's edict . . ." (*Cantos* 658). These asides, far from obscuring the issue, *become* the issue as Pound seeks to explore the close relationship between ideals of Confucian order and the variable record in which they appear. Pound's lexical asides alert his ideal, if limited, readership to the fact that history is *written* and is thus subject to the vagaries of textual scholarship.

The theme of Canto 96—like that of *Thrones* in general—is proper governance, particularly with reference to the distribution of wealth. The fascist millenium upon which he had depended in his earlier work having failed, Pound now turns to ideals of leadership based on metaphysical principles of personal rectitude and suffering. This does not mean that fascist elements have been eliminated, only that they have been dislodged from their fulfillment in a single individual (Mussolini) and redefined as a spiritual quest.[7] In the first cantos of *Thrones*, Pound pursues this theme with dizzying specificity among Migne's *Patrologiae*, *The Book of the Eparch*, and Alexander Del Mar's *History of Monetary Systems*. Pound is particularly interested in the relationship between certain leaders of the Byzantine Empire and the minting of coins. In fact, we might say that Canto 96 is his economic riposte to Yeats's idealized portrait of Byzantium, where gold represents the "artifice of eternity." In Pound's Byzantium, gold is called "money." Following Del Mar's edict, "When kings quit, the bankers began again," Pound traces the line of certain "just sovrans" whose authority is characterized by their ability to coin and distribute wealth equitably among the populace.

But money is not Pound's only theme; he is concerned with "just price" in the linguistic sphere as well. At various points in his reading of Paul the Deacon's history of the Lombards, Pound stops to grumble over certain words or phrases that do not appear in his Greek-English lexicon. Reading of Heraclius, a Byzantine emperor of the seventh century, Pound finds a footnote pertaining to the leader's coinage of "current coins and silver coins" in order to defeat his Persian adversary, King Chosroes II. Pound quotes the footnote in Greek, but then goes on to query the last word as follows:

> & melted down the church vessels & coined them
> $\nu o\mu\iota\sigma\mu\alpha\tau\alpha$ $\chi\alpha\iota$ $\mu\iota\lambda\iota\alpha\rho\iota\sigma\iota\alpha$
> (which is not in Liddell D.D.),
> The Deacon, col. 1026, thinks it "argenteos,"
> nummos aureos et argenteos, HERACLIUS versus Chosroes
> coined candle-sticks to keep off Chosroes
> $\epsilon\iota\chi o\nu o\varsigma$
> Justinian 527
> Tiberius Justin
> Mauricius 577
> Phocas
> Heraclius, six oh two, all dates approximate.
> Deutschland unter Dulles, U.S.A., slightly nostalgic
> by the boat-bridge over Euphrates.
>                                             (*Cantos* 656–57)

Pound's speculation over a Greek word found in a footnote in an obscure history may seem completely irrelevant to the larger drama of governance that informs the canto, but since the word in question is "silver" and since the issue is the use of things such as candlesticks to coin money, the speculation leads to the material forms that power takes. To some extent, a ruler *is* his image, especially when that image is represented on a coin—a fact made graphically clear by the way Pound balances the Latin phrase "nummos aureos et argenteos" against his two leaders, Heraclius and Chosroes. In the list of other late Roman leaders who precede Heraclius, they are, as Pound's use of the Greek word implies, "icons" as much as historical figures. Whatever their qualities as leaders, they lived at a time when the strength of the state depended on its ability to generate wealth, a power that has, according to Pound, diminished over the centuries—as his sneering reference to John Foster Dulles seems to indicate. The dates when certain leaders lived may be "approximate," but the words being passed on to describe their deeds are the literal "coinage" that keeps the flow of information circulating. Words taken for granted, not subjected to lexical scrutiny, so the logic goes, would be counterfeit—hence, the lexical aside as a sign of attentiveness.

Pound's remark about Liddell rhymes with other passages in the late cantos in which the authority of the record is obscure. Several pages before this passage, Pound, in speaking of Charlemagne, presents the Chinese character *hsin* untransliterated, followed by the remark: "Wang's middle name not in Mathews." Since the *hsin* character reminds Pound of his friend, the young poet David Wang, whose middle name is *hsin*, Pound is led to his Mathews dictionary—but to no avail. He discovers, from Wang himself, that the character refers to fire and intense heat, and since David Wang's family is descended from certain noble Chinese emperors (possibly the T'ang dynasty poet, Wang Wei) the association of fire with dynastic authority can be made. Since the larger frame of the canto concerns the leadership of Charlemagne ("verbo et actu corruscans," "splendid in word and deed"), Pound makes an association between the Chinese character, the noble lineage of his poet friend, and the greatest of the Carolingian kings. Pound's parenthetical aside about Mathews, like the other about Liddell, asserts that, where the dictionary is silent, a certain speculation must take its place.[8]

This speculation has been called, disparagingly, "a mumbling over of unexplained verities, the *disjecta membra* of a political and religious philosophy known only to Ezra Pound" (Surette 229). While true at one level, this remark overlooks the function of such "mumbling" as Pound shifts his focus away from the monumental, dynastic artifact toward a more personal record. Early on he had warned against regarding his epic as a "portable substitute for the British Museum" (*Letters* 257), but critics have insisted on seeing the poem as a kind of monastic library in which all texts are cross-listed, all passages coded according to unchanging principles ("repeat in history," "subject rhyme," *phantastikon*). In *Rock-Drill* and *Thrones*, Pound intrudes directly into his sources, quoting verbatim and showing himself thinking about them—even when they fail to yield necessary information.

Pound's reasons for foregrounding his research are related to the science of philology itself. In his early career, it offered the young scholar of Romance languages an image of linguistic totality, a vast, sprawling network of interrelated roots and grammars in which could be discerned the lineaments of a sleeping giant that he called the Mediterranean virtu. Pound gathered the limbs of Osiris by finding those luminous moments in history when someone bothered to translate a text, thus keeping one language alive by adding to another. Philology also suggested an ideal of scientific objectivity, modeled on the natural sciences, in which whole cultures could be isolated in a few juxtaposed phrases.

While Pound initially may have used philology to remove himself from history, it was by the same science that he was empowered to rejoin the present. The shattering events following the war—the failure of fascism, the Pisa, and St. Elizabeth's experiences—dramatized the fact that he had not kept his own house in order. He could not raise the heavenly city of Dioce out of great books alone. If his cultural program was to have any validity, it would have to recognize both the variability of the record and the interested nature of historical speculation. This recognition would thus move the *Cantos* from the realm of the monastic library into the field of history and place the burden of historical method not upon books themselves but on the speculative acts by which they are encountered. The lexical insert performs a small but vital role in signaling this revised sense of the poem. In exposing the seams of the text, the lexical insert exposes Pound in the act of making history.

## "HOW TO DANCE / SITTING DOWN"

Among poets who followed Pound's example, "lexical archaeology" has exerted a profound effect. Louis Zukofsky, Charles Olson, Philip Whalen, Robert Kelly, Gary Snyder, Robert Duncan, Johanna Drucker, Tina Darrah, and Susan Howe all have shown their dictionary research as part of the poem, not to establish cultural parallels but to validate cognitive acts in the present. While this is an important gesture in historicizing poetry—foregrounding the practice as well as the object of research—postmodern lexical archaeology often relies on an ideal of origins that violates those historicizing tendencies.

We can see some of these tensions at work in Gary Snyder's poem "Wave," where a dictionary gloss supports the poet's larger concerns with pattern and design in nature. The etymology of the title leads to parallel etymologies for "wife" and "woman":

> Grooving clam shell,
>     streakt through marble,
>       sweeping down ponderosa pine bark-scale
>         rip-cut tree grain
>           sand-dunes, lava
>             flow
> Wave  wife.
>     woman—wyfman—
> "veiled; vibrating; vague"
>   sawtooth ranges pulsing;
>         veins on the back of the hand.
>           (*Regarding Wave* 3)

The dominant image is the wave pattern as found in clam shells, tree grain, lava flow, and even in the sawtooth form of the letter "w." Though there is no direct connection between "wave" and "wife," Snyder joins them by sound and then by associated (if speciously derived) characteristics. He makes use of the root of "woman" in Anglo-Saxon "wyfman" (with man) and of the roots of "wife" in "veiled." Other words, "vibrating" and "vague," refer back to "wave," but their proximity to words for "wife" and "woman" seems to indicate some shared affinities. Snyder elides each of these images to suggest, as he says later, "the dancing grain of things / of my mind." For it is finally the interparticipation of natural forms and cognitive processes that is being celebrated here, a unity reinforced by etymology in which a word palpably has a life of its own.

Snyder packs his principal word, "wave," with resonance so that it would appear to link, sonically as well as morphologically, with other natural forms such as mountain ranges, zebra stripes, and thickets of ocotillo. The use of a dictionary definition creates the illusion of natural affinities between words ("wave" and "wife") that may validate a larger mythos based on woman's supposed relationship to oceans, waves, and cyclic nature. What is essentially a romantic myth of ecological interrelationships is given scientific authority by the use of a lexical quotation. By bracketing certain words in terms of their etymologies, Snyder may authenticate natural parallels beyond the poem by means of lexical parallels within.

Similar versions of this same use of etymology can be found in poems such as Philip Whalen's "The Education Continues Along," which is made up almost entirely of quotations from technical dictionaries and encyclopedias, or in Robert Duncan's "Spelling," based upon Jesperson's *A Modern English Grammar on Historical Principles,* or even in Snyder's "The Blue Sky," from *Mountains and Rivers without End.* These poems use dictionary definitions and etymologies to provide another rhetorical layer to the poem, one that often counteracts or subverts the authorial first person. In the case of Whalen, various quotations from dictionaries and scientific encyclopedias provide an ironic commentary on the poet's tendencies to become lost in scholarly pursuits ("How badly do I need to read one more book, whatever its price considering that I'm already half blind from too much reading anyway" [325]). It is as if the endless corrections and second guesses made possible by etymological research, rather than clarifying a given point, obscure comprehension to the point of absurdity. As for Duncan, the use of authoritative sources in his "Passages" series serves to link his language—the product of an organic as well as historical process—with his daily activities of reading, thinking, dreaming, and walking. At the same time that the dictionary is used to authenticate meaning, the act of consulting it defers that very meaning, deflecting the original intention onto a new process of speculation and conjecture.[9]

In these and other cases, the dictionary is adduced to verify a word's meaning and to provide a framing language of philological objectivity. At the same time, the act of incorporating the dictionary definition into the poem authenticates the present moment of conjecture, a moment given historical weight by its insistence on *this* act in *this* book. Thus, the dictionary gloss is caught in a tension between appeals to diachronic and synchronic poles: the word as product of cultural and historical change and the word as enactment of one such moment. To some extent, this tension is part of a larger problem in postmodern poetics based on wresting significance from unreflective acts in order for the poet to move, as Duncan says, "naked as the wind in a world of words" (*Bending* v). At the same time, quoting from the dictionary provides some historical or scientific objectivity by which to assess those acts.[10]

This interest in etymology among postwar poets is buttressed by a theory of language that treats words as extensions of physical and biological life. Meaning exists within a semiotic DNA, and every utterance taps into that great verbal pool. Poetry intensifies pre-oedipal and precultural latencies in language by referring to archaic sources but also, and more important, by activating plural meanings and sensual surfaces in the poem itself. Thus, it may participate in the field of organic ratios and natural processes from which language derives. "Logos," for someone like Charles Olson, does not mean prior reason or authorizing signification but "what is said," regardless of any appeal to its truth value.[11] His desire to antedate modern associations for words such as "myth," "history," and "truth" in Indo-European roots reflects his attempt to recover physical, material bases at the heart of all speech acts:

> Which is of course, why language is a prime of the matter and why, if we are to see some of the laws afresh, it is necessary examine, first, the present condition of the language—and I mean language exactly in its double sense of discrimination (logos) and of shout (tongue). (*Selected Writings* 53)

Olson finds that this double sense of language is available even in our most abstract verbal forms:

> "Is" comes from the Aryan root, *as*, to breathe. The English 'not' equals the Sanscrit [sic] *na*, which may come from the root *na*, to be lost, to perish. "Be" is from *bhu*, to grow. (*Selected Writings* 18)

This emphasis on physiological roots for language is part of the more general postmodern rejection of poetic diction and verbal artifice that characterized an earlier generation. Etymology forces attention on language as a system whose laws of generation and change are tied to human use. Word as object, word as action—these are the primary terms of what Olson calls "objectism": the attempt to circumvent the mediating function of the ego by returning language to the world, an Emersonian project for which the dictionary is the central vehicle.

In Olson's essays, lexicology and archaeology represent parallel endeavors, analogous to poetry, insofar as they seek to penetrate multiple layers of personal psychology and history. The tools of archaeology that Olson used during his sojourn in the Yucatan Peninsula during the early 1950s help verify cultural speculation, much as philological research helps to establish a word's sedimented associations. Olson appreciates the tools of lexical archaeology as much as what he discovers with them, and many of his poems consist of lengthy footnotes, references, and citations from his research, along with his own marginal glosses. He is not unconscious of the dangers of fetishizing research for its own sake and in "The Librarian" speaks of the difficulty of separating his historical resources from the very history he studies. In a dream vision, he sees himself looking through the window of a library: "My thought was, as I looked in the window ... / there should be materials here for Maximus" (*Collected Poems* 217). But he is "caught // in Gloucester" (as he is caught in a dream), subject to and subject of a historical process beyond him. No text can provide him with a proper vantage from which to view history since he is complicit in it. His only recourse is to reenact that process in the poem.

Such a poem is "Tyrian Business," what one might call a "dictionary dance" in which specific entries in *Webster's Fifth Collegiate Dictionary* provide a set of variations on the theme of balance. The title refers to the second century Neoplatonic philosopher, Maximus of Tyre, who is a prototype for Olson's scholar-poet-archaeologist. The "business" of the contemporary Maximus involves tracing certain words in the dictionary, an act that he likens to dancing. Lexical research becomes a dance performed while "sitting down," a conceit elaborated in an essay written just prior to this poem (1953), while Olson was the rector of Black Mountain College. In "A Syllabary for a Dancer," he associates dancing with writing, both involving "an object and an action" in which form and content cannot be separated:

> For sign, in language and in dance, is that force of representation which holds in itself always the fables of the objects which man has found important enough to give a name to, and the motion of those signs (what a verb does or in dance, the movement of the mobiles of the body) holds in itself all the wills which man has made himself capable of. ("Syllabary" 10)[12]

Both (poetic) language and dance "represent" not by reference to some prior narrative imposed from without—a condition Olson sees as a liability in Martha Graham's work—but by embodying narrative possibilities in the physical resources of the body. One suspects that Olson is finding alternate terms for Yeats's famous (rhetorical) question, "How can we know the dancer from the dance?" In Olson's terms, the question becomes how can we repossess ourselves of some

"From the Latin Speculum"    111

material presence ("the fables of the objects") immanent in every sign; how can we reunite object and action, word and thing, act and actor without turning to distancing and alienating figures of speech that maintain that dualism.

Olson's answer in "Tyrian Business" is to rummage around in his dictionary for roots of words such as "heart" and "felicity" that have become denuded of concrete associations.[13] But Olson is not content simply to use his dictionary to illustrate language's original potency; he must show his lexical research as part of the things he discovers (and as verification of his own masculine potency). "The difficulty of discovery," as he says elsewhere, is that "definition is as much a part of the act as is sensation itself, in this sense, that life *is* preoccupation with itself" (*Selected Writings* 53). Olson becomes preoccupied with the dance of the intellect among words of the dictionary so that the act of speculation and its objects become one phenomenon.

The word "heart" inaugurates one such movement:

a hollow muscular organ which, by contracting vigorously,

    keeps up the
        (to have the heart
                (a whorl of green bracts at the base

                              (ling,
    she is known as

        Weather
comes generally
        under the
            metaphrast.
                (When M is above G, all's
                well. When below, there's
                upset. When M and G are
                coincident,
                it is not very interesting)
                    (*Maximus Poems* 40)

In this admittedly cryptic section of the poem, Olson looks up the word "heart" ("a hollow muscular organ, by contracting vigorously, keeps up the"), but before he can complete the definition he becomes distracted by another word on the same page of his Webster's dictionary: "heather," defined as "A species of heath . . . having a rose-colored calyx with a whorl of green bracts at the base; ling, . . ." At this point he becomes distracted again as the word "ling" (a synonym for "heather") reminds him of Madame Chiang Kai-shek, whose nickname is Mei-ling. She has already been mentioned in an earlier section as epitomizing a certain wastefulness and opulence that this poem opposes ("as that . . . international doll, / has to have silk, when she is put up"). Up to this point, Olson's stepped lines and open parentheses seem to be illustrating a kind of heart beat of their own, shifting attentions and keeping alive the forward-moving thrust of the poem.

Olson then moves to another part of the dictionary, presumably to look up the word "metaphrast," a word referring to one who changes a text from one form into another—a reflection on the poet's own attempt to render historical materials into poetry. On the same page and below "metaphrast" is "meteorology" ("Weather / comes generally / under the / metaphrast"), and below this is the word "metacenter," which describes a position of buoyancy in floating objects. The word is accompanied by a diagram of a ship's hull with intersecting lines showing various positions relative to buoyancy, each line marked by a letter. The full definition reads as follows:

> The point of intersection ($M$ in *Illust.*) of the vertical through the center of buoyancy ($B$) of a floating body with the vertical through the new center of buoyancy ($B'$) when the body is displaced however little. When $M$ is above the center of gravity ($G$) of the floating body the position of the body is stable; when below it, unstable; when coincident with it, neutral. (*Webster's Fifth Collegiate Dictionary*, quoted in Butterick 61)

Olson collapses the entire passage into a brief quatrain, retaining just enough of the technical language to suggest its source but adding his own metaphrastic translation.

We could see the entire poem as a commentary on this passage; that is, the poem is potentially a "metacenter" that changes due to environmental conditions—like the randomly discovered glosses and diagrams found in a dictionary. Olson attempts, thematically and structurally, to achieve some kind of balance without positing an absolute center. In a later portion of the poem, this point is driven home by means of a story about Olson's old fishing ship, the *Doris Hawes*, and its captain, Cecil Moulton, who risks an entire fishing expedition in high seas to pick up loose timber for a garage that he is building. The ship runs into one of the planks, which in turn damages the screw, thus destroying the prop and, ultimately, the expedition. It is a vivid example of a man who loses sight of his primary concern, substituting his own self-interest for that of his crew. *The Maximus Poems* are filled with such figures who are distracted from the work at hand by the lure of immediate gratification and quick profits. This little story provides a frame for the terms introduced above: centrality, balance, isochrony, measurement, and buoyancy, terms that provide a highly specific context for something as abstract as "right reason" or "order" or "control." They also suggest alternative notions of "balance" such that even "sitting down" (and attendant cognitive acts) could be considered appropriate to dance.

"Tyrian Business" is built out of definitions that lead not to unitary meaning but outward to other frames of reference—"projective" as Olson felt verse should be once bodily ratios are admitted into composition. Definition is discovery, a fact given form by the poet's characteristic interrupted lineation:

> Definition: (in this instance,
> and in what others, what
> felicities?
>         "The crooked timbers
> scarfed together to form the lower part of the compound rib are
>
> futtocks,
> we call 'em
>
>         But a fylfot,
> she look like,
>             who calls herself
>                     (luck
>                         (*Maximus Poems* 44)

Here, definition is also discrimination: "futtocks" ("The crooked timbers / scarfed together" to form the rib of a boat's hull) leads to "fylfot" (a sign for luck or felicity), two terms that are linked not by any philological authority but by proximity in the dictionary and, even more important, by their relationship to Olson's ever-shifting concerns in this poem. "Fylfot" actually refers to a swastika, which, in its Sanskrit root, means luck or fortune. Given the context of the poem, it also resembles the screw of a ship, that "central" piece of machinery to which the story of the *Doris Hawes* refers. As it turns out, the poem is very much about the structure and design of ships: how they stay afloat, how they are constructed, and how they are controlled. But definition is also a matter of felicity, of what words come to the eye as it wanders over the page of a dictionary. A balance between definition, as scientific verification, and luck, as contingency, is the necessary "business" of Olson's ideal citizen/poet.

The contemporary poet's fascination with the dictionary represents a double motion: on the one hand, the poet seeks to return a word's "original," concrete meaning by an appeal to its roots or at least to some authoritative definition. On the other hand, the etymological insert insists upon the temporality in which the current word is used—as part of a discursive action in the poem itself. The poet's reference to Sanskrit or Anglo-Saxon roots deliberately foregrounds a diachronic dimension to language, but it is a gesture undermined, to some extent, by the way this historical authority is used. By using philological sources such as the dictionary, the poet may undermine any historical intent by an essentialist desire for origins. "Back is no better," Olson warns, but his own example often proves the contrary:

> The "source" question is damned interesting today—as Shelley saw, like Dante, that, if it comes in, that way, primary, from Ma there is then a double line of chromosomic giving (A) the inherent speech (thought, power) the "species," that is; and (B) the etymological: this is where I find "foreign" languages so wild, especially the Indo-European line with the advantage now that we have Hittite to back up to. (*Selected Writings* 27)

Olson's biological metaphor silently acknowledges his links to nineteenth-century philology and signals the "science envy" of the sort that marks Pound's polemical essays.

It may be that philology offers both a solution and a trap for poets of the 1950s and 1960s who seek to avoid the high cultural models of dynastic history used by the modernist generation. Pound's own example dramatizes the problem as he moves away from an ideal of seamless, philological layering to the "lexical insert," a move of great importance for the evolution of a new historical poetics. By turning to the dictionary, the poet may trace a word's earliest meaning—or, as in Olson, establish its most concrete present meaning—while sustaining the immediacy of the poetic act itself. This shift is paralleled in philosophy by the turn to existentialism and phenomenology and in the adoptions of gestalt models in theories of cognition. The importance granted to action and gesture must be set against the antiideological (and antihistoricist) moment of the Cold War. The problem with this gesture is that it may avoid both the current history of which a word is a part and the very historical process that the poet seeks to validate by such philological excursions. This paradox may be inescapable in any poetics of presence: that the desire to participate directly in the moment depends upon an authorizing agency prior to and ultimately beyond that moment.

# 4

# Dismantling "Mantis"
## Reification, Louis Zukofsky, and Objectivist Poetics

> thinking with the things as they exist. I come into a room
> and I see a table. Obviously, I can't make it eat grass.
> Louis Zukofsky, Interview

### INCIPIT VITA NOVA

Despite Louis Zukofsky's claim that he cannot make a table eat grass, at various points in his poetry he appears to have attempted just that. In *"A"*-7, for example, he turns wooden sawhorses into horses: "For they have no eyes, for their legs are wood, / For their stomachs are logs with print on them" (39). Not only do these horses bear a printed message ("Street Closed"), their triangular shape resembles the first letter of the alphabet, upon which Zukofsky erects his epic poem. Such transformations suggest that "thinking with the things as they exist" means taking tables, sawhorses, the *St. Matthew Passion*, or the letter A as they occur in their immediate circumstance, not to make them new but to discover them for the first time. Zukofsky significantly performs his sawhorse conversion while sitting on an urban stoop, surrounded by signs of the then-current Depression: "laundry to let," "brother, we want a meal," "rent in arrears." These facts are no less material than the wooden sawhorses that alert citizens to repairs being made in the city's infrastructure. To change one is implicitly to challenge the other: to return workers to the street (or a society to productive health) involves changing the value of certain fixed signs.

We could see the transformation of schematic sign into fully realized animal as the most typical example of modernist decreation, but we do so by ignoring the fatal pact between modernist objectivism and materialism. These two terms, often treated synonymously by those who elevate the former as a triumph over the latter, come together in significant ways among American poets during the late

1920s, whether one is studying writers of the Harlem Renaissance, activist poets writing in *The New Masses* and *The Partisan Review*, or the Objectivists. But it is in the last group that tensions between the two forms of materialism become a decisive issue in their poetics.

The Objectivist movement has assumed an increasingly important place in the nomenclature of modernisms as readers have begun to explore alternate canons that emerged between the two wars.[1] The movement has special relevance for a recent generation of writers who are attempting to displace the free-verse expressivism of the 1960s with new formalisms of various kinds.[2] Objectivism emerges as an extension of the poetics of Ezra Pound and William Carlos Williams, but it also attempts to address the social and economic costs of "modernization" as it was experienced in the 1930s. The fact that the Objectivists came of literary age during a time of massive unemployment and social unrest at home, with the specter of fascism emerging abroad, exerted powerful effects on their work. At one level, these events encouraged a poetics of direct presentation and clarity advocated in Zukofsky's 1931 *Poetry* essay.[3] At another level, however, history forced the Objectivists, along with many of their contemporaries, to confront contradictions between modernist formal aesthetics and left-wing politics, contradictions that ultimately caused one Objectivist, George Oppen, to stop writing for twenty-five years. What was at stake was more than a conflict over political poetry. Rather, it was a confrontation with what might be called the "ideology of form": if Pound's ideogrammatic method could be placed in the service of Mussolini's Fascism, or if Eliot's impersonality could be used to legitimate cultural imperialism and classist anti-Semitism, what did it mean for second-generation sons of Jewish immigrants to employ the same techniques in the service of progressive social views?[4]

On first glance, Zukofsky's 1931 tenets seem to reinforce modernist values of disinterestedness and autonomy, most apparent in his advocacy of "rested totality," "the apprehension satisfied completely as to the appearance of the art form as an object" (*Prepositions* 13). Yet Zukofsky's actual practice exposes the object status of the poem as a delusion, a stoppage of what is, in reality, a dynamic process. We can see a dereifying tendency in many works of this period, notably in Zukofsky's *"A"*-9, an elaborately worked variation on Cavalcanti's "Donna mi priegha" built upon Marx's labor theory of value. But perhaps the most graphic example of formalism in dialogue with modern materialism is Zukofsky's sestina "Mantis," which not only addresses the alienation of life under modern capitalism but does so by debating the "implications of a too regular form."

What is most interesting about Zukofsky's response to social crisis is that it is often conducted in formal terms that seem at odds with the material under consideration. This disparity has prompted Eric Mottram to speak of "*A*"-9's canzone structure as a kind of "dandyism" whose "strained versifying operates a trite statement of art taking its place as labour in 1938–40" (98).[5] Mottram's essay is one of the best accounts of the difficulties of forging a materialist poetics, but it fails to historicize the oppositional meaning of Zukofsky's formalism with respect to competing theories of committed art during this period. Zukofsky used formalism not to aestheticize social tensions but to return a degree of use-value to an increasingly instrumentalized poetry. Rather than solve the problem as Oppen did— by giving up poetry altogether—Zukofsky sought to provide an immanent critique within the terms of modernism itself.[6]

One way of understanding Zukofsky's formalism is to see it as a response to the larger issue of social reification. In Lukács's canonical description, reification refers to the transformation of labor power into a commodity, the objectification of "sensuous human activity" into a "second nature." Building upon Marx's notion of commodity fetishism in *Capital*, Lukács describes the process by which relations between individuals "take on the character of a thing and thus [acquire] a 'phantom objectivity'" (83). As Marx dramatizes (in a passage quoted in "*A*"-9), commodities seem to speak to each other, saying "our use-value may interest men, but it does not belong to us as objects. What does belong to us as objects, however is our value. Our own intercourse as commodities proves it. We relate to each other merely as exchange-values" (176–77). As both Marx and Lukács argue, when commodities acquire independent agency, the worker's role in creating them is occluded, leading to a sense of passivity and helplessness in the face of an autonomous, self-regulating market—"autotelic" in every sense.

Lukács is less interested in the specific economic factors contributing to reification than he is in the epistemological forces that maintain it. He describes the bourgeois philosophical tradition inherited from Kant as constructing a reflective consciousness that, while claiming power over its material surroundings, is unable to assess its own historical circumstance. The bourgeoisie, since it is implicated in this contemplative attitude, cannot rupture it; but the proletariat potentially can understand its own historical moment—and its alienation. What the proletariat "owns" is not labor power but a certain vantage by which the congealed version of that power in commodities can be seen for what it is. It is this vantage that preoccupies Zukofsky in his early poems and that becomes the focus of "Mantis."[7]

"Mantis" concerns the perspective from which material conditions become detached from an observer. Rather than being *about* commodities or labor per se, the poem uses its own status as an aesthetic object as a lens for viewing social alienation. And since the observer in this poem is also a poet, the work explores the degree to which "looking" and "writing" are implicated in a single mode of production. It is not that social reality is reproduced through the poem but that, through describing the inability of poetry to remove barriers between individuals, the poem generates a second vantage "produced" in the interstices between formal accomplishment (the poem as made thing) and social inadequacies (the absence of a unified proletarian consciousness).[8] The poem consists of two parts— a sestina and an interpretation—each of which augments and redefines the other. The sestina invokes the poet's sudden encounter with a praying mantis in a subway station; the interpretation accounts for the sestina itself, situating the encounter with the mantis within a larger meditation on writing. It may seem odd that Zukofsky chooses such a complex literary vehicle to deal with "the growing oppression of the poor," but the poem's recycling of terminal words according to a numerical formula provides a felicitous frame for rendering "The actual twisting / Of many and diverse thoughts" invoked by the mantis.

The sestina's invention is associated with Arnaut Daniel, who invented the form, but most important for Zukofsky is its use by Pound who, in *The Spirit of Romance*, described it as "a thin sheet of flame folding and infolding upon itself" (27). Pound wrote several sestinas in his early career and regarded the form as a paragon of virtuosic difficulty, a touchstone for poetic apprenticeship. Zukofsky, no longer an apprentice, uses it to address Pound at a moment

(1934) when the older poet's increasing interest in Mussolini and Social Credit threatens their relationship. By subjecting the sestina to "ungainly" issues of poverty and urban alienation, Zukofsky confronts the dangers of poetic mastery divorced from the cultural and social institutions such mastery serves. Virtuosic control, as an end in itself, quickly becomes

> Stuffing like upholstery
> For parlor polish,
> *And our time takes count against them*
> *For their blindness and their (unintended?) cruel smugness.*
> (*All* 76–77 [emphasis added])

Although Pound is not the antecedent here, a certain Victorian "smugness" associated with Pound's early personae is.

Although the title of the poem focuses on the mantis, clearly the subject is less the insect than the speaker's ambivalent response to it:

> Mantis! praying mantis! since your wings' leaves
> And your terrified eyes, pins, bright, black and poor
> Beg—"look, take it up" (thoughts' torsion)! "save it!"
> I who can't bear to look, cannot touch,—You—
> You can—but no one sees you steadying lost
> In the cars' drafts on the lit subway stone.
> (*All* 73)

The shifting deixis of these lines dramatizes the speaker's ambivalence, both to the mantis and to the poor. The ambiguity of "it" in the third line suggests that he addresses himself as much as the mantis. For Zukofsky is asking whether or how to "take up" the event, how to give it form and stabilize "thoughts' torsion," much as the insect strives to steady itself in the drafty subway. The confusion of first and second persons ("I who can't bear to look, cannot touch,—You— / You can—but no one sees you") points to the speaker's conflict about addressing those who challenge his autonomy. Deixis fails to differentiate the subject from the eyes around him, and by the end of the stanza the question of whose eyes are seeing whom is thoroughly vexed, although understandable for a poet who consistently pronounced I's as "eyes."[9]

The only witness to the poet's discomfiture is the newsboy, but he is, in Lukács's terms, wrapped in the endless circulation of commodities, an extension of the reified history represented in his papers:

> Even the newsboy who now sees knows it
> No use, papers make money, makes stone, stone,
> Banks, "it is harmless," he says moving on—You?
> Where will he put *you*?
>
> (*All* 73)

In the interpretation, the market logic introduced here is shown to be circular:

> Rags make paper,
> paper makes money, money makes
> banks, banks make loans, loans make
> poverty, poverty makes rags.
>
> (79)

It is precisely this vicious circularity to which Zukofsky's poetic form refers, even as it offers its own alternative semiotic economy for six recycled words. Likewise, the problems of deixis and perspective illustrate the difficulties of looking at another *outside* of market relationships. The mantis, by breaking through the speaker's contemplative gaze, reminds him of cultural traditions that he has forgotten but nonetheless summons to explain the insect's mythic meaning:

> Don't light on my chest, mantis! do—you're lost,
> Let the poor laugh at my fright, then see it:
> My shame and theirs, you whom old Europe's poor
> Call spectre, strawberry, by turns; a stone—
> You point—they say—you lead lost children—leaves
> Close in the paths men leave, saved, safe with you.
>
> (73–74)

The speaker's attraction to and repulsion from the mantis replicate his response to the poor, and by acknowledging "shame" he transforms self-closed revery into vulnerability and even empathy. By referring to "old Europe's poor," Zukofsky acknowledges his own ethnic origins, sustained by the affirmative nature of shared narratives. Just as the mantis is able to "lead lost children" in an old story, so it saves one modern subject from isolation.

At the end of the sestina, the poet realizes that, until he identifies his alienation with those around him, he cannot translate his subway experience for future generations. He urges the mantis to "Fly . . . on the poor," as it has alighted on him, "arise like leaves / The armies of the poor, strength; stone on stone / And build the new world in your eyes, Save it!" The paraphrase of the socialist motto ("Building the new world in the shell of the old") is varied here to include the acts of looking and identifying that have dominated the poem so far. But the final tercet presents a too-tidy conclusion to a poem that has opened up more problems than it has solved.

If "Mantis" ended here, with the ringing injunction to "build the new world in your eyes," we would have been left with the very aestheticized politics deplored by Mottram. It is for " 'Mantis,' an Interpretation" to return to the poem and dismantle the totalizing gesture implied by the form and manifested in its utopian apostrophe. Zukofsky's mandate to append an interpretation is granted by Dante, whose *Vita Nuova* offers an earlier example of poetry plus commentary (albeit in prose). And as with Dante, Zukofsky wishes to render a transformative experience by interpreting the conditions surrounding words brought to bear on it:

> *Mantis! praying mantis! since your wings' leaves*
>     Incipit Vita Nova
>     le parole . . .
>     almeno la loro sentenzia
> the words . . .
> at least their substance
> at first were
> "The mantis opened its body
> It had been lost in the subway
> It steadied against the drafts
> It looked up—
> Begging eyes—
> It flew at my chest"
>     —The ungainliness
>     of the creature needs stating.
>         (*All* 74–75)

Zukofsky includes a first-draft opening to the poem ("The mantis opened its body") to indicate his difficulty in finding words for an awkward moment. However "ungainly" these first twenty-seven words, they become the "pulse's witness" to the event, just as Dante's "new life" begins with Beatrice's look. Zukofsky's equivalent look combines the "Begging eyes" of the mantis with those of the poor.

Zukofsky refuses to treat the mantis as a symbol, but he realizes that it *"can start /* History" by calling up disparate areas of knowledge and subjecting them to experience. Like Melville's whale, the mantis can become a curriculum:

> line 1—entomology
> line 9—biology
> lines 10 and 11—the even rhythm of riding under-
>     ground, and the sudden jolt are also
>     of these nerves, glandular facilities,
>     brain's charges
> line 12—pun, fact, banality
> lines 13 to 18—the economics of the very poor ...
> lines 22 to 24—Provence myth
> lines 25 to 29—Melanesian self-extinction myth
>                                   (*All* 78–79)

This catalog, like the whimsical index at the end of "*A*" or the footnotes to "Poem Beginning 'The,'" presumes to account for topics invoked by the mantis, but the more Zukofsky includes, the less he verifies. For the listing of facts alone cannot account for the "original shock" provoked by the insect. When facts remain ends in themselves, they signal their distance from any actual exchange. What "Mantis" offers as a corrective is to provide "a use function of the material: / The original emotion remaining, / like the collective, / Unprompted" (79). For it is this "invoked collective" of disarranged and recombined facts that reestablishes contact, not to stop history with a verbal icon but to keep it alive and tangible in the present.

"Mantis" and its interpretation are one poem seeing modern history through two pairs of eyes. We could speak of the sestina as embodying the modernist attempt to secure sight through the imposition of formal constraints, the humanist achievement of mastery over the quotidian, the mantis turned into a symbol of the poor. But in the interpretation we discern a postmodern (and we might say post-Marxist) attempt to dereify the discourse of mastery in favor of internal critique. Neither poem exists without the other, just as the eyes of the mantis trade places with the eyes of its beholder. Both pairs of eyes are out of their element, the mantis removed from its natural leaves, Zukofsky, the bourgeois intellectual with a head full of facts, lost in the subway among the poor. Yet it is precisely this being out-of-one's-element that links the "simultaneous, / The diaphanous, historical / in one head" and begins the ungainly process of saving that which by becoming objectified threatens to become invisible.

### "FOR LABOR, WHO WILL SING...?"

Four years after "Mantis" was written, Zukofsky returned to Marx's theory of commodities in an even more complex fashion, using the structure of Cavalcanti's canzone "Donna mi priegha" as his formal model. As with "Mantis," "A"-9 includes, in its intertextual matrix, an implicit critique of Pound, who had translated the Cavalcanti poem twice.[10] In his essay that accompanies his first translation (1934), Pound reflects on the loss of the "radiant world where one thought cuts through another with clean edge, a world of moving energies" exemplified in general by late medieval Mediterranean culture and in specific by Cavalcanti's (perhaps heretical) philosophical poetry (*Literary Essays* 154). It is this association of Cavalcanti with the "radiant world" of enduring values that provokes the poem's second appearance in 1935 as Canto 36, this time to validate the "clean edge" of historical destiny as embodied by Mussolini. In this second version, the canzone stands as a salutary alternative to the wastage of "Mitteleuropa" presented in the previous canto. In Canto 35, Pound had paid particular attention to the ill effects of international Jewry, warning of "the intramural, the almost intravaginal warmth of / hebrew affections" and telling the story of

> ... a peautiful chewisch poy
> wit a vo-ice dot woult
> meldt dh heart offa schtone
> and wit a likeing for to make arht-voiks
> (*Cantos* 174)

Pound bemoans the destruction of ancient Italian guild traditions and the appearance of mass production and usurious banking practices:

> So that our goods please the buyer.
> Tell the Wazir that that stuff is ours only in name
> it is made by damned jews in exile ... damned jews in
> Ragusa and sold with Venetian lables.
> (176)

It is against this corruption of production through usury that Canto 36 follows with its celebration of Love held as an *"active virtue"* in the mind and made manifest in Cavalcanti's elaborate structure. For Pound, the complicated internal structure of the canzone represents work that is able to resist corruption and thereby contain "the intellect possible" in the intellect palpable (177).

Pound's anti-Semitic statements were not reserved for the *Cantos* by any means but were appearing regularly in his letters to Zukofsky during this period.[11] Zukofsky, whose father was one of those "damned jews in exile," responds with his own study of commodification by reproducing Cavalcanti's strophic pattern, rhyme scheme, and hendecasyllabics in a double series of five sonnets plus envoi. However, value does not reside "in memory's locus" as it does in Pound's Cavalcanti but in "An eye to action" that sees things as the result of human labor. Production becomes the focus of the poem, which draws on passages from Marx's *Capital* with reference to commodities. Where Cavalcanti's speaker is the reflective poet, responding to a lady's question ("A lady asks me / I speak in season"), the speaker in the first half of Zukofsky's version is the commodity form itself, a persona introduced by Marx to embody the self-enclosed world of objects produced solely for exchange. The shift in persona from Pound's romantic poet to Zukofsky's alienated product is a crucial one for understanding the latter's specific critique of modernist subjectivity. For Pound and Eliot, the poet acquires the historical sense by maintaining an ironic or endistanced vantage; in Zukofsky's view, the urban proletarian in the 1930s has no such advantage. Marx's persona, then, is more than a rhetorical device appropriated by Zukofsky; it is the condition within which the modern bourgeoisie frames its goals and horizons.

The first half of *"A"*-9 was published in 1940 in a limited edition, consisting of various texts that went into the making of the poem up to that point: Cavalcanti's canzone in Italian; selected passages from Marx; quotations from H. Stanley Allen's *Electrons and Waves: An Introduction to Atomic Physics* (which provides some of the scientific vocabulary); four translations of Cavalcanti's canzone (Pound's two included); a brief description of the form of the canzone followed by a description of the formula for a conic section (which governs the deployment of certain consonants in the translation); and finally a prose paraphrase of each strophe. The penultimate document in this forty-one-page pamphlet is the first half of *"A"*-9 as it exists in its present form, but it is important to note that its terminal position does not mean that it is given privilege of place at the expense of what precedes. In his foreword, Zukofsky reminds us that his "aids" are presented "in the foregoing order, the poem last, so that, if the intention to have it fluoresce as it were in the light of seven centuries of interrelated thought has at all been realized, the poem will explain itself. In any case, the "aids may forestall exegesis" precisely because interpretation must occur *within* the text, not outside it (*First Half* 1). "*A*"-9 is not the final *product* of its various aids; it is one of those aids itself, implicated in the creation of value and as such unable to exist separate from the conditions by which it is generated. Even the fact that Zukofsky published the book by hand and distributed it himself must be seen as an enabling aid in the text's ultimate meaning.

The goal of "*A*"-9 is utopian; Zukofsky claims that "aside from what has already been said—a Briton pronounces *capitalism* with the accent on the second syllable: ca-pit'-al-ism. '*A*'-9 may mean more if it be taken also as a sign that c*api*talism will capitulate" (*First Half* 1). If part of Zukofsky's goal is the transformation of capitalism, it will surely not be because his poem makes Marx easier to read. Rather, it is because the poem, through its multiple attempts at translation (Cavalcanti, Marx, Pound, science), will return the poem and the issues it raises about its own materiality to a world of multiple auditors. In addition to Pound's lyric translations of "Donna mi priegha," Zukofsky includes two other versions whose diction imitates that of ethnic, working-class populations. Pound's opening lines ("A lady asks me / I speak in season / She seeks reason for an affect . . .") become considerably more localized in Jerry Reisman's Brooklynese ("It's so hot an' proud comin' so often, dough / A natural freak, I'm itchin' t'speak becuz / A dame ast what wuz love") and Zukofsky's proletarian Irish ("A foin lass bodders me I gotta tell her / Of a fact surely, so unrurly, often' / 'r 't comes 'tcan't soften its proud neck's called love mm . . ."). Hence, pronunciation of "capitalism" has everything to do with the form by which it is capitulated once language is returned to its historical producers.[12]

In "*A*"-8, Zukofsky had asked, "For Labor, who will sing . . . ?" and, as Peter Quartermain observes, "the coda to ["*A*"-9] provides the answer: no one; *labour* can sing . . . of its own accord. For inspired by the abstraction 'time congealed labor' (l. 3), the poem has in the course of its writing been *forced* to turn from the abstraction to the actual and specific labour which the words themselves, in the song, embody..." (215). Zukofsky had, of course, attempted to sing *for* labor in early poems such as "Memory of V. I. Ulianov," "During the Passaic Strike of 1926," "D.R.," and the proletarian song of *"A"*-8. But in *"A"*-9, as in "Mantis," he is less interested in representing labor than in understanding his own form of production as a writer and intellectual. In Lukácsian terms introduced earlier, the poem dismantles a specific (interpretive) vantage from which a single, isolated individual regards the world as so many discrete objects. Within this logic, the poet's own poem becomes such an object, its autonomy replicating the object status of all commodities. By dismantling this vantage (and the autonomy thesis as well), the poem may, in Zukofsky's words, "fluoresce" into the relations between production and value. In order to do this, *"A"*-9 imposes an extraordinary series of limitations upon its own readability, beginning with the mapping of Cavalcanti's difficult rhyme scheme and continuing through the rendering of passages from Marx and Spinoza, to the deployment of consonant sounds according to a mathematical formula. These impositions occur less as occasions for virtuoso performance than as challenges to unitary recuperation. The "mystery" of commodities in Marx is that they "mirror for men the social character of their own labour... as an objective character attaching to the labour products themselves" (*First Half* 5). This is the first stage of fetishization, the granting of metaphysical qualities to products such that they appear to lead a life of their own. Zukofsky's formalism halts rather than enhances this kind of reification by creating a verbal surface as richly nuanced as it is syntactically compact:

An impulse to action sings of a semblance
Of things related as equated values,
The measure all use is time congealed labor
In which abstraction things keep no resemblance
To goods created; integrated all hues
Hide their natural use to one or one's neighbor.
So that were the things words they could say: Light is
Like night is like us when we meet our mentors
Use hardly enters into their exchanges,
Bought to be sold things, our value arranges;
We flee people who made us as a right is
Whose sight is quick to choose us as frequenters,
But see our centers do not show the changes
Of human labor our value estranges.    (*"A"* 106)

This opening strophe draws on phrases from *Capital* but with obvious deformations of Marx's language. Semantic values are confused by extensive modification, inversion, and deletion. Reference to Marx's original may provide a serviceable paraphrase but will not sort out the dense syntax and intricate rhyming. Where Marx says, "We are concerned only with a definite social relation between human beings, which, in their eyes, has here assumed the semblance of a relation between things" (quoted in *First Half* 5), Zukofsky condenses: "An impulse to action sings of a semblance / Of things related as equated values," playing on the rhyme of "related" and "equated" and picking up the sibilance of "impulse," "sings," "semblance," and "things." Zukofsky's condensation of prose passages creates puns and double entendres that link dissimilar terms and confuse syntactic function. Should we read line 3 as "The measure all [of us] use is time congealed labor" or "The measure [that] all use is [is] time congealed labor?" In line 10, do we read "[We are] bought to be sold [as] things [that] our value arranges" or "[Since our value arranges things according to exchange value, things are] bought to be sold [as] things?" Such confusions are not merely playful; they point to congruences between subject and object—"use" as a verb of action and "use" as an adjective modifying value—that are very much at issue in Marx's own theory of commodities.

Zukofsky provides his own paraphrase of this strophe, explaining that the "poem sings about things embodying a common denominator of past work, tho this abstract evaluation of them hides the fact that things are goods made to be used by people. If things could speak, they would point out that those who buy to sell them in the exchanges withdraw them from their proper owners who work in order to enjoy them" (*First Half* 40). The difference between this and stanza 1 (as well as the relevant passages from *Capital*) is that the paraphrase describes reification from a reified position, a social scientist's explanation of speech acts, reducing each to a semantic common denominator. The paraphrase instrumentalizes poetic language, separating it from its material form. *"A"*-9's convoluted syntax and internal rhyming *make* words into sensual objects, blurring and confusing boundaries that otherwise divide and separate. And since Zukofsky, like Marx, speaks from the standpoint of a commodity, the "we" of the poem undergoes some of the same deictic confusions of "Mantis."

If instability is the result of Zukofsky's formalism, what do we make of the scientific vocabulary and formulaic deployment of consonants? H. Stanley Allen's book on physics provides Zukofsky with his definition of "action" ("the product of energy plus time"), which could be seen as a physical correlative to Marx's ideas of social action. But Zukofsky's use of the formula for a conic section is more problematic. As he explains, "the first 70 lines [of "A"-9] are the poetic analog of a conic section—i.e. the ratio of the accelerations of the two sounds (r, n) has been made equal to the ratio of the accelerations of the coordinates (x, y) of a particle moving in a circular path with uniform angular velocity" (*First Half* 37). Barry Ahearn and Peter Quartermain have provided admirable descriptions of how Zukofsky uses the formula for a conic section to arrange repetitions of "n" and "r" sounds. Zukofsky divides the seventy-five lines of the first half of "A"-9 into into five points or sections (corresponding to the five strophes plus coda), each one of which represents 90 degrees of a circle. Within each of these five groups, words containing the letters "n" and "r" are chosen according to a formula that measures the ratio between the diagonal of a circle and a point moving around its circumference. As Ahearn points out, Zukofsky is anxious to provide an analog for the mathematical counterpoint he admires in Bach's music: "Mathematics, like music, has the advantage of relative freedom from doctrinal or didactic import. It therefore serves as a 'pure' form for combining sound so that the energy of the spoken word operates in a rigorously plotted field" (234). It would seem, from this, that Zukofsky is performing that most modernist act of imposing spatial form upon diachronic motion, turning linear prosody into a circle. But placing the word "in a rigorously plotted field" is more of an ideal for Zukofsky. The actual plotting of "n" and "r" sounds in "A"-9 is irregularly performed and gradually breaks down by the poem's end. Mathematics must remain a horizon rather than an accomplished fact since words, unlike points in Euclidean space, are subject to a philological and social history that is constantly evolving. For Zukofsky, it is enough to invoke mathematics as a discourse to emphasize his point that poems should imitate scientific rigor. And given "A"-9's subject matter, it seems clear that Zukofsky is interested less in the perfection of formal method than in the way it defamiliarizes and rematerializes. It is no accident that his most rigorous applications of the conic section formula are reserved for the two portions of *"A"* (8 and 9) that deal most directly with Marxian ideas.

Since this calculus is used in terms of ratios and velocities rather than static categories, it is useful to think of it as an analog to history. And indeed, in Zukofsky's essay on Henry Adams (based on his Columbia University M.A. thesis, completed in 1924), one may find this same geometrical formula invoked to explain Adams's theory of history. In the famous Paris Exposition passage in the *Education*, Adams describes man "as a force [who] must be measured by motion, from a fixed point" (quoted in *Prepositions* 114). In this same passage, the historian describes how, by using the Gothic era as "the unit from which he might measure motion down to his own time," he posits his own history as relative measure: "With the help of these two points of relation, he hoped to project his lines forward and backward indefinitely, subject to correction from anyone who should know better. Thereupon, he sailed for home" (*Prepositions* 115). This passage may seem irrelevant to issues of literary formalism, but it suggests an attitude toward history—and modernity specifically— in which the measurement of time is a function of two points, one of which (like the point moving on the periphery of a circle) is contemporary and therefore still under construction. Zukofsky also suggests that the reader ("anyone who should know better") may participate in this dialogue between past and present, correcting where necessary and situating his or her own subjectivity as an active agent of reinterpretation.

A further justification for Zukofsky's invocation of mathematics in *"A"*-9 is that it provides a counterpart to Marx's materialist science. The two sciences are not distinct, in Zukofsky's mind, and as a poet he is particularly aware of how poetry engages both. The poet takes the potentially "stable" system of language (as base and as superstructure, as number and as the things that it numbers) and subjects it to procedures that destabilize it, releasing congealed meanings from lexical sources. At the same time, he uses the sciences of materialism and physics against themselves as absolute descriptions of the world. They may describe the material relations between humans or between points on a curve, but they are not the same as any individual or any event. The inadequacies of both sciences as final descriptions of nature are explored in the second half of *"A"*-9.

Eight years intervened between the writing of the first part of

"A"-9 and the second, during which time World War II enacted its own terrible calculus in Europe and the revelations of Stalinist complicity with Hitler prior to the war and his brutality during the Moscow trials seriously damaged the left. During the same period, Zukofsky married Celia Thaew (1939), and their son Paul was born in 1943. When the poet returned to his epic in 1948, it was not to Marxian themes of labor but to Spinozistic ethics of love and natural generation. Most critics choose to see the second half of "A"-9 as a reply to the first, a lyric celebration of love over the alienated monologue of commodities:

> Love speaks: "in wracked cities there is less action,
> Sweet alyssum sometimes is not of time; now
> Weep, love's heir, rhyme now how song's exaction
> Is your distraction—related is equated,
> How else is love's distance approximated."
> ("A" 110–11)

There is little doubt that Zukofsky has found an alternative to "time congealed labor" in the second half, but it would be wrong to see him as rejecting politics entirely.[13] It would be more accurate to say that he discovers a more intimate arena in which to study his primary themes of labor and value. And if we consider the second half in light of "Mantis," we may recognize the poet's tendency to create a dialogue within the poem, the later portion responding to the earlier from a new perspective. Now things speak not of their exchange but of their use value:

> ... each in itself is saying, "behoove us,
> Disprove us least as things of love appearing
> In a wish gearing to light's infinite locus,
> Balm or jewelweed is according to focus.
> No one really knows us who does not love us,
> Time does not move us, we are and love, searing
> Remembrance—veering from guises which cloak us,
> So defined as eternal, men invoke us."
> ("A" 110)

Posed against modern commodification, relations of care and concern take precedence: "No one really knows us who does not love us" inverts a line in the first half, "No one really knows us who does not prove us" (107). We may see in this shift from value "proved" by exchange to value achieved through love a transformation of the social body into the human. Marx speaks of the attribution of agency to objects as a displacement of human sensuous activity onto property, and Zukofsky reminds us that the same process must happen in reverse as humans who care for one another invest nature with their own desire. This is why Zukofsky must *double* Cavalcanti's canzone—in order to "incarnate" or "flesh-out" the Italian poet's Neoplatonic metaphysics of love and resituate it in the body.[14] In short, Zukofsky writes the canzone that Pound could not, the latter being too preoccupied with making his epic serve the interests of a fascist millenium. And by choosing two (albeit heterodox) Jews for his intellectual support, Zukofsky's riposte is all the more ideologically charged.

The turn from Marx to Spinoza represents a change from a materialist definition of nature to an ethical one. It must be remembered, however, that Marx himself admired Spinoza and found in his *determinatio est negatio* ("Determination is negation") a model for the identity of production and consumption as defined in the *Grunderisse*. Furthermore, Spinoza's belief in a dynamic, active nature (*natura naturans*) involves that synthesis of creator and created that we have already observed in "Mantis" and that becomes the key to "A"-8. The opening lines of the latter draw directly on Spinoza, but with distinctly Marxian overtones:

> And of labor:
> Light lights in air,
>                         on streets, on earth, in earth—
> Obvious as that horses eat oats—
>                         Labor as creator,
>                                         Labor as creature,
> To right praise.
>                                         ("A" 43)

Zukofsky's substitution of labor for nature in the lines above suggests that he was willing to link Marx's theories of material production to Spinoza's just as Marx adapted Hegel's dialectics of spirit to the study of capitalism. In "A"-9, Spinoza reaffirms unities of subject and object, God and nature, much as Marx reaffirms the identity of laborer and product. In both seventeenth-century philosopher and nineteenth-century economist, reification begins with the invention of unattainable things-in-themselves, divorced from human action and separated from the sensual body. Zukofsky modulates the thought of each by rephrasing Marx through Spinoza in the second half, thus illustrating the inseparability of intellectual labor and material value.

## IDEOLOGY OF FORM

In his 1946 essay "For My Son When He Can Read," Zukofsky hopes that "Someone alive in the years 1951 to 2000 may attempt a scientific definition of poetry," a remark that sounds more like the words of a Russian Formalist or New Critic than that of an avant-garde poet (*Prepositions* 6). But of course Objectivism, Russian Formalism, and the New Criticism all arise as attempts to explain a new art through the eyes of science. Zukofsky's poetry following "*A*"-9 attempted to provide a practical analog for this definition, as his language became more and more hermetic and his concerns seemingly more aestheticized. Based on this (hypothetical) definition, one might regard his formulaic writing as a grand conclusion to some ultimate Mallarméan project. But the roots of this practice lie not in Symbolism or in the desire for a discrete realm of literariness but in the struggle to define the material basis of lived experience.

The formulaic character of "Mantis" and "*A*" is a hallmark of Zukofsky's work, and it has become an important feature of many later poets, from Jackson MacLow and Robert Creeley to the Language-writers. At stake in their debt to Zukofsky is a recognition of what, in my introduction, I referred to as the ideology of form—the idea that formal procedures derive from and generate critical frames. Zukofsky's use of Bach, to take one example, represents a synthesis of highly formulaic compositional practice (fugues based on the composer's name) as well as cultural values for the citizens of Leipzig invoked in "*A*"-1 who attend a performance of the St. Matthew Passion in 1729. Furthermore, the use of highly wrought structures offers alternative (and oppositional) responses to Pound's own formal practices. At every level—from the choice of Italian poets to the display of scientific knowledge—Zukofsky maps and inverts Pound's concerns. Where Vorticism was, a conic section remains.

As I said in my opening remarks, Zukofsky's use of formalism during the 1930s coincides with his interest in Marx and leftist politics. As Zukofsky said in 1938, "*A*" was to be "an epic of the class struggle" (quoted in "Notes on Contributors"), but most commentators have dismissed this intention by pointing to the lack of Marxian ideas in the later sections of the poem. More insidious is that critics have tried to protect Zukofsky from his own political commitments during the 1930s, a strategy that dehistoricizes both the poet and the movement created out of his critical remarks. I would like to reassert that intention and add that, as a "poem of a life," "A" inevitably mirrored the disillusion experienced by many Marxists in the wake of the Hitler/Stalin pact and revelations of the Gulag. This does not impugn Zukofsky's feeling, in his most vital period, that an epic poem could be generated out of (not simply reflect) Marxist principles. Furthermore, one could say that he was empowered to continue writing as he did because Marx taught him how reification had to be dismantled: by positing art not as what Adorno called a "windowless monad" in which the failed hope for community could be sequestered but as a productive enterprise in its own right. The dialogue between formalism and critique (the "Mantis" sestina and its interpretation) involves an intellectual labor in which a new kind of subject is born. The same could be said for the sonnet sequence of "A"-7 or the formulaic passages of "A"-8 and "A"-9; their formal rigor reveals writing as a process, an "action" in which things (words) cease to reflect a natural standpoint and thus stand out *as* things.[15]

But not things *only* as things. Pound had written to Zukofsky in 1935 claiming that "A commodity is a material thing or substance / it has a certain durability," to which Zukofsky angrily responded that "*labor* is the *basic commodity*. . . . What do you think labor *is* aside from what you say it does—'transmute material'—just automatic exhilaration in the best of all possible—to-day—economic worlds" (Pound and Zukofsky 171)? Zukofsky sees what Pound, the Social Credit enthusiast, does not: that labor must be more than "automatic exhilaration" or transmutation; it must be regarded as the activity of people, a dialogue between individuals who create history as they seize the forms of their labor. Zukofsky, with an eye to his own verbal action, "Forces abstraction to turn from equated / Values to labor" and in so doing makes his formal enterprise "the detail, not the mirage, of seeing, of thinking with the things as they exist" (*Prepositions* 13). It was upon this plank that Objectivism was born and upon which it must be reassessed.

# 5

## "Not Sappho, Sacco"
*Postmodern Narratives/Modernist Forms in Muriel Rukeyser and Charles Reznikoff*

> Poetry can extend the document.
> Muriel Rukeyser, Note to
> *The Book of the Dead*

> This is a nation's scene and halfway house.
> Muriel Rukeyser,
> "The Book of the Dead"

### NARRATIVE AND NATIONALITY

Recent scholarly debate suggests that poetry is once again in crisis. Conference panels, books and articles with titles such as *Can Poetry Matter?*, "Is Talk about Poetry Still Important to Us?," "Whatever Happened to Poetics?" or "Do We Still Talk about Poetry?" imply that, at least in academic forums, the significance of poetry has diminished from its more buoyant forms during the 1960s and 1970s.[1] While there are probably a multitude of reasons for this crisis, one that I would like to develop here involves a certain "narrative turn" in postmodern cultural theory, a turn analogous (and dialectically related) to the "linguistic turn" of structuralism and semiotics. Beginning with early studies in narratology, the turn toward narrative can be found in Bakhtinian stylistics, tropological historiography in Paul Ricoeur and Hayden White, Fredric Jameson's cultural theory, studies of nation formation and colonization in Benedict Anderson, Gayatri Spivak, and Homi Bhabha, and New Americanist projections of *post*national identities. It can be seen in Jean-François Lyotard's diagnosis of the "postmodern condition" (an incredulity toward metanarratives), and it informs neo-Freudian critiques of interpretation in Gilles Deleuze and Félix Guattari. It dominates cultural study's interest in marginalized and hybrid voices and new historicist readings of cultural texts.

While a comprehensive survey of this narrative turn is not my subject in this chapter, I would like to focus on one influential version of it and the ways that it excludes poetry, particularly that engaged with issues of national identity. In the work of many postcolonial critics, "nation" is viewed as a story whose plot is the growth of "a people" from common linguistic and cultural origins through stages of conquest, unification, and colonization.[2] The name of this story is "nationalism," and according to Mary Layoun it "lays claim to a privileged narrative perspective on the nation (the 'people') and thus justifies its own capacity to narrate its story" (411). Within this national narrative emerge ideologies of cohesion and consensus by which immigrants, dissidents, and ethnic others can be marginalized or suppressed. At the same time, these subaltern populations articulate their own relationships to national ideals by means of stories, thus creating counterhegemonic narratives of ethnic origin, cultural identity, and resistance. Depending on which side of hegemony one lives, poetry may serve as a civilizing agent for the dominant culture's educational and colonizing agenda or as the repository for indigenous folk myths and traditions that reinforce new nationalist movements. A poet like Yeats, as Edward Said points out, may serve both agendas, but whether his work is used as an example of high cultural (British) modernism or Irish nationalism, it is subsumed within a descriptive code based on narrative ("Yeats and Decolonization").

While this is a highly schematic description of the ways in which "nation and narration" are joined, it is based on the priority given to temporal models used to define the modern nation-state. Homi Bhabha's "Dissemination," to take the best-known example, describes nationhood as an attempt to provide the "ambivalent temporalities" of modern existence with a causal logic, a teleology of progress that will link disparate peoples and cultural backgrounds into a common historical sequence. "The scraps, patches and rags of daily life must be repeatedly turned into the signs of a coherent national culture, while the very act of the narrative performance interpellates a growing circle of national subjects" (145). When those national subjects resist these interpellations (Bhabha's example is the Harlem Renaissance), their cultural practices are nevertheless fashioned in a rhetoric of national narrativity, albeit one that "thrives on rhetorical strategies of hybridity, deformation, masking, and inversion" (144).

For Fredric Jameson, prose narrative becomes a privileged site for studying the formation of national subjects since its structure replicates tensions within the culture at large. Although prose fiction is often Jameson's primary object of study, narrative means considerably more than a literary genre; it implies a descriptive code or cognitive map by which reality is normalized. All texts—even the most resolutely apolitical ones—are informed by a political unconscious that acts on them much as the libido, in Freud's theory of repression, structures the ego. Jameson, like Adorno before him, favors moments of intimacy and introspection in modern novels because by positing a separate, private space of subjectivity they announce their distance from a more threatening public arena of capitalist exchange. Jameson feels that we can see the workings of this "internal distancing" in the novels of Gissing, Conrad, and Joyce, but we can also see it in third-world novels in which "the story of the private individual destiny is always an allegory of the embattled situation of the public, third-world culture and society" ("Third World Literature" 69).[3] To understand the political unconscious he must deny agency to the author (and by extension the political subjects being represented) in favor of the "scientific" critic able to see beyond the workings of ideology inscribed on the text's surfaces.

While Jameson's reading of narrative as national allegory could, with some modification, be applied to many modernist poems (one thinks of Pound's *Cantos* or Neruda's *Canto General* or Edward Brathwaite's *Middle Passage*), he resists doing so because for him poetry is subsumed under an ideology of modernist autonomy.[4] When he confronts poetry at all—as in his reading of Bob Perelman's "China"—he must read the text's fracturings and non sequiturs as symptoms of postmodern schizophrenia, not as a critical perspective on "the immense, unfinished social experiment of the new China" (*Postmodernism* 29).[5] One suspects that Jameson's resistance to poetry is also a reaction to its centrality for the New Criticism or the Yale school of deconstruction, in which it served as a privileged mode of linguistic indeterminacy. What links Jameson to his former colleagues at Yale is his belief that the text requires an interpreter to complete or fulfill its absences—whether rhetorical or ideological.

Jameson's theory of the political unconscious has been influential for theorists anxious to explain nationhood as a cultural, rather than strictly sociopolitical, phenomenon and who draw upon the close relationship between the formation of nation-states and the evolution of realist fiction.⁶ The unexamined term in these versions of national narrative is not "national," a category rightly being deconstructed as a self-evident term for social and political organization, but "narrative," insofar as it provides the rhetorical markers and syntax within which national identities are formed. But narrative is hardly limited to prose. From Shelley's "Mask of Anarchy" to Browning's monologues through Yeats's "Meditations in Time of Civil War" and Pound's *Cantos* to the long poems of Hugh MacDiarmid, W. H. Auden, and Charles Reznikoff, narrative becomes a vehicle for a critical reappraisal of nationhood. Unlike the romantic crisis poem admired by M. H. Abrams and Harold Bloom or the metaphysical lyric valued by T. S. Eliot and John Crowe Ransom, narrative poetry engages history over time and, at least in the cases I will be discussing, by means of documentary evidence drawn from the public sphere. To adapt Jameson's phrase, narrative poetry becomes the political unconscious of high modernist lyricism, a reminder that temporality cannot be contained in epiphanic moments. The scandal of narrative poetry for modernists was the eruption of lived history into the objective correlative; the scandal of narrative poetry for contemporary theory is the eruption of critical historiography in poetic form.

## DOCUMENTARY CULTURE

The title of my chapter is taken from Muriel Rukeyser's "Poem out of Childhood" (1935), which describes the shift among writers of her generation from "Sappho" to "Sacco," from the expatriate salon culture of the 1920s to 1930s activism inaugurated by the Sacco-Vanzetti trial. The distance covered is also from an austere lyricism, for whom Sappho was the model, to forms of documentary history and photojournalism that blur generic terms.⁷ The result is a series of hybrid works that begin to appear in the late 1920s, continue well into the postwar era, but have as their enabling moment the social crisis brought about by the 1929 crash. These works would include John Dos Passos's *U.S.A.* trilogy, James Agee and Walker Evans's *Let Us Now Praise Famous Men*, Zora Neale Hurston's *Mules and Men*, Margaret Bourke White and Erskine Caldwell's *You Have Seen Their Faces*, Hart Crane's *The Bridge*, Ezra Pound's Adams and Dynastic Cantos, William Carlos Williams's *Paterson*, Marianne Moore's pastiche poems, Charles Reznikoff's *Testimony*, Langston Hughes's *Mon-*

*tage of a Dream Deferred*, and Rukeyser's "Book of the Dead." Such works complicate our sense of high modernist formalism by relying on genres of folklore, documentary, oral history, reportage, legal testimony, and advertising. The use of such materials does more than provide texture to historical themes; it participates directly in the writing of history by exposing the institutional venues through which history is written.

Of course nothing could be more modernist than the introduction of nonliterary materials into the literary, but what distinguishes these works from Dadaist or Surrealist collage is their documentary character, their reliance on a public record and the institutions that support and uphold that record. Applied to our concerns with national narrative, we could say that quoting from documents in poetry redirects modernism's emphasis on the materiality of aesthetic language to the materiality of social speech. This tendency to foreground the materiality of the document also differentiates these works from more recognizable narrative poems of the same period—the work of Frost, Sandberg, Rexroth, Auden, or Jeffers—in which storytelling reaffirms the authority of a reflective consciousness at odds with modern materialism. Pound's cantos of the 1930s are driven by an increasing—sometimes obsessive—concern for the possibilities of a fascist aporia, yet his personal voice is replaced by the published histories of early federalist America and dynastic Chinese history, as if to solicit validating testimony for the present from other times, other places. From the opposite political perspective, Charles Reznikoff's *Testimony*, by its use of court cases, instantiates his critique of industrial America by focusing on the system of jurisprudence that mediates relations between individuals under the law. Stress in both cases is on the discursive properties of the official record in narrating social ideals.

That this record is intimately tied to the construction of national identity can be gleaned from Reznikoff's comments on the 1934 edition of *Testimony:*

> A few years ago . . . I was working for a publisher of law books, reading cases from every state and every year (since this country became a nation). Once in a while I could see in the facts of a case details of the time and place, and it seemed to me that out of such material the century and a half during which the U.S. has been a nation could be written up, not from the standpoint of an individual, as in diaries,

nor merely from the angle of the unusual, as in newspapers, but from every standpoint—as many standpoints as were provided by the witnesses themselves. (xiii)

Reznikoff rejects the idea of a unified national story based on consensus, whether through personal impressions (diary) or exceptionalist history (newspaper). Rather, he writes through the voices of multiple witnesses as they appear in legal testimony. But he does more than this; he recognizes that witness itself is bounded within a material form (a court transcript in a case report) and an ideological state apparatus (a legal system that interprets the meaning of such witness). Thus, the use of legal language retains a degree of objectivity while calling attention to the ideological field such objectivity serves.

Reznikoff's writing of American history began in the early 1930s, when, as we have seen with Oppen and Zukofsky, the spacious vistas of capitalist largesse were being severely challenged. Writers on the left such as Reznikoff and Rukeyser were part of a new documentary culture that, to paraphrase Walter Benjamin, was trying to "brush history against the grain" by reading American history not as a narrative of Adamic discovery and perfectability but as a material record of diverse constituencies. *They Must All Be Represented* is both the title of a documentary project and an imperative felt by writers of the time to write history from "as many standpoints as were provided by the witnesses themselves."

## CAMERA AT THE CROSSING: "THE BOOK OF THE DEAD"

Muriel Rukeyser's "The Book of the Dead," published in *U.S. 1* (1938), offers a striking synthesis of narrative poetry and documentary culture as it emerged through various federal agencies (Works Projects Administration, Federal Arts Project, Farm Security Administration) and through collaborative projects such as those of Agee and Evans. It is against the backdrop of the era's photojournalism and investigative reporting that "The Book of the Dead" must be read, fusing as it does techniques of modernist pastiche and montage with partisan reportage and editing. In this respect, Rukeyser's poem represents the obverse of Zukofsky's attempt to rewrite the labor theory of value as a double canzone. Whereas *"A"*-9 treats aesthetic compression as a form of unalienated labor power, Rukeyser maintains the photojournalist's perspective upon lived experience, creating a gap, as she says, between "The man on the street and the camera eye" (16). Furthermore, she builds her poem on themes of death and renewal familiar to readers of modernist poems like *The Waste Land*. The fragments she shores against ruin are not the voices of Homer, Dante, or Baudelaire but of George Robinson, Arthur Peyton, and Vivian Jones—anonymous actors in an industrial tragedy that must be included in any national narrative.

The camera eye that records the "man on the street" was more than a metaphor for Rukeyser; it was an aperture through which she often looked during the 1930s, both as a poet and as a social activist. She was intimately connected to the worlds of photography and film through her participation in the Film and Photo League and Frontier Films (for which she served on the board of directors).[8] She provided the subtitles to several films, including *The Defense of Madrid*, a silent film dealing with the Spanish Civil War. She was close friends of documentary filmmakers and writers such as Joris Ivans, Ben Maddow, Paul Rotha, Paul Strand, and Leo Hurwitz, with whom she collaborated on a number of projects.[9] For Rukeyser, film provided an ideal synthesis of individual creativity, collective work, and ethical pedagogy whose technical manipulation often served as an analog for poetry:

> One characteristic of modern poetry is that arrangement of parts which strikes many people as being violent or obscure. It is a method which is familiar enough on the screen; when you see the picture of a night-club, and then see the heroine's face thrown back as she sings, you make the unity without any effort, without even being conscious of your process. (*Life of Poetry* 16)

The poet, like the film editor, deals in "rhythms of length and relationship." In language reminiscent of Sergei Eisenstein, Rukeyser extols the "ethical" value of editing yet the collective work of commercial filmmaking—its "repressive codes and sanctions [and] the company-town feeling" put the process "at the end of any creative spectrum farthest from the making of a poem" (152, 150–51). Rukeyser's remarks about the Hollywood studio system anticipate those of later intellectuals who saw in the emerging culture industries of the postwar period the debasement of collective work—where the writer is "forced to conform to a code which dictates emotional limits, and [produces] material which can be censored and re-arranged, with or without his knowledge" (156).

Against the instrumentalized filmmaking of Hollywood, Rukeyser poses the documentary film, a medium that, however flawed, considerably influenced modern commercial filmmaking. In *The Life of Poetry* she acknowledges the importance of early documentaries such as *The River, Night Mail,* and *These Are the Men,* which were limited initially by their aestheticization of movement for its own sake— a tendency to focus on the rhythms of machinery and labor for the sensual appeal of repetitions. Quoting Paul Rotha, Rukeyser avers that early documentarians "did not . . . realize that these repetitive rhythms, beautiful to watch in themselves, raised important materialist issues of the men at the machines, of the social and economic problems lying behind modern machinery and transport" (158). But in films such as *Spanish Earth, Crisis, Native Land,* and *Heart of Spain* (which featured scores by Aaron Copland, Virgil Thomson, and Hanns Eisler), Rukeyser finds an ideal synthesis of documentary and "enacted film."

All of this has relevance for "The Book of the Dead," a poem built upon documentary techniques and materials taken from the congressional record. The poem tells of a West Virginia mining tragedy in which workers were exposed to excessive amounts of silica while digging a tunnel near Gauley's Junction as part of a hydroelectric dam project.[10] To extract the silica, a valuable mineral used in the processing of steel, workers were forced to mine the tunnel dry instead of using wet drills. The tunnel was not adequately ventilated, and workers were not required to wear masks, even though the New Kanawha Power Company, which contracted the job, well knew the deadly effects of toxic dust on the lungs. Many miners contracted silicosis and died by slow suffocation, and when survivors sued the parent company, Union Carbide, their claims resulted in minimal compensation. What little money they did receive was absorbed by lawyers' fees. The company's attempts to conceal its illegal drilling practices became the subject of a federal investigation, from which numerous testimonies in the poem are derived.

According to the British documentary filmmaker Paul Botha, Rukeyser had hoped to help him make a documentary film of the events the poem depicts, but the deal fell through.[11] Instead, she traveled to the minefields of West Virginia with Nancy Naumberg, a lifelong friend and member of the Film and Photo League whose presence was to become an important focal point for the authorial perspective of the poem.[12] Rukeyser and Naumberg visited the West Virginia site to provide photographic documentation that would supplement the use of testimony drawn from congressional subcommittee hearings conducted on the case.[13] Although Naumberg's photographs were not included in the first edition of U.S. 1, her presence as recorder is represented in "The Book of the Dead" as a locus for acts of looking, hearing, and observing that parallel the documentary form of the poem. Rukeyser is aware of the paradoxical relationship between the silicon-based glass of the camera eye and the deaths of miners from the same substance:

> Now the photographer unpacks camera and case,
> surveying the deep country, follows discovery
> viewing on groundglass an inverted image.
> (10)

This inverted image by which the photographer records the scene is, as Walter Kalaidjian points out, the camera obscura that Marx utilized to describe the workings of ideology—in which "men and their circumstances appear upside-down" (167). Rukeyser provides her own version of this figure in a note in which she explains that although "Gauley Bridge is inland ... it was created by theories, systems and workmen from many coastal sections—factors which are, in the end, not regional or national. Local images have one kind of reality. U.S. 1 will, I hope, have that kind and another too. Poetry can extend the document" (146).

Poetry can *incorporate* the document as well, as Rukeyser does, by including testimony from congressional hearings, stock reports, letters, newspaper articles, and interviews with miners and their families. These inclusions not only frame the details of the Gauley's Junction debacle but provide voices for those who were affected by it. Philip Wheelwright, reviewing the book in *Partisan Review*, criticized this strategy of presentation for its emphasis on the "excrescences of capitalism, not the system's inner nature," yet it is precisely such discursive "excrescences" that provide Rukeyser with her critical focus (quoted in Kertesz 122). At one point in the middle of the poem, she includes a stock quotation showing Union Carbide's net gain per share and the stockholders' dividend earned as a result of its silica mining operations. It is a graphic representation of the bottom line that drives industrial expansion and signals the surplus value produced by harnessing natural power at the expense of labor power. The quotation's stark presentation of figures says more than any editorializing comment could about the "inner nature" of capitalist exploitation.

The triadic relationship between economic, natural, and labor power is sustained throughout the poem. Against the diversion of water into hydroelectric power are the testimonies of Philippa Allen, Vivian Jones, Mearl Blankenship, George Robinson, and others whose stories present plural narratives of corporate insensitivity, mismanagement, and greed. Their testimonies against Union Carbide offer a fourth term of power—that of speech—against the silica that has, quite literally, closed off the breath. The nameless mother whose three sons died at Gauley Bridge and whose husband has been debilitated describes the pain that silicosis has caused her family. She quotes her dying son, who urges her to seek compensation:

> he lay and said, "Mother, when I die,
> "I want you to have them open me up and
> "see if that dust killed me.
> "Try to get compensation,
> "you will not have any way of making your living
> "when we are gone,
> "and the rest are going too."
>                                                   (28)

To some extent, Rukeyser performs the necessary operation, "opening him up" and gaining a compensation his mother would never receive. Rukeyser fuses with the woman's voice at the end of this section when she says, "He shall not be diminished, never / I shall give a mouth to my son" (30). The mythic stature achieved by this mother is marked as such by italicized lines that punctuate those in Roman:

> *I have gained mastery over my heart*
> *I have gained mastery over my two hands*
> *I have gained mastery over the waters*
> *I have gained mastery over the river.*
>                                                   (29)

In a poem in which individuals have ceded power to the power company, such claims of mastery appear to have been made in vain. But when the mother's voice is joined to the testimonies of others—Rukeyser's as well—then some of the suffering may be mitigated.

The documentary evidence of "The Book of the Dead" involves a debate over who shall "speak" for workers who have no voice. Those who are empowered to represent the needs of those workers turn out to be professionals and bureaucrats whose salaries are paid by the parent company and whose ability to speak is thereby mediated. The mother's attempt to find a doctor who will X-ray her children is frustrated by the doctor's complicity within the mining company:

> When they took sick, right at the start, I saw a doctor.
> I tried to get Dr. Harless to X-ray the boys.
> He was the only man I had any confidence in,
> the company doctor in the Kopper's mine,
> but he would not see Shirley.
> He did not know where his money was coming from.
> (28)

The mother's agonizing description of her attempt to find money for the X-ray is compounded by the unwillingness of the doctors to diagnose the illness as silicosis. The equation of powerlessness and voicelessness is focused in the next section when Rukeyser literalizes the recovery of the son's voice by quoting from a doctor's oral description of an X-ray. Lacking a photographic representation of lungs destroyed by silicosis, Rukeyser represents that visual record as reported by the voice of medical authority:

> This is the X-ray picture taken last April.
> I would point out to you : these are the ribs;
> this is the region of the breastbone;
> this is the heart (a wide white shadow filled with blood).
> In here of course is the swallowing tube, esophagus.
> The windpipe. Spaces between the lungs.
> (31)

The clinical description of organs and skeleton, the outlining of internal cavities, is punctuated by questions coming from the investigating committee ("Between the ribs?" "What stage?") and then by testimony from afflicted victims:

"It is growing worse every day. At night
"I get up to catch my breath. If I remained
"flat on my back I believe I would die."
                    (32)

This polyphony of voices—including the absent photograph itself—draws attention to the twin roles of narration, both as interpretation and as physical medium.

As Michael Thurston points out, Rukeyser's own "voice" is active in such sections by editing congressional testimony in order to "[destabilize] the authoritative voice of the local physician, Dr. L. R. Harless, and the institutional authority of the medical profession" (223). Such editing puts the voice of several witnesses into one person, as in the case of "The Doctors" when the words of separate physicians, journalists, and congressmen are fused into a common voice of authority. Such deliberate editing may violate the original record, but as in many documentaries it enables one to see complicity in malfeasance, which might be eclipsed by a proliferation of isolated documents. We see medical professionals as a group, capable of invoking scientific detachment in order to avoid responsibility for human suffering. When pressed by committee members to answer whether silicosis could be caused by external factors in the mine, Dr. Goldwater retreats into vagueness:

Dr. Goldwater. I hope you are not provoked when I say "might."
            Medicine has no hundred percent.
            We speak of possibilities, have opinions.
Mr. Griswold. Doctors testify answering "yes" and "no."
            Don't they?
Dr. Goldwater. Not by the choice of the doctor.
Mr. Griswold. But that is usual, isn't it?
Dr. Goldwater. They do not like to do that.
            A man with a scientific point of view—
            unfortunately there are doctors without that—
            I do not mean to say all doctors are angels—
            but most doctors avoid dogmatic statements.
            avoid assiduously "always," "never."
                                (40–41)

I have stressed the documentary character of "The Book of the Dead," but Rukeyser provides interpretive frames for extending the document into national allegory. She figures herself as the engaged

"Not Sappho, Sacco"   147

spectator driving through a landscape marked (and often scarred) by history. By taking literal and figurative backroads into America's industrial landscape, Rukeyser connects the current events at Gauley Bridge with the larger political history of the South. Her journey takes her past Indian sites, battlegrounds, and the marker for John Brown's raid upon Harpers Ferry. Resistance, of the sort represented by John Brown, continues in the voices of those who testified against Union Carbide, but their heroism is as anonymous as the town they inhabit. Rukeyser responds to those who want their history in romantic form:

> What do you want—a cliff over a city?
> A foreland sloped to sea and overgrown with roses?
> These people live here.
>                                      (17)

Despite her attempt to return history to the lived experience of citizens, she develops mythic implications of the mining disaster by alluding to the Egyptian *Book of the Dead*. As a modernist Isis, Rukeyser gathers the scattered limbs of the proletariat ("strikers, soldiers, pioneers") and joins them to the Republican forces in Spain ("from the hero hills / near Barcelona") and finally to the miners of West Virginia. Like previous heroic questers (and modernist poets), these miners also descend into the underworld, although their journey is not a search for lost cultural plenitude but a fatal contract with progress:

> these carrying light for safety on their foreheads
> descended deeper for richer faults of ore,
>     drilling their death.
>
> These touching radium and the luminous poison,
> carried their death on their lips and with their warning
>     glow in their graves.
>                                      (70)

In this rather stunning anticipation of more recent workplace contaminations, Rukeyser deflates the modernist mythological imperative typified by Eliot's invocation of cyclic vegetation myths. Buried in *this* waste land are the corpses of workers for whom a reading of the classics would have offered little sustenance. When ritual descent is controlled by mercantile interests, one's only defense is sight, an ability to "widen the lens and see / standing over the land myths of identity, / new signals, processes" (71).

This widening of the lens through camera and documentary testimony is figured in the metaphor of glass. As Walter Kalaidjian has noted, it is the central motif of the poem "insofar as it signifies modernization, ownership, and the spectacle of consumerism" (168). The ocularcentric world of modernist commodity culture is literally "ground down" to its basic component, silicon dioxide, thus reversing the process of industrial production to show its effects on workers. The windows, lenses, X-ray machines, and glasses that become metaphors of unmediated access to truth suddenly become clouded, obscured by a fine white powder that chokes the lungs.

This inversion of the productive apparatus has implications for narrative poetry as well, uniting two kinds of representation: the mirror and the lamp, the diachronic record and the transcendent moment. Recent attempts to revive narrative poetry—the so-called new narrative movement—have attempted to solve the anomalous character of the genre by contesting the "old" free-verse versions in Pound and Williams (and presumably in Rukeyser). Frederick Fierstein contends that by eschewing meter, earlier modernists were thrown back on "old myths or texts or ... some larger political action offstage" to drive what were essentially lyric sequences (9). What Rukeyser's example suggests is that for her generation, "larger political action" could never occur offstage but had to be embedded in the materiality—the "excrescences"—of her text. The glass in both mirror and lamp could then be seen as a chemical substance that both kills and permits sight. Such understanding of the crucial pact between medium and truth would seem congruent with the study of narrative as a socially symbolic act.

"These are roads to take when you think of your country," Rukeyser says in her opening line:

> and interested bring down the maps again,
> phoning the statistician, asking the dear friend,
> reading the papers with morning inquiry.
> Or when you sit at the wheel and your small light
> chooses gas gauge and clock; and the headlights
>
> indicate future of road, your wish pursuing
> past the junction, the fork, the suburban station,
> well-travelled six-lane highway planned for safety.
> (9)

"Not Sappho, Sacco"  149

At one level, these lines describe the literal roads Rukeyser drove with Nancy Naumberg to get to Gauley's Junction, roads that had been extensively expanded through WPA construction projects. To give a "voice" to these roads the Federal Writers' Project provided a series of guidebooks for the new automobile-driven landscape.[14] What these guidebooks revealed to their readers was that roads such as U.S. 1 are suffused with history—from the founding of Virginia in the seventeenth century to the establishment of Union military headquarters during the Civil War: "troops / here in Gauley Bridge, Union headquarters, lines / bring in the military telegraph" (12). These lines introduce a second meaning of "roads" as lines of communication, conduits of testimony and conversation that knit a larger community together. By the end of the poem, we understand that the roads also have a vertical dimension, the descent into mythological realms that provide the poem with its title. At each level, horizontal and vertical, these roads "take you into your own country," but a country "mirrored" in men and as such cannot be reconstituted in an overarching symbol of human aspiration (*The Bridge*) or an archetypal city on a hill (*Paterson*). The mirror itself—the material record of what people say—is a surface of conflicting promises and misleading statistics for which a collective pronoun is inadequate. The national narrative remains necessarily partial and incomplete, "a nation's scene and halfway house" (66).

## THE MATTER OF THE DOCUMENT

Although "The Book of the Dead" is unique among Rukeyser's poems in its direct quotation of nonliterary materials, it is consistent with her lifelong commitment to personal witness. Many of her poems derive from firsthand experiences of historical crises—from "Mediterranean" (1938), written while attending the antifascist Olympic games in Spain, to "The Gates" (1978), inspired by her visit to South Korea in support of dissident poet Kim Chi Ha. What links the documentary imperative to acts of testimony is the fact that eyewitness reports retain some vestige of the unique individual; they testify that someone was actually present when such-and-such happened, and *this* document is its record. Shoshana Felman observes that testimony is like writing; both extend solitude—the fact that a witness can report on only his or her experience—to others. "As a performative speech act, testimony in effect addresses what in history is action that exceeds any substantialized significance, and what happens in impact that dynamically explodes any conceptual reifications and any constative deliminations" (5). Felman is speaking of testimony by Holocaust survivors for whom the horrors of concentration camps are beyond any category of "truth." She could be speaking for many works written if not "after Auschwitz" at least within its orbit—the Depression, World War II, the Holocaust, the atom bomb, the highly technologized wars of more recent history—in which the ability of the private voice to provide adequate testimony has become attenuated.

The disparity between private witness and historical trauma marks testimony as a Janus-faced phenomenon pointing both at the integrity of the speaker and at the discursive frame within which he or she speaks. Something of this dual character of witness can be found in Charles Reznikoff's *Testimony*. Compared to Rukeyser's use of the Egyptian *Book of the Dead* to mythologize the Gauley Bridge disaster, Reznikoff's austere use of legal briefs makes this a very different kind of text. Kenneth Burke, in his introduction to the 1934 edition of the work, observes that such spareness offers a salutary alternative to the world-historical syntheses of someone such as Spengler. "[Reznikoff's] bare presentation of the records places us before people who appear in the meager simplicity of their complaints" (Reznikoff, *Testimony* [1934] xiv). At the same time, the standpoint from which these complaints are made is that of the law court, in which the objectivity of documentary evidence is mediated by the institution of jurisprudence:

> In this respect Mr. Reznikoff's work embodies in miniature the
> problem of the "whole truth" as it arises in civilization marked by
> many pronounced differences in occupational pattern. There arise the
> "doctor's point of view," the "accountant's point of view," the "salesman's point of view," the "minister's point of view". . . . Much of
> Mr. Reznikoff's "testimony" is clearly local to his profession; but the
> vein of sympathy that underlies his work is not similarly local. (xvi)

Burke's canny recognition of the duplicit character of legal testimony—its claims to objective truth while reflecting occupational and class positions—speaks not only to *Testimony* but to Objectivist poetics in general. Reznikoff's oft-quoted remark about the Objectivist poet being one "who is restricted to the testimony of a witness in a court of law" has permitted many of his readers to assume a correspondence between poet and witness, thus effacing the poet's active role in selecting materials and interpreting relations between one subject and another ("A Talk" 99).[15] The example of *Testimony* suggests, on the contrary, that the poet serves not as witness but as editor—a witness of witnesses—whose arrangement of legal documents supplies a social narrative for acts of private observation.[16] *Testimony* provides an extreme example of negative capability; Reznikoff stated as much in his interview with L. S. Dembo: "Something happens and it expresses something that you feel, not necessarily because of *those* facts, but because of entirely different facts that give you the same kind of feeling" (106). The localized suffering of laborers in factories, of blacks in Jim Crow America, or of children in abusive families may not be experienced by the general populace, but testimony to these conditions in court cases produces a kind of collective witness that transcends local conditions. To this extent, Reznikoff's objectification does not escape empathy but rather provides a series of surfaces upon which identification can be built.

By basing his poem on summaries of court cases, Reznikoff stresses the legal structure of history, the reported character of events as framed by the law court. The cases upon which *Testimony* is based were found by the poet in volumes of the federal and state reporter system, developed by West Publishing Company in the nineteenth century to provide a record of all published decisions of cases that reach the appellate level. As a writer for the legal encyclopedia *Corpus Juris*, Reznikoff would have used these summaries on a daily basis, and in his papers can be found photocopies of pages from individual volumes from which he derived sections of the poem. The volumes of West's national reporter system are divided into seven districts—Pacific, North Western, South Western, North Eastern, Atlantic, South Eastern, and Southern—and are supplemented by individual reporters for fourteen states. This regional division provided Reznikoff with his somewhat abbreviated division of the poem into four cardinal compass points and allowed him, as we will see, to link various cases by region. The poem is further subdivided by categories ("children," "the machine age," "negroes") relating to the type of injury or individuals involved. According to an unpublished "Prolegomena" found among his papers, Reznikoff utilized the reporter system to organize not only the geographical location of cases

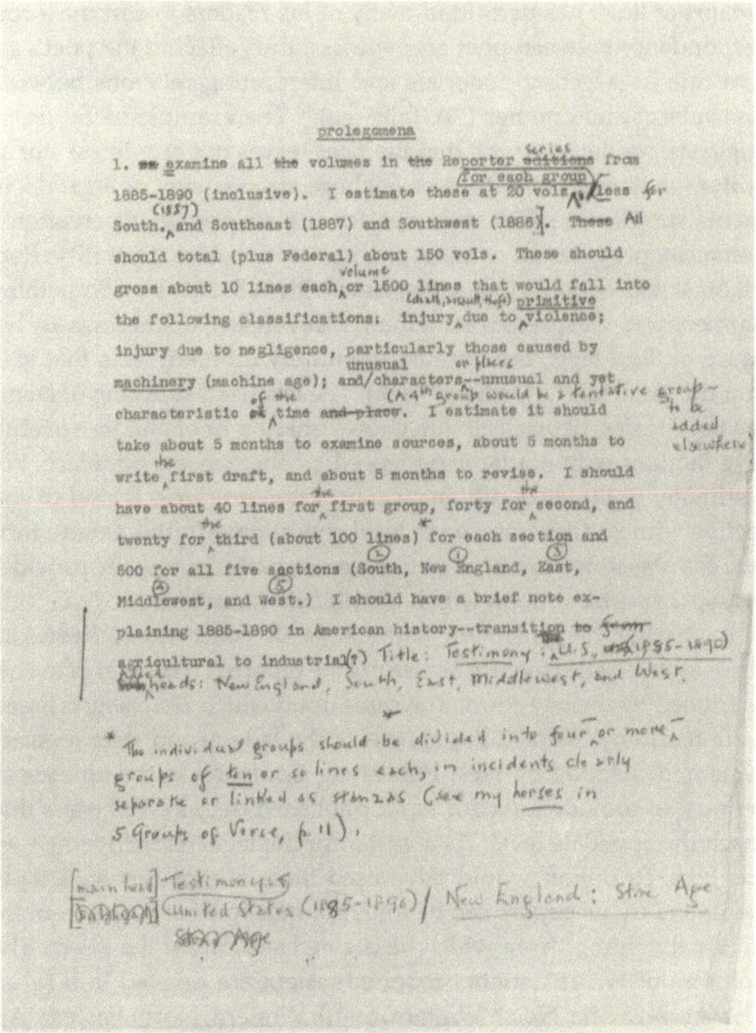

> prolegomena
>
> 1. examine all the volumes in the Reporter series from
> 1885-1890 (inclusive). I estimate these at 20 vols.
> South, and Southeast (1887) and Southwest (1886).
> should total (plus Federal) about 150 vols. These should
> gross about 10 lines each, or 1500 lines that would fall into
> the following classifications: injury due to violence;
> injury due to negligence, particularly those caused by
> machinery (machine age); and/characters—unusual and yet
> characteristic of time and place. I estimate it should
> take about 5 months to examine sources, about 5 months to
> write first draft, and about 5 months to revise. I should
> have about 40 lines for first group, forty for second, and
> twenty for third (about 100 lines) for each section and
> 500 for all five sections (South, New England, East,
> Middlewest, and West.) I should have a brief note ex-
> plaining 1885-1890 in American history—transition
> agricultural to industrial(?)

Figure 9. Charles Reznikoff, "Prolegomena."

but the number of lines devoted to each jurisdiction. He even estimated the amount of time it would take to read all 150 volumes (including the federal reporter series) and how many lines should be derived from each volume (Fig. 9). Thus, not only does the poem draw its language from court cases, its formal structure is determined by the arrangement of cases as they appear in a library of books.[17]

The continuity linking the several editions of *Testimony* is the act of translation, whether from witness to judge, from court transcript to case report in the reporter volumes, from first-person testimony to third-person narration, from prose to verse.[18] We can see the complexity of Reznikoff's translation by comparing a case found in the reporter volumes with its subsequent typescript and printed transformations. Under the subheading "Machine Age" appears a brief poem based on a Maryland case in which a young woman sued the American Tobacco Company for damages incurred as a result of an accident she suffered while working there. The *Atlantic Reporter* describes the case as follows:

> When she first went into the company's employ, in January 1897, she worked on a sieve . . . but her employment was subsequently changed to sweeping the floors of the factory, and she was so engaged in May, 1897, when she was injured. Among other places she was required to sweep was a room in which there was a smooth, revolving vertical shaft which ran from the floor to the ceiling and which was in an aisle or passageway between the wall and a stationary machine, being about 28 inches from the former and 10 inches from the latter. The shaft is 3 inches in diameter and at the time of the accident it made about 170 revolutions a minute. It was the duty of the plaintiff to sweep around this shaft as well as other places where the dust collected on the floor; and in doing so on the morning of the accident, her apron was caught in some way, and was drawn around the shaft. She was whirled around and violently striking such objects as were in her way (probably the wall and machinery) had her clothing torn from her and received injuries which confined her in a hospital for nine weeks. (*American Tobacco* 1,084)

The reporter summary goes on to discuss the $6,000 award that the girl's family received, the appeal filed by the company, and a motion to dismiss the appeal on various technicalities. In Reznikoff's version, however, only the details concerning the accident and the workplace are retained:

> All revolving shafts are dangerous
> but a vertical shaft,
> neither boxed nor guarded against,
> most dangerous.

> The girl's work for the company was changed
> to sweeping the floors:
> among other places the floor of a room
> where the shaft in a passageway—
> between the wall and a machine—
> ran from the floor to the ceiling.
> In sweeping around it one morning
> her apron was caught
> and drawn about the shaft
> and she was whirled around
> striking the wall and machinery.
> <div align="right">(<i>Testimony</i> [1978] 238)</div>

The opening quatrain is drawn from another portion of the case in which an expert witness, a machinist, in response to a question concerning the dangers of unexposed shafts, says "All shafts are dangerous; but I regard a vertical shaft, passing up through the floor unprotected, as the most dangerous character of shaft" (1,085). Reznikoff, by appropriating the witness's first-person testimony as his own, combines the third-person perspective of the court report ("The girl's work for the company was changed") and the first-person witness into a single, omniscient point of view. The machinist's sentence is parsed into its component parts, one line for each grammatical unit, as if to reduce the sentence to its barest essentials. This rephrasing provides the poem with an introductory thesis that the next lines validate.

The second stanza not only substantiates the machinist's remark but creates a verbal environment as blunt and frontal as that faced by the young plaintiff. Reznikoff's elimination of excess verbiage "exposes" the rotating shaft, and his lineation reinforces the violence of the accident by isolating individual verbs on separate lines. The more elliptical phrasing of the summary ("and in doing so on the morning of the accident her apron was caught in some way . . . striking such objects as were in her way [probably the wall and machinery]") is transformed into a series of parallel verb phrases: "her apron was caught / and drawn about the shaft / and she was whirled around / striking the wall and machinery." The use of repetition dramatizes the shaft's circular movement, and the repeated three strong stresses in the final three lines embody the violence of the injury. An earlier draft of the poem reveals that Reznikoff had thought to frame the poem by quoting the children's rhyme "Ring around the rosy" but thought better

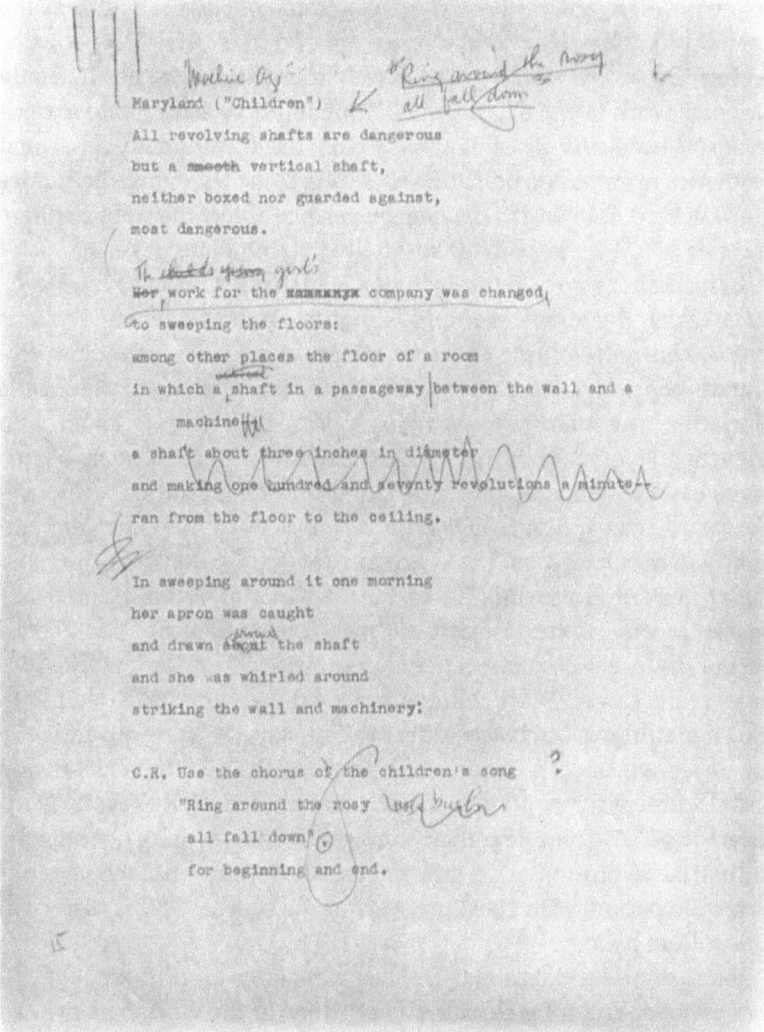

Figure 10. Charles Reznikoff, *Testimony*, manuscript page.

of it, realizing perhaps that the stark language describing the workplace would drive home his message (Fig. 10).

This brief example is typical of Reznikoff's compositional technique. By drawing its language from a public document, it challenges the supposed "aura" of originality in art while redirecting attention to the surface features of legal language. As Kathryn Shevelow notes, Reznikoff provides an example of classical *inventio*: the poet *discovers* his poem in the language of others (291). If he edits or revises the source text, it is not simply to make a more aesthetically pleasing work but to expose the distinction between private experience and public forum, a distinction that has traditionally separated aesthetics from public policy. By lineating court testimony, he frames the venues within which private experience enters the public sphere and relates the materiality of social life to that of language.

In his editor's note to the 1978 Black Sparrow edition of *Testimony*, from which the above example is drawn, Seamus Cooney explains that the current volume contains the previous New Directions edition of 1965 and most of a privately published version of 1968. "Thus Black Sparrow will finally bring into print the results of more than ten years devoted labor by Charles Reznikoff." But *Testimony* begins much earlier than 1965, appearing first in William Carlos Williams's *Contact* of 1932 and in the *Objectivist Anthology* of the same year and finally in the Objectivist Press version of 1934. Cooney is correct that the 1978 edition reprints all of the versions of *Testimony* that appeared in verse, but these earlier prose versions must be considered part of the larger project—a poem upon which Reznikoff worked for most of his career. Most commentaries on the work have dealt with the later editions, but by considering *Testimony* as a text grounded in the 1930s we can see continuities between Reznikoff's social vision and documentary projects of the sort that influenced Rukeyser.[19] Furthermore, we can see Reznikoff's project as documenting not only the industrial revolution of the late nineteenth century (the later versions cover the period from 1885 to 1915) but the sources of this history in antebellum history.

Regarded as a palimtext, *Testimony* contains all of these levels, a fact made abundantly clear in the portions of the work first printed in *Contact* magazine. Here, under the title of "My Country 'Tis of Thee," Reznikoff foregrounds the performative aspect of his poem by prefacing it with a cartoon showing a man displaying "Oratorical and Poetical Gestures" (Fig. 11). Reznikoff implies, sardonically, that there is a relationship between history and histrionics, between private acts and a public forum of persuasion and seduction embodied by the courtroom. Reznikoff is also elaborating on the tension between history as lived and history as represented in its Fourth of July trappings, a tension reinforced by his original title. In the *Contact*

Figure 11. Charles Reznikoff, *My Country 'Tis of Thee*, title page.

version, Reznikoff accompanies his prose vignettes with entries taken from a dictionary of affective states, complete with accompanying cartoons. These images provide a sardonic commentary on the more sober material within the text and illustrate the gap between concrete incident and moral law derived.

We can see the merging of these various frames, textual and visual, in a section that tells the story of a black man accused by a (presumably white) woman of making advances to her. He is then cruelly beaten and shot by "white men of the neighborhood . . . with negro whips in their hands" and left to die (103). It turns out that the man was not the one who approached the woman, but once this fact is discovered no attempt is made to save the injured black man. This section is juxtaposed to a second story of a mulatto woman who serves as a concubine for her master, a role that leads to accusations by the housekeeper of laziness and diffidence. Framing these two passages is a dictionary entry on "Love &c." accompanied by a cartoon of a woman whose face displays expressions of intense emotional rapture, "a soft serenity to the countenance, a languishing to the eyes, a sweetness to the voice, and a tenderness to the whole frame . . ." (Fig. 12). The contrast between the sentimental treatment of love and the brutal face of sexuality within racist society foregrounds the ideological complicity between the two realms. At a moment when the Scottsboro trial had drawn the nation's attention to relations between white males' sexual fears and racist stereotypes, such stories of antebellum plantation culture became all the more resonant.

When Reznikoff collected various sections of "My Country 'Tis of Thee" in its Objectivist Press edition, he eliminated the cartoons, withdrew reference to sentimental moral rhetoric, and changed the title to *Testimony*. He also organized his sections by region based on regional divisions of the national reporter volumes. And whereas in "My Country 'Tis of Thee" he ran the various sections together, in *Testimony* (1934) he began to number each section and arrange them under general headings ("Of Murder," "Of Slaves," "Depression,"), thus joining cases under a common topic. In its *Contact* version, we see a Reznikoff very much part of a New York avant-garde magazine culture in which the more daring use of montage and pastiche coincided with Dada and Surrealist experimentation. With the 1934 edition of *Testimony*, Reznikoff submits "the matter of the document" to handcuffed, and a chain, hanging from the wall, fastened around his neck. He was so frightened, as the white men of the neighborhood gathered to question him with negro whips in their hands, that his master, standing near him, could hear his heart beat . . .

The negro was taken from the house to the road, where Mr. Harley and others were waiting for him. He was struck in the face, and, turning away, tried to run from them, but was shot down.

He was put on a wagon by Mr. Harley's friends and taken to Mr. Harley's house. While lying in the wagon, one of the men put a pistol to his heel and shot him, the ball coming out at the calf of the leg. Mrs. Harley was called out to see him. She said he was not the negro who had struck her, and he was taken a little way up the road and thrown into a fence corner to die . . .

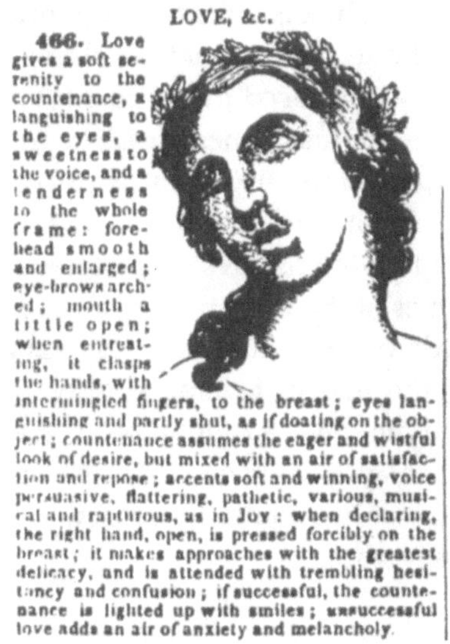

LOVE, &c.

466. Love gives a soft serenity to the countenance, a languishing to the eyes, a sweetness to the voice, and a tenderness to the whole frame: forehead smooth and enlarged; eye-brows arched; mouth a little open; when entreating, it clasps the hands, with intermingled fingers, to the breast; eyes languishing and partly shut, as if doating on the object; countenance assumes the eager and wistful look of desire, but mixed with an air of satisfaction and repose; accents soft and winning, voice persuasive, flattering, pathetic, various, musical and rapturous, as in Joy: when declaring, the right hand, open, is pressed forcibly on the breast; it makes approaches with the greatest delicacy, and is attended with trembling hesitancy and confusion; if successful, the countenance is lighted up with smiles; unsuccessful love adds an air of anxiety and melancholy.

Moser, her master, seemed fond of the mulatto and was often in the kitchen with her when she was cooking, and she was often in his store. One morning, Martha Wood, the housekeeper, saw her come out of the store with some white homespun which she said her master had given her. Martha Wood went to the door of Mosser's room, and saw for the third time where two had been lying on the bed and two headings.

Figure 12. Charles Reznikoff, page from *My Country 'Tis of Thee*.

the legal history of the United States and aligns himself with other documentarians of his era.

### A POINTED INSTRUMENT: *TESTIMONY* (1934)

The short vignette that concludes *Testimony* (1934) could serve as an emblem for the entire book:

> As the case was turned over upon the wharf, a rattling was heard inside. The looking-glass was broken. The pieces were wedge-shaped; the cracks radiated from a center, as if the glass had been struck by a pointed instrument. (71)

The looking glass, instrument for bringing the distant close, is broken; attention is drawn to the glass of which it is made, the design of cracks radiating from a center, the "pointed instrument" necessary to break it. Although the looking glass could serve as a metaphor for Reznikoff's interest in precision and focus, in this context it is a commodity, found in a packing case on a wharf, damaged in some kind of shipping or storage accident. As such, it is linked to the stories of trade and shipping that make up the second half of the volume. The lack of any reference to context—who caused the accident, the intended use for the glass—removes the instrument from its instrumental purpose, defamiliarizes the commodity from its purveyors and purchasers. Since this prose fragment is contained in a larger section called "Depression," the radiating fissures of shattered glass extend into the economic hard times of the 1930s.

As this example indicates, little of the actual trial summary remains from the original entry in the state or federal reporter. Legal language—its Latinate syntax and diction—is diminished, reference to judicial precedent is stripped away, and at no point is the verdict mentioned. The only evidence that we are reading a transcript is the occasional highlighting of certain words:

> Jim walked behind him stepping in his prints until they came to the "piney" woods. (7)

> They went to the "steeragedeck" late Saturday afternoon, and screwed the nut back again after three hours. (29)

These brief references to the court transcript permit the collision of two narratives—one provided by the original witnesses and one rearticulated by Reznikoff. Quotation marks are the material residue of an oral record whose idiosyncratic diction and phraseology announce the presence of a historical witness. In his *Contact* version of the work, Reznikoff thanks the "reporters and judges not only for the facts but for phrases and sentences" (14), and on a legal-sized page found among his papers Reznikoff created a catalog of interesting language from his reading in the reporter system, some of which made its way into the text:

> "I have your age in my pocket" (said while placing hand in pocket in which was revolver)
>
> "he made a *clip* at me" (with a club)
>
> (of an old man) active and "smart on his feet" (Fig. 13)

Reznikoff's listing of interesting linguistic flora and fauna extends to the choice of case itself. Often he gives us little information about the particular crime but focuses on a discrete moment within it. Industrial accidents, like the one mentioned earlier, are metonymically represented by reference to the tools and machines that create hazards for the worker:

> His work was to carry rolls of wet cloth from a machine called an "extractor" to a hoist outside the building. On one side of the passageway to the rolls of wet cloth were the "extractor" and the shaft propelling it and on the other a fan and the shaft and the shaft upon which it turned. The fan was used for drying wool and turned about seven hundred times a minute—so fast that it looked like an object at rest. The "extractor" was not so swift as the fan, but ran with much more noise, so that one would be likely to keep farther away from it. The passageway was about four and a half feet wide. As he walked along, his hand-barrow under his right arm on the side next to the "extractor," and in his left hand a handful of ropes, used in binding the rolls of cloth together for hoisting, a rope caught and wound around the shaft of the fan. (67)

The worker here is anonymous, dwarfed by machines whose ominous propensities are embodied in the clinical description of the narrow passageway in which he must walk. The reiteration of the ominous word "extractor" in quotation marks is like the machine itself, noisier and more threatening than the fan that turns so fast "it [looks] like an object at rest." But this silence proves deadly, as we learn in the last sentence. Reznikoff's reticence in describing the actual injury

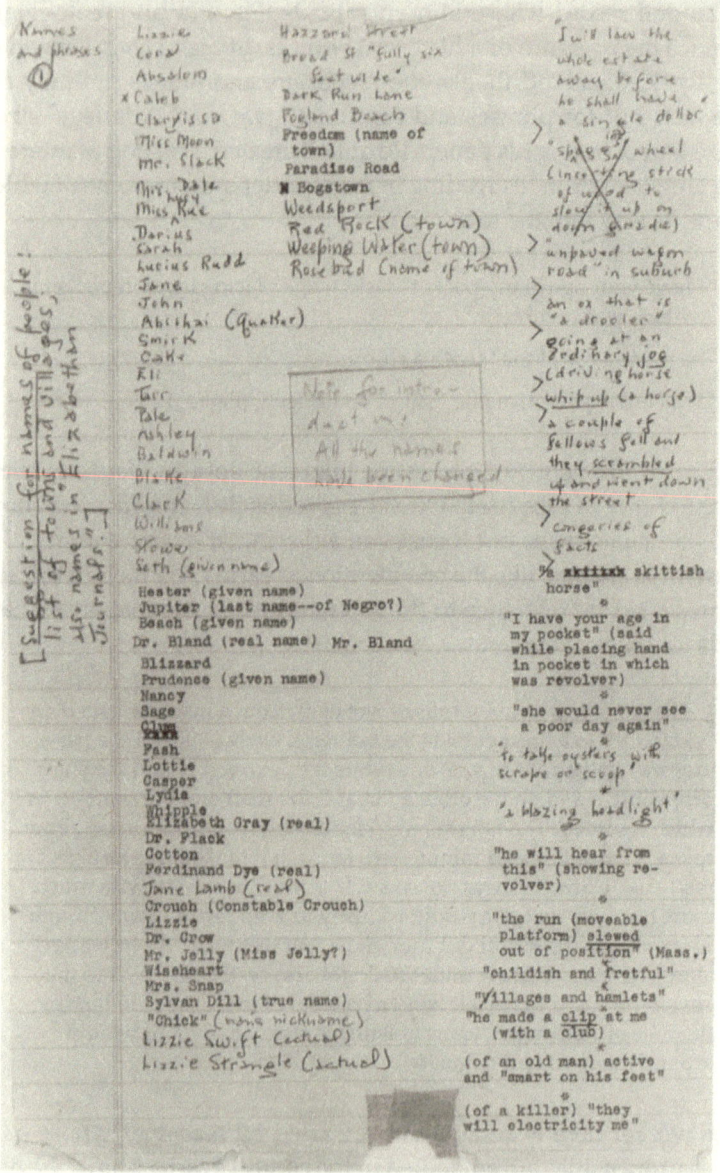

Figure 13. Charles Reznikoff, list of words for *Testimony*.

dramatizes the silent threat posed by a machine whose danger is hidden in its efficiency. He is less interested in the worker's particular claim than in the conditions within which he works, his relationship to machines that "extract" life on several levels. The clinical spareness of Reznikoff's language replicates the functionalist mentality by which men become subjects of their machines. This is not the Victorian Henry Adams reflecting on the modern dynamo's theological primacy but a modernist embodying the dynamo's secular threat.

If the legal system provides a larger narrative for these small stories of human suffering, an even larger frame is provided by the Depression itself. In these 1930s versions of *Testimony*, the cases from which Reznikoff draws are from the antebellum period. References to slavery, paddlewheel steamers, sailing ships, and early technology provide a historical reference to the emergence of the United States as a republic following the revolutionary period. Although later versions of *Testimony* deal with industrial expansion during the Gilded Age, these cases from pre–Civil War America suggest that the metaphor of master and slave, as used by Hegel and later by Marx, finds its focus in slaveowning America. Reznikoff did not circulate in the Communist and fellow-traveling orbit of Muriel Rukeyser, but his ability to read modern forms of reification against their historical sources linked him as much to work being published in *The New Masses* as it did to that in *Contact* and *Broom*.

Reznikoff's treatment of "Southerners and Slaves," as he titles his first section, is a bottom-up view of plantation culture. Poor whites and slaves both participate in seemingly unmotivated acts of violence; bodies are whipped, violated, and penetrated without provocation; slave women are forced into concubinage while their children are sold to the highest bidder; bodies are the sites of injustices that eliminate all human traces:

> The body was in a clump of post-oak bushes, ten or twelve feet from the road, the left foot over the right one. It was on its back. From the eyes down all the face was gone, the face bones were gone, and the brains had been eaten out of the skull by the hogs. The hogs were eating the body when it was found. (7)

Kenneth Burke complains about the "gruesome aspect" of such passages, but he fails to read individual vignettes in relation to each other as they build their own internal narratives (xv). The passage above, for example, is preceded by the story of "Jim" and "Ranty," who mercilessly kill a local storeowner for some whisky. When Jim is arrested and put in jail, he dreams

> that his two hands were tied together, and were on fire; there was a book hung before them—it had a leather cover just like the one they swore him on at the trial—the book caught fire and all the leaves were burning. (7)

The "burning book" in Jim's dream refers both to biblical and legal forms of justice—the refining fire of God's vengeance against sinners and the purifying fire of blind justice. In the pages of both books, Jim is found guilty. The anonymous, half-eaten body found near the road must be contrasted to the religious and legal definitions of humanity as they come together in Jim's dream. By juxtaposing these two stories, Reznikoff seems to be showing victim and murderer in their primal moments of flesh and spirit—the body turned back into earth and the body dreaming of its transcendence.

The two vignettes that follow the description of the faceless body help place the violence done to it by contrasting two kinds of narrative. The first tells of a plantation owner, Kelly, whose material success is based on slaves and oxen but whose imaginative life is improved by reading histories of the kings of England, "big men [who] ruled over the people" (8). The second story is a letter from a young girl to her uncle describing her emergence into ladyhood: "How my heart grows sick at the idea of leaving school in five months. Can it be possible that I am no longer to be a wild prattling school-girl" (10). As a sign of her new maturity she renounces novel reading:

> So great an influence have these fictitious tales on my mind, that I cannot be as a rational being under their influence. Such contempt have I for novel-readers, I intend reading all the histories that I can obtain and all valuable works of the distinguished authors. (10)

Both plantation owner and girl achieve a level of "rationality" by reading histories. Kelley reads stories of "big men" who dominate others, thus reinforcing his right to own slaves. In the second case, the impressionable white girl measures her newfound maturity by her dismissal of novelistic fantasy. But the framing cases involving slavery provide a counterdiscourse to this rationalist scenario, suggesting that contemporary history is no less fantastic than that in novels—and a good deal closer to home.

The young woman's emergence into ladyhood contrasts with the next sequence of vignettes, which describe the lives of female slaves. Ever vulnerable to rape and beatings, unprotected against the sale of their children to other families, these women present lives antithetical to the spirited ingenue. The story of "Sophia" tells of a slave who has been a faithful servant to her mistress but who becomes intractable once her son is given away to the mistress's daughter in order "to pick up chips and be company for me" (15). Without her child, Sophia ceases to be obedient and is subsequently sold to a series of neighbors. She continually runs away to be with her children but is found, beaten, and resold. After she has run away once more, her new owner catches her and punishes her:

> He had her stripped and staked down on the ground: her feet and hands spread and tied to the stakes, her face downward. Mr. Spencer was calm and took his time; he whipped her from time to time with a plaited buckskin lash about fifteen inches long. He drew some blood, but not a great deal, and then he took salt and a cob and salted her back with it. (16)

Reznikoff's prose reinforces the inhuman treatment of Sophia by its detailed reference to Spencer's method of torture—the length of his lash ("about fifteen inches long"), the fact that he whipped her "from time to time," his exculpatory remark that he "drew some blood, but not a great deal"—all of which paves the way for the final salting of her wounds. The anonymous body eaten by animals with which I began this discussion of slavery now returns within a system of discipline and punishment that equally dehumanizes the body and exposes its internal organs. Regarded as a linked sequence, Reznikoff's section on slavery exposes the close relationship between reading and the racialized and sexualized body that is often its subtext.

The second section of the book is titled "Sailing Ships and Steamers," a subject that may seem removed from that of plantation society but that manifests many of the same hierarchies and brutal conditions: cabin boys and deckhands are routinely beaten for disobeying orders; harsh weather combined with extended periods at sea exacerbate bad treatment; passengers and crew are neglected or cheated; captains are often called "Masters"; and workers on the lower decks often resemble slaves. Reznikoff's linkage of these two spheres emphasizes the fact that antebellum American society was based on twin forces of mercantilism and slavery, both intertwined in their common origins in oceanic passage. The Atlantic slave ships and the steamers that probed the new continent's inland waterways constituted a "middle passage" of entrepreneurial growth, the ill effects of which were being profoundly felt during the period that Reznikoff was writing.

Although Reznikoff provides examples of mistreatment at the hands of higher officers, the most troubling passages in this second section deal with neglect. In a section entitled "Hands," Reznikoff draws on the case of a crewman named Cresswell, whose legs are broken when he falls from a topsail during a storm. His bones are set—badly, as it turns out—by the "master" and the first mate. He is then placed in his hammock to wait until the boat docks: "This was on the 30th of March. The ship did not come to Boston until the 10th of June. All this while Cresswell lay in his hammock, helpless, swinging in the unceasing motion of the ship, and for a time in great pain" (34). When the ship finally arrives in port, the crew disperses, and the master leaves the ship for the weekend. When he returns on Monday, Cresswell is finally taken to the hospital, where his legs are treated. Reznikoff's understated conclusion stresses the tension between Cresswell's physical pain and the neglect with which he has been treated: "His left leg was found to be somewhat twisted, but the right was much worse—the foot was turned out at right angles from the way it should have been" (35). The "way it should have been" describes both the shape of bones but also the proper course of care to which Cresswell was entitled. The phrase also alludes to itself as testimony whose understated quality defines the gap between incident and remedy.

The inhumanity chronicled in these sections—whippings, torture, and neglect—is ameliorated somewhat in the last section, entitled "Rivers and Seas, Harbors and Ports." Here Reznikoff puts aside his legal briefs for a Whitmanian catalog of ships and their names, cargoes, and ports. While this strategy may seem to restore the romance of sea-going erased by the preceding chronicle of human cruelty, it also serves to emphasize on another level the ideology of romance that keeps such inhumanity in place. The heroic and mythical names of ships—*Harvest Queen, Seaflower, Sparkle, Sea Nymph, Silver Spray, Comet, Fair American, Golden Age, Jewess, Laurel, Mist, Fawn, Serpent,*

*Jerusalem*—contrast with the inhuman conditions on board. The same can be said for Reznikoff's catalog of captains' names—Captain Proud, Captain Percival, Captain Ivory, James Fortune—which ring with suggestions of national promise and manifest destiny.

From the names of boats and captains, Reznikoff moves on to the various cargoes of the ships—"cases, trunks, bales, casks, kegs, and bundles"—of everything from tea and coffee to lambskins, indigo, and lead from ports with names such as Rattlesnake Shoal, Pelican Shoals, Flapjack Reef. And concluding the section is a long, lyrical chronicle detailing the varieties of sailing conditions:

> The sound calm and the night starlight; the vessel anchoring in the bay about nightfall, the snow turning into rain, the wind, about midnight, coming out of the northwest and blowing heavily on shore, the weather growing cold; the ship moored in the channel, the moon shining through a slight haze, on the easterly side a high bluff jutting into the sea, to the west a low sand-spit, in front of the sand-spit the shore line of the bluff curving into a bight; bays, inlets, rivers, harbors and ports. (56)

Kenneth Burke feels that in this section Reznikoff gives himself over to "embellishment of the 'poetic sort,'" but I see this as offering a series of vantages from which the more documentary testimony can be reassessed. The grim record of mercantile history that precedes this section offers no insight into the narratives that produce violence and legitimate the master/slave system. This passage provides that history with a national narrative made out of ships and captains with heroic names and romantic places in which adventure and magic occur. Taken on its own, this passage defines the moonlit magic that Hawthorne felt was necessary for the romance, the mystic twilight of Whitman's "Out of the Cradle, Endlessly Rocking." But in contrast to the rest of the book the passage details the ill-fated, even tragic mood that dominates the American narrative. It is no surprise that the first boat named in the catalog is "The sloop Hamlet, heavily laden with stone" (52).

## IMAGINED COMMUNITIES

In my opening remarks, I suggested that poetry is once again in crisis. I was obviously drawing upon associations with an earlier literary crisis, that of the lyric in an age of mechanical reproduction (and, not coincidentally, consolidation of national identities within colonial empires). As we pass the centennial of Mallarmé's Oxford lectures (1894), in which these problems were first diagnosed, we might feel that poetry has been in a state of crisis ever since. The more recent rhetoric of crisis, however, is marked less by changes wrought by the introduction of free verse than by worries that poetry in general—the expressive lyric in specific—can adequately represent emerging constituencies and political identities at a transnational moment. When Paul de Man used Mallarmé's lectures to speak of an analogous crisis in the criticism of the 1970s, it was to define crisis in essentially linguistic terms: "The rhetoric of crisis states its own truth in the mode of error. It is itself radically blind to the light it emits" (16). De Man set out to show how error is implicit in the arbitrary nature of the sign, a fact of which poetry is constantly reminding us even as it aspires to unmediated expression. Although most cultural theorists have eschewed any relationship to de Man or his colleagues, they have sustained his belief in the critic as the one capable of sorting ideological error from surface intentions. Furthermore, they have equated ideas of simultaneity, repetition, and consensus that serve to solidify national identity with aesthetic theories of spatialization, of which the Symbolist lyric is the supreme example. But as Homi Bhabha points out the "narrative and psychological force that nationness brings to bear on cultural production and political projection is the effect of the ambivalence of the 'nation' as a narrative strategy" (140). This ambivalence testifies to the inadequacy of terms such as "a people" or "a nation" to address the lived realities of individuals gathered under such terms. It also creates an alternative "space" in which to assess poetry's particular role in addressing issues of national identity.

A counter to Bhabha's inscription of nation within narrative can be seen in the two epigrams with which I began this chapter. They summarize a trajectory taken by both Muriel Rukeyser and Charles Reznikoff as modernists whose poems on U.S. history extend from textual practices intimately tied to progressive social programs of the 1930s. "Poetry can extend the document" is Rukeyser's recognition of poetry's ability to provide a voice for individuals who live at the margins of a national scene. Their voices go unrepresented not because they lack a forum (the fact that Rukeyser draws on congressional hearings testifies to the fact of such venues) but because the nature of the forum neutralizes critical perspective on the conditions that prompt one to speak. Although she is referring to her own poem, which *does* "extend" documents, Rukeyser could be speaking for a larger context of artists during the 1930s for whom public life as represented in photodocumentaries and films drew on forms of montage and pastiche first developed to serve aesthetic ends.

Rukeyser's other epigram, "This is a nation's scene and halfway house," describes the literal landscape of Gauley's Junction, West Virginia, which stands as a complex hieroglyph for an allegory of industrial dominance and corporate greed. But her line also puns on the word "scene," referring to the fact that this landscape is *seen* by those who depend upon it for their livelihood. Their stories temporalize what is otherwise a static image or map. "What two things shall never be seen? / They: what we did. Enemy: what we mean." Rukeyser wants to make visible a record that cannot be summarized by a collective "they" or demonized by a faceless "enemy." What constitutes nationhood is a scene of writing—*this* writing here—in which voices of testimony describe actions usually lost to the historical record. The national scene is neither a ceremony nor a monument but a "halfway house" on the way to community.

By subsuming Reznikoff's project under Rukeyser's epigraphs, I want to indicate his participation in a common documentary project of the 1930s. The fact that the first stages of *Testimony* were written in prose should not disqualify the work from entering our debate on the genre of nationhood. In fact, it is precisely because *Testimony* unites several genres—prose narrative, court testimony, epistolary novel, narrative poetry—that it best serves our purpose in challenging certain assumptions about the generic limits of national narratives. In an era defined by the lure of grand narratives (New Deal or Popular Front), Reznikoff's emphasis on "petits récits"—contingent and partial stories—places his project far in advance of his era. While not trying to make *Testimony* a distinctly postmodern poem in the terms outlined by Jean-François Lyotard, I feel that in its various forms from 1932 to 1978 Reznikoff's magnum opus argues for a more expansive view of narrative, one truly heteroglossic and hybrid in its impulse.

By writing his history out of the national reporter system, Reznikoff foregrounds the institutional legal structure within which a national history is written. Likewise, by drawing upon oral testimony from congressional hearings Rukeyser links private testimony to national politics. If, as Benedict Anderson points out, nationhood is an "imagined community" constituted through print culture, such overt manipulation of printed documents toward alternative histories would seem a significant intervention in any totalizing view of nationality. Furthermore, it should suggest that the importance granted by cultural theorists to narrative as the self-evident vehicle for a nation's story perpetuates its own exclusions and colonizations, removing certain storytellers and historical subjects from their own histories. If poetry is in crisis, it is perhaps because, like a postcolonial community, it is still being imagined in its imperial form.

# 6

## Marginality in the Margins
### Robert Duncan's Textual Politics

POSTMODERN MARGINS

A preoccupation of postmodern cultural theory is its almost theological interest in transgression. Violation, cross-dressing, abjection, subversion, and infection have become tropic alternatives to various forms of totalized discourse. In its attempt to undermine hierarchies implicit in binary structures, postmodern theory searches for the occluded or effaced term (*écriture*, the subaltern, the semiotic) whose marginality contests the authority of unitary sign or subject. Far from simply inverting the poles of the Saussurian model in a kind of negative theology of the signifier, recent theory has focused on the space between poles as a kind of fractal landscape where heterogeneity and eroticized play reign. At stake in much of this discussion is a spatial metaphor—whether in the form of a map, a body, or a text—whose autonomy is challenged by the existence of an unspecified outside or *hors texte*.

A recent museum lecture series, announced as "Rethinking Borders," could be seen as symptomatic of this trend.[1] It attempted to study the relationship between map and boundary by featuring art historians, social scientists, and artists discussing the cartography of postmodern culture. The series' theme was adumbrated by the poster's design, which juxtaposed a human brain upon a map of the world, implying that changes in the so-called outside world are being lived in the so-called inner. Despite this provocative image, one of the series' events, a lecture by Jean Baudrillard, presented the view that such oppositions are bankrupt in postmodern society. His main points reiterated themes that have been a staple of his work since his analysis of commodity society in the late 1960s: communication is obsolete, based as it is on outmoded models of addresser and addressee; computer screens have eliminated information, turning either/or systems into logics of the same; history is over, hence any dialectical edifice based on it is condemned to endless circularity; political opposition is meaningless because it only replicates the dualisms of hegemonic culture; the only possible politics in a world of simulacra is indifference. Baudrillard's own indifferent responses to (often angry) questions following the lecture displayed his belief in the latter. If Baudrillard's grim vision is any indication, the museum's project of "rethinking borders" is irrelevant since it depends upon an epistemological apparatus that has been retrofitted by Warner Communications. How can one "rethink" something that exists only as an image?

While Baudrillard's description of the modern wasteland is by no means the only map of postmodern culture, it is one that has had surprising currency within the artworld. It serves as an explanation of a certain flattening of expression, "the waning of affect," as Fredric Jameson calls it, and explains the turn toward simulationism as a critique of the auratic object.[2] It also describes the "implosive effects" of television culture, by which the distance between viewer and screen is eliminated, leaving only a recursive circuitry where once was a subject (see Crary). Given this tendency for maps to consume their borders, it might be well to return to the spatial model that provokes such speculation and consider the individuals who are marginalized within it.

For certain historical subjects, crossing borders is more than a cartographical metaphor, viruses are more than a cybernetic phenomenon, and marginalization is more than a reference to nongeneric art. In the case of gays and lesbians, for example, these terms resonate well beyond the act of writing, and yet writing has often been the site of their thematization. Robert Duncan noted this fact more than forty years ago in his essay "The Homosexual in Society," in which he attacks a pervasive homophobia within the artworld and links it to more overt forms of racial prejudice in society as a whole. Speaking openly (and courageously) as a homosexual, Duncan also criticizes the gay community for its willingness to repeat these same prejudices in a cult of exclusivity and superiority. In this respect, Duncan acknowledges his own culpability in speaking of his early gay experience:

> Faced by the inhumanities of society I did not seek a solution in humanity but turned to a second outcast society as inhumane as the

first.... In drawing rooms and in little magazines I celebrated the
cult with a sense of sanctuary such as a medieval Jew must have
found in the ghetto; my voice taking on the modulations which tell
of the capitulation to snobbery and the removal from the "common
sort"; my poetry exhibiting the objects made divine and tyrannical as
the Catholic church has made bones of saints, and bread and wine
tyrannical. (quoted in Faas 321–22)

Duncan's reference to sectarian cults suggests the way that marginal societies may fetishize their outsider status in parodies of the dominant culture, thus preventing self-criticism and resistance. The evil of prejudice is not so much its exclusion of others as its tendency to become normalized *by* the other in self-exculpatory strategies of denial. Resistance is made all the more difficult when, to adapt the terms above, the margins resemble the text. In 1944, in the wake of Stalin's and Hitler's final solutions to marginal populations, these remarks had a special importance in explaining how ideology does its work.

"The Homosexual in Society" represents the complicated relationship of the pre-Stonewall gay writer to both the political and cultural left. First published in 1944 in Dwight MacDonald's magazine *Politics*, the essay reflected the editor's own nondoctrinaire socialism as well as the young poet's close identification with the anti-Stalinist left. As a result of its publication, John Crowe Ransom, editor of *The Kenyon Review*, rejected Duncan's poem "An African Elegy" for what he saw as its "advertisement or... notice of overt homosexuality" (Faas 153). Since Ransom and his editors at *The Kenyon Review* had already accepted the poem for publication, their post hoc reconsideration based on "The Homosexual in Society" can be seen as a significant contradiction of their New Critical attitudes toward disinterested reading. Moreover, their rejection can be seen as a manifestation of a moral panic that emerges when an ideology of the text can no longer contain meanings that surface in the page's margins.

Ransom's rejection of the poem was based on new, homoerotic meanings that he could now read into it. The following lines, for instance, could be seen as describing a homosexual mise-en-scène:

those Negroes, all those princes
holding to their mouths like Death
the cups of rhino bone,
were there to burn my hands and feet,
divine the limit of the bone and with their magic

> tie and twist me like a rope. I know
> no other continent of Africa more dark than this
> dark continent of my breast.
>
> (*Years* 34)

Ekbert Faas observes that the possibility of a sadomasochistic ritual "with the speaker cast in the role of the victim" no doubt caused Ransom some distress, but he adds that this reading could only be accomplished by a rather extreme Freudian approach (152). I cannot see how anyone, Ransom included, could avoid the homoerotic imagery of this passage, nor do I think that the darkness that pervades the poem can be simply assigned to psychological indeterminacy, "'the mind's / natural jungle,'" as Faas feels it is. From his earliest poems to his last, Duncan invokes a sexual and erotic "underside" that is violent at its core and whose sources must be found in the larger homophobic culture. As I will point out, this violence has a specific historical source in the poet's early sexual awakening, and it became formative in his conception of field poetics.

Despite Duncan's imprecations against cultishness in "The Homosexual in Society," he gained a good deal of his polemical energy from establishing an apostate relation to what he perceived as orthodoxy. He wrote self-consciously as an outsider to the literary establishment, a gay writer in a homophobic society, an anarchist within the anti-Stalinist left, a bookish poet among bohemians, a bohemian among academics, a formalist among free versists, a field poet among closed formalists. He identified with heresies, whether Albigensian, Kabbalist, Manichean, Black Mountain, or Protestant and saw his poetic vocation as part of a brotherhood of poetic adepts, locked in battle against the establishment.[3] Even his relationships with friends and peers such as Charles Olson, Jack Spicer, Denise Levertov, and Robin Blaser were charged with conflicts over violations of (imagined or real) orders. "I am a poet, self-declared, manque [sic]," he said in a remark that provoked an angry response from Charles Olson ("Against Wisdom" 67–71). "I have never been and never will be baptized, converted, psychoanalyzed, initiated, graduated, endowed, sacramented or insured" ("Pages from a Notebook" 3).

This commitment to marginality was, to some extent, derived from his upbringing in a theosophical household where esoteric texts and spiritualism were part of everyday, middle-class life. For his family, reality was treated as a vast, corrupt text that needed translation, and reading involved an active subversion of the text's surface to reveal heretical meanings beneath. Duncan adapted this inversionary hermeneutics to his own poetic (and sexual) formation. For Duncan, poetry instantiates a ritual "scene of instruction" that inaugurates the poem and then becomes one of its central subjects. In its most common form, the scene opens with the poet engaged in reading (or, in some cases, in writing) a text, whereupon lexical or philological questions of the sort described in chapter 3 disturb concentration and permit entry into a deeper level of comprehension. The poet returns to a "place of first permission" where suppressed meanings intrude onto the surface text. Those meanings include archaic survivals of cultic and atavistic religions whose doctrines propose a unity of spirit and form, of soul and eros. The material text itself becomes an agent in this transition, providing both the means (pens, paper, typewriter) and resources (reference materials, scholarly editions) in the unfolding design. The ultimate meaning of this "field" of origins is often a sexual mystery—an allegory of homosexual or bisexual love—that has been suppressed within canonical books. The fact that this mystery often includes an element of violence and violation means that all efforts to recuperate origins must remain partial and incomplete.

The scene of instruction, both as theme and as textual practice, occurs often in Duncan's oeuvre: in *Medieval Scenes*, the poet "receives" poems in a series of poetic séances based on prose quotations; in "Two Presentations," the poet is interrupted from writing a poem on the bus by "the hysterical talk of a school-girl," which breaks into his concentration, "dictating fragments of a message that seemd meant for me" (*Roots and Branches* 74); "My Mother Would Be a Falconress" is preceded by an explanatory prose poem ("A Lammas Tiding") in which the poet describes being wakened in the middle of the night with the first lines of the poem ringing in his head, whereupon he takes his notebook "into the kitchen to write it out at the kitchen table" (*Bending the Bow* 51). The most famous instance of this scene occurs in "A Poem Beginning with a Line by Pindar," in which the opening of the Wade-Gery and Bowra translation of Pindar's first Pythian ode introduces puns and double entendres whose decoding generates a meditation on the loss of love to the forces of commodification (*Opening of the Field* 62–69). Duncan witnesses a "god-step at the margins of thought" that is both prosodic (Pindar's meter as ritual dance) and thematic (sexual desire as disturber of disinterested contemplation). All of these moments of instruction occur in marginal states of consciousness that, as I will point out, often utilize the literal margins of the page for their enactment.

Like the romantic crisis poem that is its forerunner, Duncan's variation situates the speaker in a passive relation to a text that is suddenly exposed to its vertical or hieratic implications. What differentiates his poetry from its predecessors in the nineteenth century is its deliberate foregrounding of intertextual layers as they impinge upon a single moment of reading—what in this book I have been describing as the poem's palimtextual surface. At times, philological research and etymological speculation take on the character of a quest romance. In "An Interlude of Winter Light," for example, the poet meditates on the aging process and on the possibility of encountering "the Times of Man" in one's own quotidian existence. The opening is lyrical and reflective, but this tone is suddenly broken by a passage in brackets:

> it is the seminal glow of royal dark
>     within the sea of light
> shown in the visionary stone a flame
>     arrested there, it is . . .
>
> [ *Here the interruption of the poem came.* "What does 'Idumaean' mean?" *the old crone sitting next to me turns to ask, pointing to her program notes. It comes into the poem then, even as I dread it. The initiation has to do with what I cannot name.* "Who is the child of Idumaean Night?" *she asks as if I should know. . . .*]
>
> (*Ground Work* 150)

The interruption, presented as marginal commentary, refers to a performance of the Béjart Ballet dancing to Pierre Boulez's *Pli selon Pli*, a composition based upon Mallarmé's poems. Sitting in the audience, Duncan is accosted by the woman sitting next to him who draws his attention to the word "Idumaean" ("l'enfant d'une nuit Idumée" [151]) in the Mallarmé text upon which the Boulez composition is based. This "old crone" who intrudes out of the ballet is the facilitator for the rest of the poem, a weird or fairy-tale witch disguised as a member of the audience. From this point on, Duncan as questor tries to answer her question, identifying "Idumaean" first with

Mt. Ida, then as a king of Crete, then as a statue dedicated to Zeus, then as the child of Helios—each association taking the poet further back into classical mythology and history. Finally, he turns to the Pleiade edition of Mallarmé, where the editorial commentary (in Duncan's paraphrase) explains

> that Idumée is the land of Esau, Edom, and that the Kabbala relates that Esau and the kings of Edom (Zeus, then, and the kings of Crete) were pre-Adamic, presexual, reproducing themselves without male or female, not being in the image of God. (152)

I have quoted at length from the marginal material of this poem to point out that the etymological and philological speculations within brackets *become*, in a real sense, what they propose to uncover. The hidden poly- or bisexuality of Duncan's idealized pre-Adamic world merges with polylingual associations in the mind of a receptive listener: "such is the Demon of the Psychopathology of Daily Life" (151). This potentially heretical meaning rises to the surface of a ballet based on a musical composition based on a poem that is, itself, based on other poems. Mallarmé's phrase "pli selon pli," from which Boulez derived his title, represents the textual layering with which Duncan's poem is made, a fold upon fold of associations for which there is no clear origin. As a meditation on aging, the poem introduces its own "time" by violating the discursive, reflective narrative with which it opens. By permitting the "foreign matter" of contingency to disturb discursive logic, the poem quite literally shows how "Time works" by giving dramatic instances of the quotidian. The theme emerges as a question raised in passing whose answer is thus removed from its place in a book and returned as a process to the reader.

## A POET IS BEING BEATEN

During the period in which "An Interlude of Winter Light" was written, this reader did not, in any practical sense, exist. In 1968, following the publication of *Bending the Bow*, Duncan declared that he would not publish another book for fifteen years, preferring instead to distribute typescript copies of his work in progress to friends.[4] It was a daring (and professionally dangerous) move for a poet whose reputation had been secured with *Bending the Bow*. Duncan felt that the demands of writing "toward" a book (many of his previous books had been composed as unified texts rather than selections of poems) limited his ability to compose at random. Furthermore, he chafed at editors' design requirements and typesetters' errors. Duncan's printed page was becoming increasingly complicated with the advent of the "Passages" series, and he wanted to ensure that spacing, typography, and lineation reflected his design. Olson's "Projective Verse" had approved of the typewriter's ability to register minute fluctuations of attention and vocalization, and Duncan was exploring exactly how far the hand-printed page could take him.[5]

Duncan's dissatisfaction with publishers and printers is spelled out in a long letter printed in the special issue of *Maps* devoted to his work. Here, Duncan excoriates Graham MacIntosh, who typeset *Bending the Bow*, and John Martin, who published *Tribunals* (Passages 31–35), for slighting the poet's specific instructions with regard to spacing. To complicate matters, Duncan conducts his debate with yet another publisher, John Taggart, the editor of *Maps*, who was unwilling to print the essay from the author's typescript. Against these various (male) publishers and printers, Duncan posits the model of Virginia Woolf who, in *Three Guineas*, links the writer denied control over her means of publication to other social outcasts. Woolf is writing against the historical backdrop of Hitler, who, by remaining unnamed in her essay, becomes a generic term for patriarchal authority:

> And abroad the monster has come more openly to the surface. There is no mistaking him there. He has widened his scope. He is interfering now with your liberty; he is dictating how you shall live; he is making distinctions not merely between the sexes, but between the races. You are feeling in your own persons what your mothers felt when they were shut out, when they were shut up, because they were women. Now you are being shut out, you are being shut up, because you are Jews, because you are democrats, because of race, because of religion. (quoted in Duncan, "Pre-Face" 7)

Against the genocidal "monster," Woolf posits the independent writer, working on her typewriter or manipulating the printing press as she and her husband, Leonard, did at the Hogarth Press: "Typewriters and duplicators are actual facts and even cheaper. By using these cheap and so far unforbidden instruments you can at once rid yourself of the pressure of boards, policies and editors" (quoted in Duncan, "Pre-Face" 13). Duncan draws upon Woolf's model, relating his refusal to publish to a long tradition of independent poet/

designers, from Blake through the Arts and Crafts movement of Victorian England to the present small press revolution. Where Woolf invokes World War II and Hitler, Duncan invokes the Vietnam era and the fulfillment of a "permanent war economy" that infects all aspects of life: "You publishers have your Tonkin Gulf crisis approaches to herd us into line," he warns in a somewhat extravagant analogy between publishing schedules and prosodic features.

This debate with publishers is conducted not only against the backdrop of war but within a system of sex/gender relations. Textual politics—the seizing of one's means of literary production—coincides with social marginality, and by speaking *with* or *through* the voice of Virginia Woolf Duncan speaks as well for his own homosexual identity. The "unforbidden instruments" not only include mechanical means of publication, they suggest aspects of the body whose freedom of expression is equally vulnerable to instrumentalization and legislation. And to add a further dimension to this gender debate, we must consider Duncan's own historical role as a professional typist by which he supported himself throughout his younger life. It was a profession, as he said on several occasions, dominated by (underpaid) women and homosexual males. Duncan's argument over the necessity of utilizing typewriter copy may seem peripheral to the larger social concerns of his poetry, but within the specific context of gay and lesbian culture and its problematics of self-presentation, the issue takes on greater urgency.

This urgency is especially prominent in Duncan's late work where his attempt to control the material text coincides with his growing realization of an inability to control his physical body. *Ground Work: Before the War* appeared in 1984, published by New Directions Press in the author's typescript version. The second volume, *Ground Work II: In the Dark*, was typeset and published in 1987 when Duncan's physical condition (kidney deterioration resulting in a debilitating regimen of dialysis) could no longer permit him to be active in the publishing process. Within the two books, the scene of instruction is literalized in the form of poems written as marginal notes to other authors, living or dead. Suites of poems based on the work of Paul Celan, Thom Gunn, Baudelaire, Mallarmé, Dante, the metaphysical poets, Rumi, Empedocles, and others predominate, often beginning as notebook entries on the poets in question and then extending into sustained series.

*Dante Etudes*, to take the most obvious example of this tendency, is a series of poems inspired by passages in Dante's prose, but they are also reflections on modernism, insofar as it was influenced by the work of Italian Renaissance poets. *Dante Etudes* reflects on Pound's affection for the Tuscan phantasmagoria, the "spirit of romance" that dominates his early poems. The "outworn Pre-Raphaelite mode" of *Lustra* is posited against the clean, straight lines of the international style of Brancusi or De Stijl:

> Go, my songs, then in zealous
>    liberality, no longer mine,
> but now the friendship of the
>    reader's heart and mind
> divine;
>         (*Ground Work* 122)

Duncan's "envoi" is derived from several sources, the most immediate being Pound's *Hugh Selwyn Mauberley* ("Go dumb-born book") and the Renaissance lyric tradition to which it refers. He also quotes the Australian poet Robert Adamson, whose lines provide a contemporary version of this tradition:

> *Keeping in mind voice-prints that came before you again I say to those who have forgotten*
> *Go. . . .*
> *Go, my songs, to the lonely and the unsatisfied*
> *. . . Go out and defy opinion,*
> *Go against this vegetable bondage of the blood*
>                          (121–22)

Duncan maintains a dialogue with Adamson but also with Dante, Pound, the Pre-Raphaelites, and "the spirits of Whitman and Shelley" in order to summon up past and contemporary voices, "convivial" in their romantic persuasion. In these predecessors and contemporaries, Duncan hears "voice-prints" of his own emergence into poetry, an experience in which the poem appears not as a female muse but as a male author whose writing of the poet is as violent as it is empowering:

>                  And he
> as if moving his hands across taut
>    strings of me, commanding keys
> he turnd   and struck
> demands that straind toward
>    harmony.
>             (123)

We could read these lines as examples of Duncan's characteristic lush diction, but we must not miss the rhetoric of tension and violence in which it is conducted. The extreme, even excessive Pre-Raphaelitism within the formation of modernism implies a repressed sensuosity that Duncan sees as essential to his own emergence into poetry, just as he wants to foreground modernism's origins in the romantic movement. For sexual and poetic emergence are complex acts of reading by which the poet is ravished by a language he cannot, as yet, understand. Duncan appropriates the romantic lyre to speak of speech so eroticized that it seems to come from someone else. And since these poems *do* come from another source, the poet may "send" them back in the expectation of some response.

Wayne Koestenbaum has described this form of collaboration as a kind of "double talk" in which men who write together engage in a "metaphorical sexual intercourse," producing a figurative child in the form of the text they exchange between them (3). Koestenbaum speaks of same-sex collaborations in the late nineteenth century as producing a homosocial reality distinct from (or in opposition to) the "sanctioned male bonding that upholds patriarchy" (3).[6] Although the double talk in Duncan's poems is rather one-sided, his collage texts often engage another male in acts of literary intercourse that transform the source text into a more dialogical entity. For Duncan, collaboration occurs not with another living author but with a book in whose physical pages he inscribes a relationship of which the collaborator could not be aware. Other critics (including myself) have pointed out that this act of revision permits Duncan to write himself into a tradition, but I would add that such writing also refigures the tradition as sexual.[7]

The most obvious place in which this double talk occurs is in "Poems Written in the Margins of Thom Gunn's *Moly*," in which the poet uses the physical boundaries of a book in order to record a scene that instructs even as it receives instructions. Duncan's *Moly* poems, true to their title, were written on the pages of Gunn's 1971 volume (Figs. 14–17). What is especially interesting about this suite is the coincidence of material and textual marginality with a thematics of sexual isolation and desire. Gunn's poems address his own homosexuality in terms that are strikingly frank and unconstrained in comparison to his earlier books. They also confront his participation in the drug/youth culture of the early 1970s, a "rite of passage," as he calls it, into a realm of blurred boundaries and confused social

# MOLY

## Thom Gunn

*And From Whose Margins*
*An Expectation Grows*

*Robert Duncan*

FABER AND FABER
3 Queen Square London

Figure 14. Title page of Robert Duncan's copy of Thom Gunn's *Moly*. Photo credit, Norma Cole.

When I was near the house of Circe, I met Hermes
in the likeness of a young man, the down just
showing on his face. He came up to me and took my
hand, saying: 'Where are you going, alone, and
ignorant of the way? Your men are shut up in
Circe's sties, like wild boars in their lairs. But take
heart, I will protect you and help you. Here is a
herb, one of great virtue: keep it about you when
you go to Circe's house.' As he spoke he pulled the
herb out of the ground and showed it to me. The
root was black, the flower was as white as milk; the
gods call it Moly.

> Not far from Circe's house I met a man,
> derelict, swept by the winds, to whom I was
> I knew the apparition of some plan
> half-forming in his mind he and I were
> as if driven to by assembling fates
> and "Where are you going?" I asked:
> "You are so alone my own life
> which was eternal and self-contained
> opens up vast breaches of promise in the
> thought of you you know nothing of.
> Behind me as I speak to you I hear
> all your men, your ship mates,

Figure 15. From the opening of Thom Gunn's *Moly*, with the beginning of Duncan's "Near Circe's House."

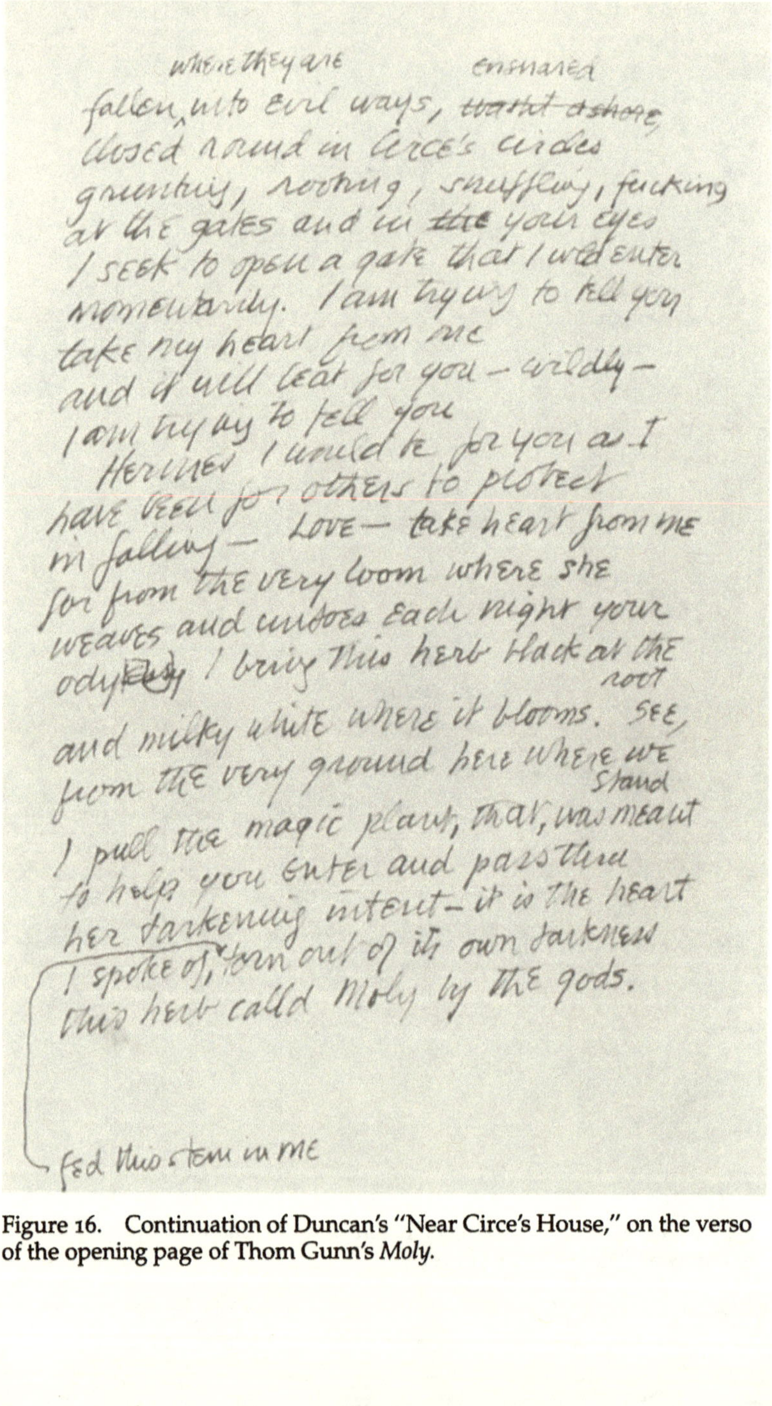

                    where they are            ensnared
fallen into evil ways, washt ashore
closed round in Circe's circles
grunting, rooting, snuffling, fucking
at the gates and in ~~the~~ your eyes
I seek to open a gate that I will enter
momentarily. I am trying to tell you
take my heart from me
and it will beat for you — wildly —
I am trying to tell you
    Hermes   I would be for you as I
have been for others to protect
in falling — Love — take heart from me
for from the very loom where she
weaves and undoes each night your
ody~~ssey~~    I bring this herb black at the
                                          root
and milky white where it blooms. See,
from the very ground here where we
                                    stand
I pull the magic plant, that, was meant
to help you enter and pass thru
her darkening intent — it is the heart
I spoke of, torn out of its own darkness
this herb called Moly by the gods.

⎣ fed this stem in me

Figure 16.   Continuation of Duncan's "Near Circe's House," on the verso of the opening page of Thom Gunn's *Moly*.

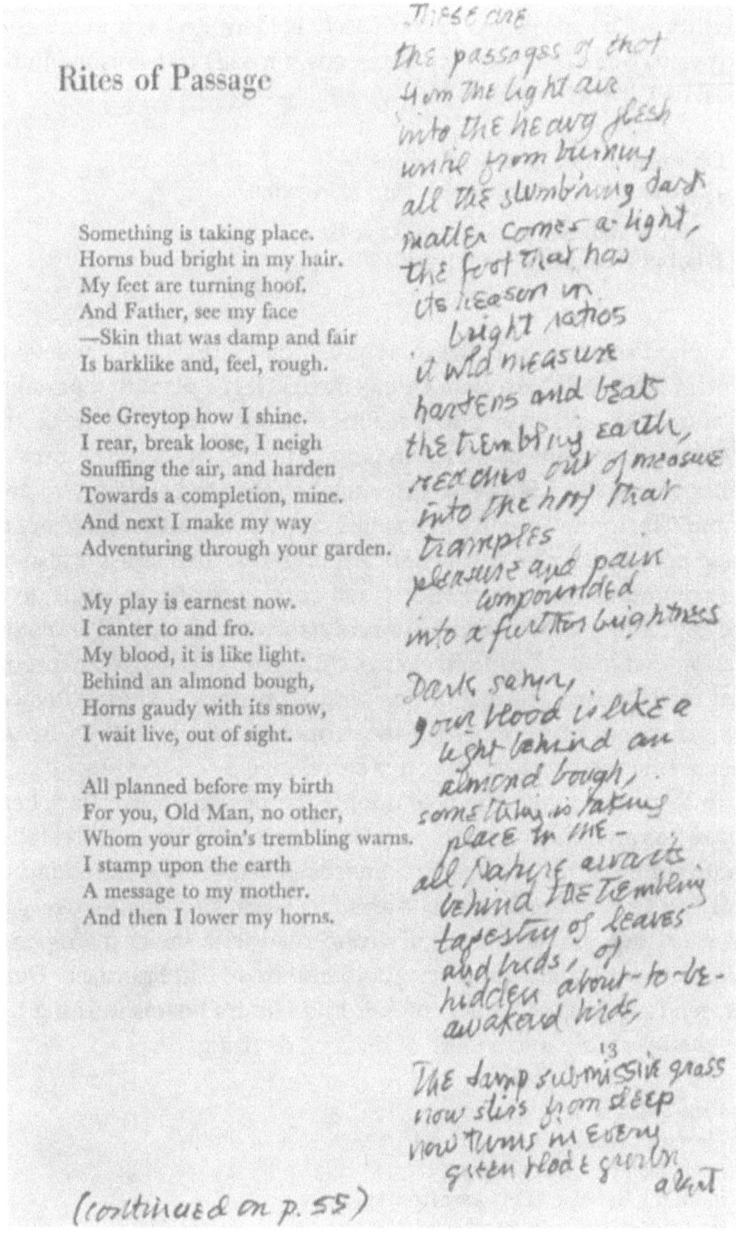

## Rites of Passage

Something is taking place.
Horns bud bright in my hair.
My feet are turning hoof.
And Father, see my face
—Skin that was damp and fair
Is barklike and, feel, rough.

See Greytop how I shine.
I rear, break loose, I neigh
Snuffing the air, and harden
Towards a completion, mine.
And next I make my way
Adventuring through your garden.

My play is earnest now.
I canter to and fro.
My blood, it is like light.
Behind an almond bough,
Horns gaudy with its snow,
I wait live, out of sight.

All planned before my birth
For you, Old Man, no other,
Whom your groin's trembling warns.
I stamp upon the earth
A message to my mother.
And then I lower my horns.

(continued on p. 55)

*[Handwritten marginalia, approximately:]*

These are
the passages of that
from the light air
into the heavy flesh
until from burning
all the slumbering dark
matter comes alight,
the foot that has
its reason in
bright ratios
a wild measure
hardens and beat
the trembling earth,
reaches out of measure
into the hoof that
tramples
pleasure and pain
compounded
into a further brightness

Dark satyr,
your blood is like a
light behind an
almond bough,
something is taking
place in me—
all nature awaits
behind the trembling
tapestry of leaves
and buds, of
hidden about-to-be-
awakened birds,

The damp submissive grass
now stirs from sleep
now turns in every
green blade quiver
alight

Figure 17. The beginning of Duncan's "Rites of Passage: I" in the margin of Gunn's poem of the same title.

identities. The speaker of Gunn's *Moly* is identified as a member of Odysseus's crew (or perhaps Odysseus himself) transformed into a beast on Circe's island:

> Oh a man's flesh already is in mine.
> Hand and foot poised for risk. Buried in swine.
>
>    I root and root, you think it is greed,
> It is, but I seek out a plant I need.
>
>                            (14)

The plant referred to is the moly given by Hermes to Odysseus to protect the Greek hero from Circe's power. It is a plant that partakes of animal as well as spiritual realms—whose "root was black, the flower was as white as milk." In Gunn's hands, the plant becomes a hallucinogen like LSD, which, during the 1960s and early 1970s, produced "Terror and beauty in a single board." But although many of these poems describe psychedelic experiences, their stress is also on the communal and social effects that such experiences bequeath—the tourism, sexual cruising, communalism, and familial transformation that marked cultural change during this period. Most important for Duncan's reading of homosexual themes is Gunn's invocation of scenes of sadomasochistic eroticism, of which the Circean transformation serves as objective correlative.

In Duncan's series, the poet adopts the persona of Hermes, here figured as an older man (whereas Gunn presents him as a streetwise youth) offering his own early homosexual experiences as a kind of moly to Gunn's confessions. Although Gunn's poems invoke gay identity, they are more centrally concerned with the changing consciousness of Haight-Ashbury youth culture in San Francisco. Duncan tends to project sexual content into Gunn's poems, turning the psychedelic moly into a plant of his own devising:

> I am trying to tell you
> Hermes I would be for you as I
> have been for others to protect
> in falling in Love, take heart from me
> for from the very loom where She
> weaves and undoes each night your odyssey
> I bring this herb, black at the root
> and milky white where it blooms.
>                      (*Ground Work* 65)

Duncan's posture is not that of an avuncular Socrates to a naive ephebe but of an aroused Pan whose satyric character is as erotic as it is violent. He recognizes that behind the carefully measured lines in Gunn's poems lie acts and occasions that are, in the most literal sense, unspeakable. "The voice we raise in poetry" is enthralling because it participates in a physical response beyond (or within) language:

> so that it seems lovely to be enthralld
>     by words and truth
> to be in soaring numbers and in rimes
>     thickens and
> goes down into the throat,
> gagging, rooting in the grass,
>     fertilities of sound,
> snuffling, snorting, snared in a
> delirium of snout and watering mouth
>     incapable of speech,
> all animal tongue and panting breath, the lungs
>     sucking the psychedelic air.
>                                           (68)

In these lines, fellatio, psychedelic experience, and poetry are linked as acts that challenge measure. And yet it is measure that focuses the issue as Duncan is brought back, through Gunn's iambic cadences, to his own early verse—and to the homosexual ambience of Berkeley in which he lived. In the work of the 1940s, Duncan often turned to Milton, Herbert, and the metaphysical poets for a kind of rhetorical diction and blank verse that embodied passional states held in check. We can compare Duncan's and Gunn's series for their metrical parallels, but by looking at the physical page upon which Duncan imposed his hand we may see how directly the former's cadences extend out of the latter's printed text.

Writing in the margins imposed specific restraints on Duncan, both thematic and textual, as he sought to project homoerotic issues suggested by Gunn. The physical limits of the margins in which he wrote forced Duncan to accommodate his lines to them (see Fig. 16). Appropriately enough, measurement and meter become a theme of the poem:

> the foot that has
> its reason in bright ratios
> it would measure

> hardens and beats
> the trembling earth,
> reaches out of measure
> into the hoof that
> tramples
> pleasure and pain compounded
> into a further brightness
> 
> (66)

Duncan projects onto Gunn's more formal verse a desire for a measure that might accommodate sexual and psychological states beyond measure. The "literate" speech of Odysseus, hardened against Circe's authority, is matched by the "illiterate / Underbelly of Man where / Violence at last comes home." This violence, Duncan implies, is a common bond between the two poets, even though their literary antecedents are rather different.

Nor is violence strictly a metaphor. In the opening poem of the series, Duncan refers to himself at age sixteen as "wounded mouth, / a stricken thing unable to release its word," a reference to an act of literal violence that happened to Duncan while growing up in Bakersfield. The event introduces another variation on the "scene of instruction," one whose information comes from a marginal landscape with which the poet identifies:

> O deepest Unrest, indelibly engraved in me,
> the wilderness beyond the edge of town, the riverbottom road,
> the lingering, the wandering, the going astray,
> to find some wanton promise the derelict landscape most
>      portrayd in me,
> the fog's sad density of cold,
> in me, the solitary and deserted paths,
> in me, the marshy wastes, the levee road
> where day after day as if driven by the wind
> I impatient strode, day driven after day,
> until the rush of impending weather was most me
> in me, the dumb about-to-be, the country way
> incapable of speech driven toward impending speech.
> 
> (63–64)

This is Duncan's version of "Out of the Cradle, Endlessly Rocking" in which the poet's sudden recognition of loss as a young child inaugurates poetic vocation. Duncan's variant identifies this coming-into-speech with an act of physical violation in which he is both the victim and perpetrator. The unnamed event is described at length in his *Gay Sunshine* interview conducted in 1976. At age sixteen, Duncan found himself walking along "the levee road" in a "derelict landscape," being pursued by an older boy. It was Duncan's first sexual encounter, but it ended violently when the boy produced brass knuckles and attacked him, leaving him bleeding. According to Duncan's account, the boy had already killed several other young men in the area, and during the police inquiry that ensued Duncan was forced to acknowledge his own complicity in the seduction. Thus, his inauguration into sexual knowledge is accompanied by his participation in institutional discourses of sexuality that "otherize" him and that he is forced to reject. Out of this sense of double marginality—being beaten and then being forced to reject his "victim" status—came Duncan's sense of having been permanently transformed:

> But the feeling that there was a momentous moment that would be like the mysteries; and certainly even if you go back to where I'm walking along the river bottom waiting for an experience to occur, a Pan-like figure to materialize out of the winter—a winter Pan would be a hobo—where is this solitary man who is the landscape, where is he? ("Interview" 5)

The "marshy wastes" described here reappear often in Duncan's poetry as the "field" to which the poet is admitted during the act of writing, but, given this biographical context, we understand that returning to a "field of first permission" is far from benign. The "wilderness" in which the adolescent poet wanders is an otherness within himself for which society has no map.

In the *Moly* poems, Duncan seizes upon another poet's confession and wrests from it a version of his own charged entry into homosexuality at age sixteen. He may play Hermes to Gunn's Odyssean crew, only because he has played the other role himself. The act of writing in the margins of Gunn's poems offers a literal transgression of the source text's boundaries, much as Gunn's poems transgress the proprieties of his own previous work. Duncan recognizes this shift in Gunn's poetry, seeing it prefigured in his own youthful career. Duncan also acknowledges "irregular meters [that] beat between your heart and mine," for which the poem cannot be an adequate image. These are irregularities (psychedelic, sexual, psychosomatic) that cannot be consigned to some presymbolic, nonlinguistic state any more than they can be tempered in verse. They live literally in the margins of books where "all the slumb'ring dark / matter comes alight" (66).[8]

## IN BLOOD'S DOMAINE

Thus far, I have described Duncan's scene of instruction as a sexualized one in which the "body" of the text represents the body of the poet, passively awaiting to be "informed." In the language of the Pindar poem, the poet/text represents a naive Psyche prior to seeing the naked body of Eros. When Duncan speaks of the poem "ravishing" him or of writing as wrestling with the angel, we must understand such metaphors as involving both sensual excess as well as sexual violence. In an age when homophobic violence is perpetrated upon gay males, this "dark/matter" must always be read into the theosophical or Orphic contexts of Duncan's language. By writing in the (literal or figurative) margins of other writers, Duncan may turn the textual field and ground of the page into a psychosocial grid whose boundaries are by no means fixed. His marginal commentary on other poets is "original" insofar as it makes origins its theme. By refusing to publish (that is, to remain marginal to the cash nexus and public reception), he may eliminate the general reader in favor of the companion, the lover, the correspondent. Finally, the field of ancestral and atavistic origins recovered is an actual field at the borders of town where a sexual knowledge within merges with the wilderness without, where Persephone's rape (a central topos in Duncan's poetry) is more than a story of seasonal change.

Many of these themes come together in the poet's last book, which describes "the beginnings of an age in [his] body." This theme is given poignance by an opening sequence, "An Alternate Life," which describes a love affair with a much younger man. While it is testimony to an enduring erotic impulse, it is also a realization of its abject consequences. The poet sees himself

> moving over to the other side of the picture.
> An old man's hand fumbles at the young man's crotch.
> An old man's body is about to tremble.   The painter
> is almost cruel in his detail to make clear
> this shaking.   I am talking of a voice shaking.
>                                                               (*Ground Work II* 1)

In this affair, Duncan recognizes himself as the Dantean lover, "alone before a hand that holds forth / the burning of a heart . . . to eat again" (*Ground Work II* 2). But it is out of this solitude that he remembers his permanent companion, Jess, whose permission and acceptance sustain and revivify him, even though his presence ("The painter") provokes humbling self-reflection ("almost cruel in his detail"). The poet returns to a household in which the everyday rituals of sleeping, eating, and talking reestablish temporal coherence:

> Seven o'clock in the morning renews itself over breakfast
>    —the richness of coffee, the full flavor of the bread
> toasted, the assorted jams and marmalades— we
>       initiate the naming of the day
> with the institution of a choice of   things
>    and repetitions of our way,   yet
> altering minutely the course of decisions   thruout
>
>      design   and unalterable variations.
>                        (11)

The contrast announced here—between the erotic body in time and the domestic body that endures through time—reappears often in the book. We could define this contrast as one between the biological body, invaded by disease, and the translated body, revived by language. The dark angel of this theme is Baudelaire, whose syphilitic decline provides an example of biological invasion with which Duncan now identifies. And just as Baudelaire's life is identified with decay and disease, so is his poetry obsessed with spiritual malaise or ennui. Speaking "To Master Baudelaire," Duncan acknowledges

> . . . the brutal
>    facts in which this unity
>       —grand illusion of what is lovely—
> takes hold.   What I know
>    makes fierce indeed the drive
>       of my striving here.   Hatreds
> as well as loves flowd thru as the
>    sap of me.   And we too,
>       my life companion and I,
> entertaind our projects and fancies,
>    playd house and kept company

>                    upon the edge of what we never knew then
>                 you made clear was there
>                          in the human condition—your *Ennui*
>                                  (17)

Duncan addresses Baudelaire, himself, and the reader as co-conspirators in an idealized and idealizing project of affirmation inadequate to "brutal / facts" that underlie unity. Baudelaire's address to his reader at the beginning of *Les Fleurs du mal* ("Hypocrite lecteur") forces us to recognize "La sottise, l'erreur, le perche, la lesine" (the stupidity, delusion, selfishness, and lust) that are part of the human condition and to recognize in ourselves a vice "plus laid, plus méchant, plus immonde" (more ugly, nasty, and foul) because more capable of absorbing everything (*Oeuvres complètes* 43). Ennui, for Duncan, is a "sickness of living" (69) that has a chemical analog in the toxicity of his own body. Whitman's vast and absorptive body gives way, in these late poems, to Baudelairean spleen.

The invasion of the body by disease is a primary drama of many poems in this last volume, and it is worth remembering that they were written at a time when many of Duncan's friends and fellow poets were dying from AIDS. What I earlier described as a scene of instruction now becomes a "scene of invasion" as the permeable walls and membranes of the body are violated by a nightmare of microscopic "foreign matter." Although AIDS is never mentioned in the book, other sexually transmitted diseases are, and they become models for the poet's own sense of infection. In "In Blood's Domaine," Duncan addresses Baudelaire, Nietszche, Rilke, and Swift as prophets whose syphilitic sufferings cannot be excised from their propositions of unity. He remembers Rilke's final decay, "—where black the infected blood / gushes forth from Rilke's mouth, from his nose, from his rectal canal / news his whole body bears as its truth of the septic rose" (68). The idealization of the sexualized body is inverted to reveal a body swarming with new cells, "spirochete invasions that eat at the sublime envelope," and in describing such invasion Duncan takes the idea of the unrecuperable sublime to its farthest reaches. What strikes Duncan as the greatest irony about infection is that these cells are generated within the body itself, "not alien, but familiars," and thus must be incorporated into our picture of the body itself. In terms I have already developed concerning the material text, the margins of the page become porous, yielding access to the body of writing.

Duncan's expanding sense of the body's vulnerability—an almost clinical interest in bodily functions—haunts these poems, permitting him to link the death of his own life with the political destruction of nature beyond:

> Link by link I can disown no link of this chain from my conscience.
>> Would you forget the furnaces of burning meat     purity demands?
>> There is no ecstasy of Beauty in which I will not remember Man's misery.
>> Jesus, in this passage     —He is like a man coming forward in a hospital theater—
>> cries out:     I come not to heal but to tear the scab from the wound you wanted to forget.
>> May the grass no longer spread out to cover the works of man in the ruin of earth.
>
> (69)

As in his Vietnam War passages of the late 1960s, Duncan is enraged by warfare so ultimate and efficient that it renders war (by which he means dialectical thought) too terrible to wage.[9] Here, the "chain" of genetic information leads from his body to larger, social wounds. Rather than regarding Christian charity as offering solace and succor—Christ as healer—Duncan urges fierce, painful recognition that in the apprehension of beauty "Man's misery" is remembered.

Duncan's powerful complaint is rendered in lines so long that they fill the page, beginning deep in the gutter and extending to the outer margin.[10] It is as though these last passages mimic the cellular invasion that is their subject, creating lines so long that their ability to sustain a "measure" is neutralized.

Lines without end, syntax without period, and page without margins all represent an attempt to measure forms of annihilation in the biological and social bodies. Referring both to the "psychosis" of genocide made possible by nuclear devices as well as to the destruction of the poet's own body by disease, Duncan sees that " 'Nothing' is happening in these words in their accumulating sentence but the mounting delusions of a compulsive psychosis" (69). Duncan juxtaposes a Mallarméan *néant*, unrepresentable in its purity, with lines that "in their accumulating / sentence" embody the sense of expanding *im*purity. To explain the presence of these very long lines, one must revise Duncan's scene of instruction as one in which the border between text and margin, body and desire, has been erased. The margin no longer separates the text from the *hors-texte*, print from white page; rather, the margins become the text. One is reminded, in this regard, of Jack Spicer's poetics of dictation in which the poet receives the poem from outside rather than from within an egocentric subjectivity. Duncan's application of this compelling metaphor rejects the psychologically constructed self of traditional humanism as well as the socially constructed self of newer historicisms in favor of a marginal or performed self constructed out of "the / patently irreal" (84).

## THE UNDER SIDE

I see always the under side turning
Duncan, *Opening of the Field*

In my introduction, I spoke of the difficulty of rethinking boundaries, whether epistemological or cultural, without considering those historical subjects who are marginalized within them. Robert Duncan saw himself as a boundary walker who took Hermes, god of the margins, as his totem figure. In his late works, as his own sense of biological vulnerability increased, Duncan projected onto the page—and onto the problematics of the textual—his own growing awareness of what marginality ultimately means. The page, far from being a notation for a subsequent performance, served as a map for a contested territory. Whether writing to another poet or permitting other writings to interrupt his conversation, Duncan saw the boundary between text and margins as a shifting one, in whose instability lay the hope of abolishing the totalized authority of other texts. Critics have defined this textual conversation as a dimension of Olson's field poetics and have adduced sources in gestalt psychology, non-Euclidean mathematics, and contemporary biology as sources. But as I have pointed out with reference to Duncan's biography, the spatial metaphors of field and ground, text and margin, do not accommodate the historical field of sexual violence and gender identity that animate so much of Duncan's work—and that often differentiate it from the work of his Black Mountain peers.

It may seem that my rather literal use of marginality to refer to the page has little application to political issues raised in my opening paragraph. But those issues—AIDS, for example, or the plight of the undocumented worker or the homeless—are often raised in spatial metaphors that depend upon a clear demarcation of boundaries: an "inner city" and the suburbs; the "home" and the homeless; the healthy body and the infected. Duncan's homoerotic politics coincides with a textual politics that blurs such boundaries, not to dismiss them, à la Baudrillard, but to make what is at stake in their transgression visible. By treating his poem as a field in which the margins may be invoked as a central fact of the poem, he may give voice to a population that has no voice and to voices within his own writing that, until experienced as a dialogue with others—another homosexual poet, for example—remain isolated. This is the communal possibility of field poetry that is seldom admitted into the field.

# 7

## Technologies of Presence
*Orality and the Tapevoice of Contemporary Poetics*

### CONSTRUCTING THE ORAL TRADITION

By ear, he sd.
But that which matters, that which insists, that which will last,
that! o my people, where shall you find it, how, where, where shall
   you listen
when all is become billboards, when, all, even silence, is spray-
   gunned?
Charles Olson, Maximus Poems

In this passage from *The Maximus Poems*, Charles Olson delivers an impatient jeremiad to his New England townsfolk, urging them to *listen* in a world in which advertising and commercial interests have reified information, where "even silence, is spray-gunned." Elsewhere in his epic poem, Olson complains about the wallpaper music beginning to be piped into public buildings and conveyances, the "musickracket / of all ownership" that lulls a citizenry to sleep (18). As a corrective, he advocates taking "the way of / the lowest, / including / your legs" (19). Walking and listening keep the individual in touch with the resilient character of quotidian life and force attention on the unique demands of a given moment. Play it "by ear" he urges in a metaphor that unites both the ideals of immediacy and acoustics in one imperative.

Olson's concern for the virtues of hearing is part of a pervasive phonocentrism that dominates contemporary poetics. For poets of the 1950s and 1960s, a new oral impulse served as a corrective to the rhetorically controlled, print-based poetry of high modernism. Whereas "voice" for Eliot and Pound is a rhetorical construct produced through personae and irony, for postwar poets it becomes an extension of the physiological organism. "Speech," as Robert Creeley says, "is a mouth" (*Collected Poems* 283). Orality signifies unmediated access to passional states, giving testimony to that which only *this* poet could know. We can see this oral imperative in Olson's essay "Projective Verse," Allen Ginsberg's theories of mantric breathing, Jack Kerouac's "spontaneous prose," Frank O'Hara's "personism," Michael McClure's "beast language," and Denise Levertov's organic form. The recovery of the oral tradition can be felt in movements such as ethnopoetics, performance poetry, and sound poetry, which stress not only the sounded qualities of language (their phonetics and pragmatics) but their supposed atavistic origins. Acoustic features play an important role in African American writers such as Amiri Baraka, David Henderson, Jayne Cortez, and Sonia Sanchez, who base their poems on jazz and blues motifs where vocalization is an essential component. Each of these tendencies articulates an ideal of immediacy based on the body and its expressive rendering through speech.[1]

Literary historians have explained the origins of this new oralism as a revival of romantic immanence and expressivism in reaction to New Critical ideals of impersonality and distanciation.[2] While these aesthetic contexts are relevant, they do not take into account the fact that many of these developments were made possible by technological advances in typography, offset printing, and—most significant for our purposes—magnetic recording that would seem the very antithesis to any poetics of unmediated presence. In "Projective Verse," Olson celebrates the advantages of breath and breathing in scoring the line, but he recognizes that the notation of such physiological functions is made possible by a machine. The typewriter provides the poet with the same "stave and the bar" as the musician:

> It is the advantage of the typewriter that, due to its rigidity and its space precisions, it can, for a poet, indicate exactly the breath, the pauses, the suspensions even of syllables, the juxtapositions even of parts of phrases, which he intends. (*Selected Writings* 22)

Although Pound, Williams, and cummings had exploited the resources of the typewriter in creating a visual page, Olson links the machine directly to phenomenological and cognitive processes for which breath and voice are the vehicles. Likewise, the new technologies of photo-offset printing offered the magazine editor flexibility and speed in layout and design not available to slower, more cumbersome technologies of letter-press printing. If the little magazine revolution of the 1960s was fueled by a neoromantic poetics of testimony and protest, it was enabled by photographic processes that returned the poem to its producer in a most palpable way. Thus, the immediacy advocated in the poetics of the period was materialized via forms of photomechanical reproduction and printing.

When historians speak of "literary culture," they usually mean the history of print technologies of the sort I have just described.[3] Even a committed oralist such as Walter Ong treats the advancements in media technology as something based "on the use of writing and print." What he calls "secondary orality"—that produced electronically—depends on a prior script and is, as such, only a simulacrum of spontaneity and communality (136–37). With the advances of magnetic recording during the 1930s, however, the tape recorder began to exert its own impact on modernist literature—and I would contend on the concept of voice itself. For the first time, poets could "hear" their own voices and use that hearing to develop notational and performance strategies. With the rise of poetry readings in jazz clubs, coffee houses, and college auditoriums in the late 1950s, the tape recorder returned a kind of oral aura to poetry at a point where it had been, as Olson phrased it, removed from "producer and reproducer" ("Projective Verse" 22). The tape recording could render the authenticity of the occasion—ambient noise, interlinear commentary, coughs, and catcalls—by which the uniqueness of the event could be measured. Tape recordings of these readings found their way into private and institutional collections, providing a significant oral history of a phonocentric era. In such archives (and in the sheer fact of their existence as acoustic records), one can "hear" as well as "see" the profound challenge posed by postmodern art to the authority of ocularcentrism in Western modernism.[4]

I have discussed the uses of tape recordings for literary criticism elsewhere ("'By Ear'"), but I would like here to speculate more broadly on the cultural meaning of this technology. For technology exists in a complex web of social articulations that extend far beyond instrumental ends. Rather than merely serving human interests—the neutral recording of acoustic data for purposes of storage and verification—technology helps produce its users. The emergence of magnetic recording during the postwar period transformed the notion of voice from something "heard" into something "overheard" such that its invocation by poets as natural or unmediated becomes increasingly problematic. Deconstruction has had a great deal to say about the limits of a phonocentric model of language—its dependence on a voice metaphysically prior to any inscription—but it has not investigated the relationships between this model and the technologies that "speak" it into being. I would like to make such an investigation by examining what we might call, following Foucault, "technologies of presence," those systems of production and reproduction within which the voice achieves enough autonomy to regard itself as present-unto-itself (*History of Sexuality* 116).[5] The paranoid versions of these technologies—in Samuel Beckett and William Burroughs, for instance—project the tape recorder as an ultimate agent of mind control, a machine capable of replacing human communication with a prerecorded script.[6]

For the poets who took up the cause of orality in the mid-1950s, voice was a contested site in a battle over identity and agency. The rediscovery of formulaic oral traditions by Milman Parry, Albert Lord, and Eric Havelock provided a link between avant-garde literary practices and earlier tribal cultures. These traditions offered an alternative not only to print culture but to the era's tendencies toward standardization and uniformity—"when all is become billboards," as Olson says. In their recuperation of an oralist, phonocentric imperative, poets hoped to suture together a social body by recovering a private body of significant sounds. But "technologies of presence" will always offer a hybrid voice—a voice in a machine—that cannot speak entirely for itself, even though it posits self-presence as its ground. It is this divided character of orality that informs the paranoid testimony of Ginsberg's "Howl," the self-tracking of Kerouac's novels, and the epic apostrophe of Olson's *Maximus*. When the complicity between presence and technology is acknowledged, in the work of William Burroughs, David Antin, Laurie Anderson, or Steve Benson, the tape recorder ceases to be a passive receptacle for a more authentic speech and becomes an active agent in its deconstruction.

## SURVEILLANCE CULTURE

Although the idea of storing acoustic information by magnetizing a metallic surface was first patented in 1898 by the Danish inventor Vlademar Poulsen, it was not until the late 1920s that practical applications of magnetic recording were put into practice.[7] With the advent of alternating-current bias that amplified the signal, possibilities for magnetic recording were expanded, first to wire and then to metallic tape. The biggest advance in this technology was the German development of the Magnetophone, which reached levels of acoustic clarity previously unrealized. First viewed at the 1936 Berlin Radio Fair, the Magnetophone was linked first to the synchronization of sound in motion pictures and then to the propaganda efforts of the Nazis during the war. It joined with phonographic technology to create the first major break in the long history of print hegemony.[8]

The fact that both forms of sound recording and reproduction were developed as part of the war effort has an important bearing on the voice that was naturalized in the process. Alice Kaplan has discussed the ways in which the Nazis exploited the radio, loudspeaker, and other forms of electronic media to reach a mass audience. She points out that for Nazi propaganda it was the "reproduced voice, rather than the voice itself, that conveyed the archaic values demanded by so-called antimodernist fascist rhetoric" (134). The voice of Hitler at mass rallies or on the radio was a powerful instrument in the "conversion experience" of many Germans, French, and Italians. Through the tape recording, the voice of the Führer or his operatives could be heard simultaneously in every country within the Axis powers, thus achieving a global presence for a single speaker. Far from retaining the "aura" of the original, these technologies offered an endistanced voice that spoke from no place yet was omnipresent. *Je suis partout* (I am everywhere) was both the title of a major fascist newspaper as well as a recognition of the new media's ability to penetrate all corners of social space. The alienation of voice from speaker contributed to the aestheticization of politics of which Walter Benjamin warned in "The Work of Art in the Age of Mechanical Reproduction"; the tape recorder's ability to repeat this voice over and over again was no small agent in this process.[9]

With the advent of the Cold War, the tape recorder came to occupy a very different role in the Western cultural imaginary. No longer associated with broadcasting a voice to the masses, the tape recorder, in the hands of the new postwar surveillance services, could now invade the private space of the individual, gathering information during a period of unprecedented suspicion and secrecy. The expansion of a "surveillance ideology" coincided with the formation of numerous federal agencies, beginning with the OSS (Office of Strategic Services) in 1941 and continuing through the

NIA (National Intelligence Authority) in 1946, the CIA (Central Intelligence Agency) in 1947, the IAC (Intelligence Advisory Committee) in 1950, the NSA (National Security Agency), in 1952, the Hoover Commission Task Force on Intelligence in 1955, the DIA (Defense Intelligence Agency) in 1961, not to mention special congressional committees such as the HUAC (House Un-American Activities Committee) in 1938 and the McCarthy Committee of 1954. These agencies gained greater access to private individuals through new, miniaturized eavesdropping devices and by the easing of the search-and-seizure prohibitions of the Fourth Amendment. Periodicals celebrated the virtues of the "martini olive" transmitter, the detectaphone (which could listen through walls), and the "spike mike" (which could be implanted in the foundations of buildings). Bugging and listening devices could be found everywhere; one was discovered in 1960 hidden in the Great Seal of the United States in the U.S. embassy in Moscow.[10]

Surveillance ideology was promulgated through a series of court cases involving civil rights, especially the prohibition against "unreasonable search and seizure" of the Fourth Amendment. In the days of the red scare and the McCarthy Committee, the ability of CIA, FBI, and other federal agencies to collect damaging information on undesirables was hampered by restrictions, first brought to light in *Olmstead v. US* of 1927 in which the Supreme Court upheld a State of Washington conviction against a bootlegger captured by the use of a wiretap. Since Olmstead's residence was not physically violated, the court ruled that the wiretap could not be seen as a form of search and seizure and therefore did not violate Fourth Amendment provisions. Dissenting opinions by Justices Brandeis and Holmes warned of the dangers of such intrusive, if silent, searches and reinforced "the right to be let alone."[11] These warnings were taken up in earnest in the 1934 Federal Communications Act, which stated that "no person not being authorized by the sender shall intercept any communication and divulge or publish the existence, contents, substance, purport, effect or meaning of such intercepted communications to any person."[12] While the 1934 act limited the admissibility of evidence obtained through wiretaps and other surveillance techniques, such evidence could serve in the "fishing expedition" that would lead to an indictment. Throughout the 1950s and 1960s, states and federal agencies tested the limits of Fourth Amendment restrictions, publicly repudiating the electronic invasion of households while privately and institutionally condoning eavesdropping.[13] The upshot was the Omnibus Crime Control and Safe Streets Act of 1968, which sanctioned the use of electronic surveillance once and for all. While the proponents for legalizing eavesdropping based their arguments on the need to defeat organized crime, these techniques of investigation became increasingly useful in the surveillance of antiwar, counterculture activists during the Vietnam era.

The climate of paranoia established during this period has been well documented and finds its cultural representation in works such as Orwell's *1984*, written in the 1940s, and in the popular imagination through movies such as *Walk East on Beacon* (1952), *The Manchurian Candidate* (1962), *The Conversation* (1974), and *Blow Out* (1981). In such films, surveillance destroys the barrier between interiority and exteriority as technology invades all areas of psychic life. The voice that one expects to hear more clearly becomes permeated with conflicting messages—the ideological static bred by surveillance itself—until the listener and the "bugged" exchange places. This entropic view of surveillance is brilliantly shown in Francis Ford Coppola's 1974 film *The Conversation*, in which Harry Caul (Gene Hackman), the super technician, realizes that, whereas throughout his professional career he has been able to listen in on any conversation, his own is now being overheard by forces he cannot identify. In the last scene, he begins methodically to dismantle his apartment, searching for the hidden mike. His role, as Kaja Silverman says, is reversed from occupying "a position behind the camera and tape recorder to one in front—from a position 'outside the door' to one 'inside the door'" (97–98).

Ironically, it was this same obsession with tape-recorded verification that led to the demise of one of the Cold War's most famous orators, a president so much in love with surveillance ideology that he bugged his own office.[14] No one had been more consumed with the fear of ideological contamination than Richard Nixon, and so it is all the more ironic—or inevitable, if my example from *The Conversation* can be extended—that he should have been "othered" by the sound of his own voice. The technologies that caught the voice of subversives and opponents also trapped the one running the machine. In a world where presence is increasingly verified by information storage and retrieval, the distinction between producer and consumer of information breaks down.

Surveillance ideology, by treating voice as something overheard rather than heard, creates a secondary level of presence, a simulacrum in which identity is revealed as something having already been recorded. This voice cannot generate information by itself; it is only the conduit for ideological messages that precede articulation. Far from the self-present voice of the new orality, the voice constructed in surveillance ideology is entirely fabricated within the laws of secrecy, covert action, and damage control. It is little wonder that when disclosures of the Watergate cover-up got closer and closer to the White House, Nixon in his public responses to the press spoke of himself in the third person.

## TAKE A SIMPLE TAPE FROM ALL YOU ARE (ALLEN GINSBERG)

By speaking of surveillance ideology in the context of poetry, I do not mean to imply that poets necessarily thematized surveillance in their work or that they were more thoroughly investigated than others of the McCarthy period. The best minds of Allen Ginsberg's generation were indeed more likely to be subjects of surveillance, but their voices were raised against larger targets than Ampex or the Bell Labs. The connection I would establish between the worlds of surveillance and poetics is that the virtues of orality become increasingly significant in a world where technology is capable of separating voice from speaker, conversation from community. Apprehension of this alienation animates the writing of many writers during this period. But far from rejecting the tape recorder as an agent of reification, they embraced it as an accomplice in the recovery of more authentic speech.

Among the Beat writers, the tape recorder held a particular fascination, both as a sign of Cold War surveillance and as an instrument for personal confession. The bulk of Jack Kerouac's *Visions of Cody* (1960) is devoted to a taped conversation between Neal Cassady (Cody) and Kerouac, followed by a satiric "Imitation of the Tape" that serves as a kind of auto-critique.[15] The stoned, unrehearsed dialogues between the two men offer a kind of verbal immediacy that contrasts with the stifling conformism of middle America. By substituting recorded conversations for fictionalized dialogue, Kerouac celebrates the dynamic possibilities of "lived speech" as a palliative for the deadened newspeak of square society. And in William Burroughs's *The Ticket That Exploded* (1962), the tape recorder is viewed as a panoptical vehicle for total mind control, capable of entering the body through the ear and transforming informational diversity and difference into bureaucratic master codes. "We don't know who is doing it or how to stop them," one of Burroughs's agents says: "Everytime we catch up with someone . . . we capture a tape recorder" (20). Against such communicational invasion, Burroughs splices and intercuts diverse acoustic materials to create his novel, much as he collaged printed materials together in *Naked Lunch*. In an afterword to *The Ticket That Exploded*, Burroughs points to the defamiliarizing function of such techniques:

> take a political speech on television shut off sound track and substitute another speech you have prerecorded hardly tell the difference isn't much record sound track of one danger man from uncle spy program run it in place of another and see if your friends can't tell the difference it's all done with tape recorders consider this machine and what it can do. (205)

Burroughs's reference to the popular television series *The Man from U.N.C.L.E.* suggests not only that all television programs are the same but that surveillance culture has provided its own forms of self-representation (and parody) to neutralize its more insidious practices.

One poet who thoroughly considered what "this machine" could do to recover the voice was Allen Ginsberg. In *The Fall of America*, he traverses the United States in a Volkswagen, speaking his observations into a tape recorder and singing the requiem of Walt Whitman's democratic vistas. The book was written in 1966 during the first major escalation of the Vietnam War, and Ginsberg was among the first to register the enormous impact of global telecommunications on that conflict. One poem in the volume, "Wichita Vortex Sutra," captures the bizarre contradictions between distant Indochina and middle America. Ginsberg is literally in a vortex of recorded speech as he drives (or is driven) from Macpherson, Kansas, to Wichita, where he is to give a poetry reading. He describes himself being surrounded by high tension wires, telegraph poles, and invisible radio waves:

> News Broadcast & old clarinets
>    Watertower dome Lighted on the flat plain
>       car radio speeding acrost railroad tracks—

> Kansas! Kansas! Shuddering at last!
>       PERSON appearing in Kansas!
>       angry telephone calls to the University
>       Police dumbfounded leaning on
>            their radiocar hoods
>       While Poets chant to Allah in the roadhouse Showboat!
> Blue eyed children dance and hold thy Hand O aged Walt
>       who came from Lawrence to Topeka to envision
>          Iron interlaced upon the city plain—
> Telegraph wires strung from city to city O Melville!
>       Television brightening thy *rills of Kansas lone*
> I come
>                                   (394)

Ginsberg views himself as a "lone man from the void" like Whitman, who has been sent to identify himself as a "PERSON" in Kansas. His isolation is contrasted with a world of electronic sound—news broadcasts, crank telephone calls protesting his appearance on college campuses, police in their "radiocars," and television signals. Ginsberg is driving through Bible-belt America, where religious broadcasts merge with news from Vietnam and then-current patriotic songs such as Sergeant Barry Sadler's "The Ballad of the Green Berets" (Miles 384). It is against this electrical interference that the salutary voices of Whitman and Melville are remembered, voices forged in a different America and a different auditory sensorium.

As Ginsberg rolls through middle America, he records the voices of radio announcers broadcasting the daily body count of the dead in Southeast Asia. Newspaper headlines, billboards, and other forms of highway signage add to the general information blitzkrieg as Ginsberg strives to retain a voice capable of prophecy:

> "We will negotiate anywhere anytime"
>       said the giant President
>    Kansas City Times 2/14/66: "Word reached U.S. authorities that Thailand's leaders feared that in Honolulu Johnson might have tried to persuade South Vietnam's rulers to ease their stand against negotiating with the Viet Cong.
>    American officials said these fears were groundless and Humphrey was telling the Thais so."
>                AP dispatch
>                The last week's paper is Amnesia.
>                              (400)

Quoted material from newspapers, far from clarifying the ambiguities of the historical moment, creates further confusion. The speech of Johnson or Humphrey, filtered through AP journalese, convinces neither the Thai leaders who want further assurance of American support of South Vietnam nor the poet who wants the opposite. Against the doubletalk of Washington or the newspaper, Ginsberg poses the prophetic voice of Whitman's "Democratic Vistas." In a world so riven by undirected sound, Ginsberg yearns for a sign or an icon that participates directly in the physical character of its source. He finds it, partially, in the Chinese character for truth as defined by Ezra Pound, "man standing by his word":

> Word picture:      forked creature
>                          Man
>           standing by a box, birds flying out
>                 representing mouth speech
> Ham Steak please waitress, in the warm café.
>                        (400–401)

Ginsberg wants a voice that has not already been heard, one equivalent to Pound's ideogram that captures in an instant what the canned voice of the media cannot provide. The voice as "word picture" would be as immediate as birds flying out of a box or a request from a lunch menu. For Ginsberg the orality of the tapevoice stands in direct opposition to the reproduced heteroglossia of incorporated sound. Newsmedia, press reports, advertising, and police radio transmissions are all implicated in an information blockage against which the low-tech, Volkswagen-driven cassette recorder stands as alternative. Prophecy no longer emanates from some inner visionary moment but from a voice that has recognized its inscription within an electronic environment, a voice that has seized the means of reproduction and adapted it to oppositional ends. "I sing the body electric," Whitman chants, but the literal possibility for such a song had to wait for Ginsberg and his generation.

### WHAT AM I DOING HERE (DAVID ANTIN)

Ginsberg's generation included a loosely knit group of poets living in New York's lower east side during the 1950s and 1960s for whom the tape recorder became an increasingly important element in composition. Paul Blackburn, LeRoi Jones (Amiri Baraka), Jerome Rothenberg, David Antin, Armand Schwerner, Robert Kelly, and Jackson MacLow linked tape recording to European avant-garde experimentation. Within the group could be found an interest in projectivist and "deep image" theories, applications of John Cage's chance operations, religious and ritual uses of the voice, Russian Futurist and Dadaist theater. The tape recorder participated actively in all of these areas.

Perhaps no one believed more fervently in the advantages of the tape recorder than Paul Blackburn. He brought his small, portable machine to readings at Le Metro, Les Deux Magots, Dr. Generosity's, and St. Mark's Church. He conducted his own poetry show on WBAI radio, thus bringing the new writing out of the clubs and bars of the lower east side and making it available to a wider audience. Furthermore, he turned on his tape recorder during informal drinking sessions with poet friends at his apartment, and the desultory conversations that resulted offer their own interest for the literary record. Beyond this, he used the machine to record world-historical events such as the moon landing or the reports of the Kennedy assassinations and collaged them informally among poetry readings, telephone conversations, and spontaneous raps.[16]

Blackburn is important to our concerns for a number of reasons, not the least of which is his synthesis of Mediterranean lyric tradition (in its Poundian transformations) with new electronic recording media. He was the first American poet to use the tape recorder as an archival vehicle for poetry, much as Alan Lomax and other rural ethnologists had used it for recording folk music. But Blackburn's omniscient tape recorder was more than a vehicle for retrieval; it became a dimension of his material text, as immediate as pen and paper had been for previous generations. It was a device for testing the page and its notation against the voice and, in some cases, for generating new materials that would be incorporated into the poem. And because it was invariably on stage with the poet, the tape recorder became synonymous with the body of the performer.

It is in the work of Blackburn's friend, David Antin, that we see magnetic recording subjected to a directly countertextual imperative. Antin's work since the early 1970s marks a decisive break with the oralist and tribal ideas of Olson and Ginsberg and points to a new, problematized attitude toward the voice. In his "talk" pieces,

Antin inverts the traditional, phonocentric relationship between text and voice by speaking first and writing it down later. He enters the gallery or auditorium, takes out his portable tape recorder, turns it on, and begins speaking. The talk is conducted without text or notes and gives the appearance of being spontaneously delivered. The talk is over when Antin turns off his tape recorder. Later, he transcribes the talk into his own, highly idiosyncratic notation, which utilizes unjustified left and right margins, lowercase letters, gaps between phrases, and little or no punctuation. Although I have referred to the printed version as a "transcription," it is in no sense a replica of the talk itself. Antin freely edits and modifies the talk so that it becomes a representation, not a mimesis, of speech.

However spontaneous these works may appear, they do follow certain patterns. The title often establishes the general territory that subsequent anecdotes, stories, and examples elaborate. When Antin gives the same talk piece in several venues, he uses the same materials and sequencing of stories, much as a standup comedian repeats a pattern of jokes. And there is a good deal of borscht-belt humor in Antin's work. He relies extensively on timing—the incremental building of a metaphor, the deferral of the punch line—and combines it with the subtle creation of himself as a schlemiel in a world of slick impresarios. These verbal strategies and postures have their antecedents in classical rhetoric as much as in Henny Youngman, and Antin often exploits the fuzzy boundaries between the two realms. Antin exploits the dialectical method of Socrates, not the spatial logic of Aristotle or Quintilian, and like Socrates he asks questions for which he already has the answers.

As other commentators have noted, many of Antin's talk pieces are about themselves.[17] It is less often recognized that they are also about the status of voice in an age of electronically reproduced information. In his three books, *Talking at the Boundaries, Tuning,* and *What It Means to Be Avant Garde,* each talk is framed by brief prefatory and concluding remarks concerning the actual circumstances leading up to and following the talk. These remarks introduce the event organizers, art patrons, and gallery curators who make the talk possible. Within the talk itself, however, are other self-reflexive comments regarding audience expectations that often initiate the larger subject of the talk. For the "subject" of the talk is very much the pragmatics of the talk environment, the manipulation of positional relations between a putative speaker and his listeners.

A good example of Antin's self-conscious manipulation of deixis occurs in "whos listening out there," delivered on radio station KPBS, a National Public Radio affiliate in San Diego. Since most of his talk pieces during the early 1980s had been delivered in public spaces, the challenge of addressing a potentially large but absent audience offered a chance to explore another dimension of his technique. In his printed version, Antin adds a preface that describes the format of the radio show on which he appeared. This particular program featured a first half hour devoted to poems by Dante Gabriel and Christina Rossetti, read by the show's moderator and other guests. These recitations, "burnished by elocution lessons," are the very antithesis of Antin's oral style and procedure. They represent a late-nineteenth-century notion of dramatic recitation in which ornate rhetoric is enhanced by histrionic vocal inflections.

In his performance on the radio, Antin explains to his host

> i didnt read anymore    that i talked as the occasion
> required     but i dont think he really believed me
> until he saw me setting up my cassette recorder
> i explained it was my habit to record my talks
> to find out what id said     but he pointed out that
> the station engineer regularly recorded the show
> and that the quality would surely be better     so i
> put away my tape recorder and prepared to listen
>                                                    (268)

This offhand remark—or, as we shall see, this *representation* of an offhand remark—sets up a dialectic of technology and orality around which many of his talks are based. The technological expertise of professionals (in this case, the station engineer) is posed against the naiveté of the oral poet who relies on his voice and his improvisatorial skills. In the talk itself, Antin utilizes the anonymity of his audience to explore the ways in which radio fictionalizes the presence of its auditors. He assures his audience that although he is not reading from a script,

>     ... you people out there you shouldnt be afraid either"
>   i wont say anything so surprising that youll have to turn    the set
>   off      and i know that you have confidence in that
> at least you generally have confidence in that     otherwise you
>   wouldnt have your radio on ....
>                                                    (270)

This assurance does exactly the opposite of what it proposes by calling into question the pact between radio listener and announcer. By addressing himself directly to the listener's fears that something out of the ordinary will *not* happen, he causes that something to happen. Such intervention is what speech act theorists would call violations of appropriateness or felicity, which occur when the contract between addresser and addressee is broken.[18] At such moments, attention is distracted from the progressive line of argument onto the utterance itself; communication becomes recursive performance. And while much of modernism is engaged with breaking criteria of appropriateness, Antin situates its problematic within the orbit of technology.

In order to illustrate further the fictions of appropriateness that radio makes possible, Antin stages a fanciful image of himself for the listeners:

> ... you cant see me running
> my hand      nervously through my greying hair
> .............................................
>
> resting my lean      almost gaunt chin in the cup of my right
> hand      regarding with mild amusement from my one good
> eye   the somewhat bemused expressions on the faces of my two
> companions in this radio booth      who might have expected
> some greater degree of decorum from a lean and tweedy
> english-looking gentleman with a black eyepatch
>
> (270, 272)

Needless to say, such a portrayal does not correspond to the "real" David Antin any more than the news received from authoritative voices of the media corresponds to events upon which it reports. But the fictive pact upon which audition is based is circular. Just as his audience cannot know him, so Antin cannot know his listeners. To imagine his interlocutors he creates a sequence of possible auditors drawn from his neighbors. The bulk of the talk piece is taken up with reimagining some of these local figures:

> so maybe its mr canton im talking to "hello mr canton
> are you out there?"      mr canton was a red faced frenchman
> tall and straight      from montreal and he rented a room
> further on down the bluff
>
> (276)

*Technologies of Presence* 211

On the one hand, such apostrophes personalize the address, turning an anonymous vocal medium into an intimate one. These characters really *could* be listening since their personalities are so vividly rendered. Yet each story concludes with Antin's recognition that each of his potential auditors is out of range in some way: Timmy, who is living "too far north to pick up our transmission," or Cindy, who does not listen to "anything but music on the radio," or Mrs. Harris, whose "hearing [is] beginning to go," or even Mr. Canton, who has probably died by this time. So the potential for hearing, offered by the personalized address, is withdrawn in each case as if to illustrate how limited each construction of presence really is.

The dialogue between technology and voice in Antin parallels a debate between professionalism and amateurism. A dominant theme in many of his talk pieces is the authority of technicians, museum curators, doctors, scientists, critics whose claims to knowledge are legitimated not by innate competence but by the discursive fields they occupy. Against the professional, Antin posits the amateur, the autodidact, the untutored citizen who, like himself, is simply trying to find answers to fundamental problems. By posing himself as the humble seeker-after-truth, Antin most resembles his Socratic ideal.

In "whos listening out there," this debate over professionalism is presented via a lengthy anecdote about doctors and their claim to be members of a scientific rather than a service community. The anecdote concerns a cocktail party that he and his wife attend consisting largely of doctors who spend much of the evening bemoaning the threat to medicine from the rising costs of malpractice insurance. Antin and his wife intercede in this debate, asking embarrassing questions about medical ethics and making nuisances of themselves. Antin argues that by regarding themselves as scientists, doctors exempt themselves from responsibility, living according to a professional ethos beyond the reach of blame. In reality, they should regard themselves as members of a service economy in which, like plumbers and contractors, they have clients who have legitimate interests in the success of their work. In Antin's view

> ... a patient comes to a doctor with a complaint    not with a disease and what the doctor offers him is a disease    a disease is the doctors prospective gift to the patient    which is then followed by other gifts    since one gift leads to another a course of therapy    drugs surgery    who knows    and

> these are more securely attached to the disease than the complaint
> as the doctor is more securely attached to the treatment and
> to the disease than he is to the complaint or the patient
>
> (281)

The problem is not that doctors are incompetent but that they invest their work with an image of their professional calling to the exclusion of the patients' needs. To this extent, the anecdote about doctors extends the earlier discussion about radio audiences. In a discourse situation in which there is no feedback (e.g., the patient is only the recipient of a "gift" of a disease; the listener has no basis upon which to validate his/her image of the announcer), the effectiveness of a diagnosis is based on the authority vested in the voice. The way to illustrate the limitation of this discourse situation is to imagine it as a radio in which an announcer could address specific listeners and in which listeners could attach a body to speech.[19]

However critical Antin is of professionals, he constantly reveals himself to be a competent amateur. In fact, his talk pieces show him to be an authority on many things—from mathematics to foreign languages to carpentry to baseball. Antin restages the Platonic dialogue in which the naive dialectician speaks, often deferentially, to "real" professionals—rhetoricians, rhapsodes, critics—who claim to know but who have no practical experience of the objects of their knowledge. By speaking, rather than by writing, Socrates is revealed to be closer to the truth because he argues directly, unhindered by a script. For the contemporary talk poet, writing (or printing) is the transcription of speech, a second degree of performance rendered as such by the use of spacing and indentation in the printed text.

The validation for Antin's distrust of professionals is provided at the end of his talk piece when he reveals that the engineer who had promised to make a tape of the broadcast somehow neglected to record it. But the piece was not lost:

> *... the next day i got a call from the artist*
> *reesey shaw who told me that she and her husband*
> *david had been listening to me on the radio the*
> *night before     david was experimenting with*
> *recording and reesey wanted to know if id like*
> *a tape of the show*
>
> (296)

This last frame draws together all of the themes discussed in "whos listening out there." The ineptness of the professional is countered by the artist and amateur who, because of her investment in what is being said, makes a tape and offers it to the poet. Thus, the hermeneutic circle has been entered the right way, through a tapeloop in which voice is understood not as something preserved but as something always already reproduced, something made in unmaking itself as truth.

## PLAYING THE BODY ELECTRIC
## (LAURIE ANDERSON)

Despite Antin's interest in the frames of voice, he nevertheless believes in one individual's ability to wrest truth from illusion. His use of electronic media is distinctly low tech, the appropriation of electronic media to serve certain minimal goals (transcription) and validate authorial presence through the presentation of a voice grounded in debate. At the same time, Antin realizes that any proposition of a "more real voice" is constructed in highly specific discursive contexts. Hence, he tailors his talks to the audience at hand (or, in my example, the lack of audience). That the audience is seldom given an opportunity to respond limits the dialogical possibilities of the talk but does not alter Antin's faith in poetry's public character.

In the work of Laurie Anderson (at least in her videos and CDs), there is no live audience and therefore no claim to dialogue. Technology becomes both the subject (in both the ontological as well as thematic sense) and the means of reproduction. In a recent "sampler" of her videos (*Collected Videos*), Anderson is shown at home, surrounded by the synthesizers, mixers, tape recorders, electric keyboards, and microphones on which she constructs her performances. She moves from one electronic gadget to another, describing each one affectionately as she flips switches or speaks into mikes—a parody, perhaps, of the 1950s domestic worker displaying her new labor-saving kitchen. But if her self-presentation as technician is ironic, her skill at using these devices is evident in all of her work.

Through her use of synthesizers—synclavier, harmonizer, contact mike—Anderson creates a cyborg voice, partly her own and partly that of technology itself. Unlike with earlier performance artists (and this would include Antin), the identity of voice with presence can no longer be presumed. As Craig Owen says, Anderson's uses of these filters "amplify, distort and multiply her actual voice in such a way that it can no longer be identified as hers" (122). Instead, voice is an index to certain ideological messages for which the body serves as a conduit. And while she projects a vision of technological dystopia akin to that of William Burroughs or Thomas Pynchon, she retains a critical perspective upon the state and corporate apparatus from which these messages extend. "Language," as she quotes from Burroughs, "is a virus from outer space," not a vehicle that emanates from within.

By speaking of her voice as a "cyborg" projection, I am inflecting Anderson's critical perspective with specifically feminist implications. Rather than recruit nature or biology as woman's realm against the deadening effects of technology, Anderson explores, in terms strikingly similar to Donna Haraway's, her constructed nature within both areas. By utilizing her body and voice as instruments for manipulating electronic signals, Anderson treats herself as a conductor of sound, a "vessel" in the most literal sense: a stretched skin whose internal spaces resonate and vibrate. And in her more recent work she uses video and audio synthesizers to lower her voice and distort her features into a male "clone" of herself, a comic straight-man who writes her lyrics and sings her songs. Although in her performances Anderson speaks through a phallic microphone, the voice that emerges is a multiple, choric construction. Since Anderson's voice is often both the soloist *and* the chorus, her performances literalize what Julia Kristeva and others thematize as a psychoanalytic paradigm for describing gender.[20]

The full implications of this cyborg presence are explored in Anderson's 1983 work *United States*. In this six-hour opera, Anderson projects a technological wasteland where the relationship between Big Science (fusion, nuclear weapons research, star wars) and Big Signs (infomatics, telecommunications) mediates all relationships.[21] Much of *United States* (both the performance and the geopolitical entity) is based on processed information such as phone messages, computerized voices, tapeloops, advertising jingles, and techno-jargon. These are voices without origin, detached from bodies, yet by their anonymity they are capable of controlling their listeners. Anderson seems to be asking how these simulacral voices gain their power if they have no agency. In one section ("Language of the Future"), for example, she tells the story of being in an airplane that loses an engine and begins a sudden, precipitous descent:

> A voice came over the intercom and said:
> Our pilot has informed us that we are about to attempt a crash landing. Please extinguish all cigarettes.
> Place your tray tables in their upright, locked position.
> Your captain says: Please do not panic.
> Your captain says: Place your head in your hands.
> Captain says: Place your head on your knees.
> Captain says: Put your hands on your head
>     Put your hands on your knees!
>     (heh-heh)
> This is your Captain.
> Have you lost your dog?
> We are going down.
> We are going down, together
> 
>                                                  (Part I)

In her recorded version of this section, Anderson reads the voices of flight attendant and captain in the same, deadpan manner, creating an even more sinister quality to her narrative. The calm, reasonable words of the flight attendant merge with the voice of the captain, whose assurances turn demonic when he plays a game of Simon says over the intercom: "Place your hands on your head / Put your hands on your knees!" By confusing the voice of the traditionally female flight attendant and the masculine voice of authority, Anderson exposes how gender is ventriloquized within technological instrumentation. The adequacy of voice to message cannot be based on anything said but upon the auditor's willingness to accept the technological mise-en-scène. "Jump out of the plane," the voice commands; "There is no / pilot. / You / are not / alone." The source of such messages is difficult to locate since it, like Anderson's voice, is electronically mixed. If there is no pilot—no source for voice—then the subject is truly "not / alone" in her paranoia.[22]

Many of Anderson's vignettes in *United States* concern an addressee who, like the passenger in the airplane, is the passive recipient of potentially violent and threatening imperatives. The same Orwellian tapevoice that we find in 1950s surveillance ideology reappears here; the phone rings, and a voice on the other end says

Please do not hang up.
We know who you are.
Please do not hang up . . .
We've got your number
                (Part I)

And in a brilliant piece of concrete poetry, Anderson renders the circuit from phone to phonetap:

```
            R           ING
            R           ING
W           ARE         IN                          LINE
WE          ARE         A PING      YOUR            LI E
WE          ARE         TA PING     YOUR            LI E
WE          ARE         TAPPING     YOUR            LINE
```

Here the larger dimensions of the phone message become clear as more letters are added: from "We are in line" to "We are taping your lie" to "We are tapping your line." Each message increases the metaphor of invasion—from the ring of the phone to the beginning of the voice to the phonetap itself. At each stage, information is added through a digitalized matrix of letters and spaces—one letter added to a space, a space filled by a letter. "This / is the language / of the on-again / off-again / future. And / it is Digital."

But this paranoid scenario does not end in some anonymous printout. The next sequence features Anderson playing a tape recording of a violin solo through a "pillow speaker" hidden in her mouth. By modulating the shape of her lips, the violin solo is modified, thus offering an analog alternative to the digitalized network of the printed script. Her voice circumvents the "on-again / off-again" world of commands and responses, figured in the intercom voices of the airplane or the surveillance message, and sends back its own message shaped by the internal workings of the body.

The same confusion of genders that we see in "Language of the Future" appears again in "O Superman (For Massenet)," in which the nurturing voice of "Mom" blends into the Voice of Authority associated with corporate America. "O Superman" begins with the most pervasive form of invasive tape recording: the phone message:

Hi. I'm not home right now. But if you want to leave a message, just start talking at the sound of the tone.

> Hello? This is your mother. Are you there? Are you coming home?
> Hello? Is anybody home.
> (Part II)

Having established that no one is home, the mother's solicitous query quickly takes on ominous overtones:

> Well you don't know me
> but I know you
> And I've got a message to give to you.
> Here come the planes.
> .......................
> And the voice said:
> this is the hand, the hand that takes.
> This is the hand. The hand that takes ... Here come the planes.
> They're American planes made in America. Smoking or
>    non-smoking?
> (Part II)

As Henry Sayre points out, in this section Anderson uses the harmonizer to lower her voice, linking the identities of technological authority and masculinity (150). And just as female performer and male voice are united through technological manipulation, so the maternal caller ("Mom") is linked to the sinister "hand that takes." The recipient of this message—presumably the daughter—must accept Mom's message and ask for comfort, not in filial terms but in those offered by corporate rationality:

> So hold me Mom, in your long arms,
> in your automatic arms,
> your electronic arms,
> .....................
> your petrochemical arms,
> your military arms ...
> (Part II)

Critics of Laurie Anderson have objected to a certain depthlessness and redundancy to her performances, yet such criticisms ignore the ways that she implicates such depth models as part of her critical project.[23] *United States* deals with the voice as a vessel for technological rationality—of "electronic arms," "smart bombs," and "friendly fire"—where the rhetoric of nurturance and comfort is electronically imprinted onto the voice of authority. Such rhyming of rhetorics—

of "mom" and "bomb"—occurs in the larger media to be sure (as it was during the Persian Gulf War, when "smart bombs" were delivered to oppose "The Mother of all wars") but finds its local occasion in the tapevoice of the phone machine, where absence is signaled by a repetition of presence.

### RELEASED FROM INEXPLICABLE CODE
### (STEVE BENSON)

As we have seen with Ginsberg and Olson, the creation of a new lyric, performative voice was the first stage in contesting surveillance culture, even though its creation was aided by the very technologies that the voice hoped to displace. In a paradox developed by Foucault and de Lauretis, a poetics of immanence becomes a technology of presence. For Ginsberg, the spontaneous recording of his own voice into the tape recorder becomes the aural equivalent to the romantic diary, the retention of a quotidian realm threatened by the "narcotic tobacco haze of capitalism" (as he says in "Howl"). Antin also privileges the immediacy of voice as the site of real-time experience, a voice made all the more present by its address to a specific venue and audience. It is important for both Ginsberg and Antin that the tape recorder maintain a low profile as the agent of transcription. With Laurie Anderson and, as I will point out, Steve Benson, the tape recorder becomes an active agent in composition, modulating the voice, permitting its duplication, and assisting in its fragmentation. In place of lyric testimony, Anderson creates a hybrid, electronically modified voice, in which gender identity has been confused and technological complicity in gender hierarchies foregrounded. Steve Benson uses the tape recorder to achieve many of the same results as Anderson in calling the self-sufficient speaker into question, yet he does so by some of the more process-oriented ethos of poets such as Ginsberg or Frank O'Hara.

Benson shares with many of his Language-writing colleagues a distrust of the expressive voice that dominated much 1960s writing, but he utilizes the latter's interest in real-time experience to create what Barrett Watten calls "dissonances of scale that call the speaker into account" (111). He does this by orchestrating interruptions in his performances that require him to improvise on the spot. Since 1977, he has used the tape recorder as a collaborator in this process.

In various performances, Benson wears headphones, listening to a tape on which he produces a spontaneous commentary. Whereas Laurie Anderson thematizes technology's intrusion into the quotidian, Benson *produces* the quotidian by his edgy, often uncertain response to the interrupting material. By an odd reversal of terms, technology allows him a greater degree of presence by forcing him, as both speaker and receiver of his own message, to respond to and interact with the printed page. At the same time, since the audience is a party to only one portion of his performance—that being improvised—it must fill in or re-create the silent "other" voice available only to the one wearing the headphones.

A brilliant example of Benson's performance style can be seen in "Echo," a work that involves the recursive properties of a text endlessly recorded, played back, and responded to. Because "Echo" is first and foremost a performance, its transcription into a book (*Blindspots*) represents less the final product than a stage in what is a potentially infinite process of recording and rereading. The structure of the work is deceptively simple. Benson begins by reading a poem called "Echo." He then improvises a desultory rap with reference to the poem he has just read. He records this rap and then rewinds the tape, during which time he reads sections from a notebook or journal.[24] He then plays back the previously recorded tape through headphones and responds to it orally. By occasionally switching the public address speakers on and off, he controls the amount of prerecorded tape that the audience can hear, thus confusing the border between private and public hearing. The "new" version, incorporating both improvised and prerecorded materials, is simultaneously being recorded, and when he is finished Benson rewinds this new tape while once again reading from journals. He then plays the new tape—now containing all of the previous material—back through earphones and, once again, responds to it. In the performance on which the published version is based, the "original" tape is subjected to three rereadings, although the number could be extended indefinitely.

While these complex procedures may resemble chance-generated techniques of Jackson MacLow or John Cage, they differ in the degree of affective response they require. Benson is trying not to circumvent intentionality through randomness but to show one sort of intentionality thwarted by another. Nothing is random in the performance since every new element is based on something that has already appeared. The audience witnesses a person trying to stay on top of an accretional information overload that threatens to overwhelm him. As a result, much of the text is devoted to rhetorical "filler"—the desultory wandering of everyday speech: "and the sort of I don't know I mean I wonder you know if listening to that you get the experience of a kind of a *haze* or you know does like there's nothing like Kirby was saying the 'it'" (32). It is this aimless quality of lived speech—the "it-ness" of real time—that interests Benson; he wants to find the intersection of a presence already heard (and recorded) with a presence immediately coming-into-being.

As an illustration of Benson's accretional mode, we might look at the opening lines of the four recorded variations. The first rap comes in direct response to the poem "Echo":

That was, like many things, not really so much something that I
would want to deem an abstraction
or
something that necessarily came across
began to appear with a purpose to belong in some idea about
(32)

It was, like many things
   I decided that, the most
  casual and appropriate plan would be to
                 sort of, step out of
some kind of a black forest that I'd imagine myself to be in
and without any particular purpose or a sense of trying to make
          a case for my belonging, in the situation
   I would find some use for myself
(35)

*It was  ,   like many things*
  *I decided that, the most*
               So— if      if there isn't a
*casual and appropriate plan would be to*
          model that attaches to that kind of
            *sort of, step out of*
    practice of heading into
*some kind of a black forest that I'd imagine myself to be in*
    white noise
(39)

>     **I decided that, the most**
> that we knew what that was and that if we got started
>             *if there isn't a*
>     **casual and appropriate plan would be**
> into it we would inevitably be sort of propelled along as a
>        *model that attaches to that*
>                     **step out of**
>        a madness, but in fact there wasn't
>     *practice of heading into*
>             **a black forest that I'd imagine myself to be in**
> anybody there other than some other people who basically were
> *white noise*                                              (47)

From a meditation on the poem "Echo," Benson imposes in part 2 a mythic narrative onto his composition—"a black forest" inspired perhaps by the story of Echo and Narcissus. In part 3, he acknowledges that the dark forest that he hopes to escape is, in fact, a narratological model, a transformation of the writer's mimetic imperative into a social construct. In this section, the emphasis is on his choice of certain semiotic elements to hold off "white noise," to deflect the obliteration of significant sound. In the fourth section, the dark forest of self-reflection is revealed as potential "madness" and the white noise revealed as the sound of "other people."

Of course to impose such a linear, developmental model on this work does violence to the performance experience. The tapevoice, its complexity notated by different typefaces, challenges the improviser's abilities to make sense. The overall recording of the performance displays Benson's nervous attempt to find "the right word" or to generate the "apt response" to a splintering informational field. It is, as his references to the dark forest indicate, a latter-day equivalent to Dante's journey into the *selva oscura*. At times, he becomes aware of the tension between the desire to keep the present moving forward and the desire to write it down: "It's odd how I think / I *do* sort of tend to generate certain themes / and so you know immediately there's the impulse to / escape, to try to write it down" (41). But this impulse, as he says, *"preposterously* informs the present with a / manic reaction against what in fact was originally / improvised" (41). What Benson seems to be saying in such passages is that the impulse to treat the text as stabilizing the present is a vain endeavor since all utterances are an improvisation within specific discursive limitations. By imposing several restraints upon his ability to "go on," Benson achieves a Beckett-like stoicism in the face of temporal diffusion and disorder. But unlike Krapp, whose tapes provide a mnemonic for reflection, Benson re-creates the past by retaping the present.

## ECHO AND NARCISSUS: THE TAPEVOICE RETURNS

Echo is the nymph whose fate it is to fall in love with Narcissus, a figure who can only love his own image. Her attempts to declare her love are complicated by the fact that she can only repeat his words. She is the tapevoice who is forced to speak by respeaking the language of others. Her voice is the simulacrum of voice, a speech without origin. By using the myth of Echo, Benson seems to be asking whether a truly reflective voice is possible in a technological age. Is Echo's private voice different from her public speech or is it always a mirror of Narcissus's? In Vygotskyian terms, does her inner speech merely replicate the public sphere, or does thought constitute a fundamentally different mode of knowledge, and can that be represented? Benson tries to answer some of these questions by manipulating the tape recording such that each repetition of information contains a supplement of new material. Or to put it another way, each generation of new information always contains a residue of the past. Echo does not repeat herself in a solipsistic circle; she also generates a new subjectivity out of her debate with the other. As she announces in the title poem

> You are trying to *be* the sunset. You are trying to make a person out of me. A person you might know.
>
> Know me but do not meet me. Hold me up to this tree and see the light I shed.
>
> (29)

Echo's crisis is that of the post-technological cybervoice: how to generate authentic speech while recognizing one's inscription in prior voices. The fixed gender roles of Echo and Narcissus are broken down in the interplay between I and you, poet and beloved, poet and reader. By manipulating the frames between poem and tape, improvised voice and tapevoice, Benson situates his readers in the position of Echo, suspended "between" voices—our own and that of the addressee—just as Benson, wearing his headphones and pacing anxiously between one side of the performance space and the other, is between layers of tape.

Benson's attempt to create a modern, technological version of Ovid's tale represents an extreme version of presencing, one in which poetry is generated by submitting to the machine's reification of the voice. Although an earlier writer such as Burroughs demonizes submission to the tape recorder of surveillance, Benson sees in such vulnerability a way of opposing the machine's panoptical control. By using the tape recorder to create contingency (rather than store it), Benson reestablishes an uneasy relationship to his own voice. And in the four decades since the "golden age" of surveillance, Ginsberg, Antin, and Anderson have provided, through the tape recorder, an alternative to the flattening of affect lamented by postmodern cultural theorists. Rather than search for forms of presence in peasant shoes or the windowless monad of aesthetic autonomy, these writers have heard in the tapevoice, to adapt Wallace Stevens, "ghostlier demarcations, keener sounds."

# Afterword
## *"Ghostlier Demarcations"*

"Ghostlier demarcations, keener sounds." Wallace Stevens's faith in the poem's ability to establish an idea of order at Key West (or Tennessee or Tallapoosa, for that matter) is declared by means of a gothic trope that haunts this book: a wraith of voice that sings "Like a body wholly body, fluttering / Its empty sleeves" (128). The phantasmagoria of modern writing often frames an oxymoron in which faces in a crowd become apparitions, in which objects in shop windows seem to speak on their own, as they do in *Sister Carrie:*

> "My dear," said the lace collar she secured from Partridge's, "I fit you beautifully; don't give me up."
> "Ah, such little feet," said the leather of the soft new shoes; "how effectively I cover them. What a pity they should ever want my aid." (Dreiser 75)

But what is this voice (gendered feminine in Stevens's poem) that, to sing on its own, needs the imposition of the mind's orders upon it? The poet's "rage to order words of the sea" offers a humanist ethos of proportion and artisanal control against the collective babble of undifferentiated sound. Stevens's metaphor also suggests that whatever idea of order will be imposed at Key West will be one both seen and *heard*, a fact that may come as a surprise to audiences acquainted with Stevens's leaden reading of his own poems on his Caedmon LP recording. "Keener sounds" may refer to water washing on the shore, but it does not necessarily translate into the sounded vocables of the poet. The modernist voice in 1934 remains an elocutionary device—an amanuensis to the text—whose presence on a long-playing record presents no adjunct to the muses' diadem.

There is another ghost in this poem. What I described as the collective babble against which Stevens's poet orders "words of the sea" is that social body whose poverty and despair posed problems for the player of the blue guitar. Stevens's poetry of the 1930s, as Alan Filreis says, is a sustained debate with critics on the left who felt that poems such as "Sunday Morning" and "Mozart, 1935" offered aesthetic refusal in the face of social crisis. On the subject of mass culture, the poet seemed reticent, if not obtuse. "Poet," Stevens apostrophizes, "be seated at the piano. / Play the present, its hoo-hoo-hoo. . . . If they throw stones upon the roof / While you practice arpeggios, / It is because they carry down the stairs / A body in rags" (131–32). If Stevens played "arpeggios" while Depression America burned, he did so in poems that resonate with contention, that incorporate the "hoo-hoo-hoo" of the present in their desultory strivings toward a supreme fiction. The confident iambic cadences of his lines ("She sang beyond the genius of the sea") are undermined by the "cries" they cannot contain, the rage they cannot order. In 1971, Louis Zukofsky, ex-Marxist and admirer of Lenin, approved Stevens's ability to deliver "an instant certainty of the words of a poem bringing at least two persons and then maybe many persons even peoples together" (*Prepositions* 26–27).

As I indicated in my introduction, the ideology of modernism is written within two materialities—one aesthetic, one socioeconomic—that cannot easily be separated. The interdependence of these two realms can be seen in modernist poets' self-conscious use of the material text—its existence as holograph manuscript, printed page, codex book, recorded voice. The ideal of aesthetic autonomy, inherited from romanticism, offered the possibility of an object separated from relations of exchange and detached from psychological dynamics. But the ideal of autonomy was underwritten by market considerations for which disinterestedness was the hallmark of entrepreneurial expertise. Texts could choose *not* to be associated with such considerations, but they would record their "investment" in them by privileging the object status of their medium and the genius of their creator. Gertrude Stein in the 1930s is my model for the writer caught in such contradictions.

To delineate various ghosts that inhabit modernist texts, the critic needs to be aware of presuppositions that determine in advance what form these shapes will assume—to continue my Stevensian metaphor, to anticipate the "nothing that is not there and the nothing that is" (10). In the case of orality, it means reconsidering one's reliance on certain acoustic models to describe a poem's ability to "speak" and be heard. What readers hear as "keener sounds" will be different, say, for leftist critics in 1934 than for readers accustomed to technologies of vocal transcription in the 1960s. My ability to summon up certain lines by Stevens is aided by the fact that I have *heard* him read them a number of times; they have become part of my acoustic mnemonic archive. When we speak of "hearing" what the author may not have intended, we infuse hermeneutics with a body, and that body cannot be taken for granted. When the critical body is defamiliarized and made strange, the specular relation of critic to autonomous object undergoes a sea change, a fact that I can illustrate by a personal anecdote.

In the process of writing the previous chapter on the tapevoice, I lost half my hearing due to the removal of a tumor from my left auditory canal. Another tumor is still growing on the right side and will have to be removed at some future date, posing the possibility of total deafness. While I am not particularly superstitious, I was conscious of the uncanny coincidence between my operation and my investigation of orality, my attempt to relate surveillance ideology to the production of voice. Was I being covertly investigated by cultural conservatives for proposing that the voice is not natural, that it is produced in a cultural marketplace among tape recorders, contact mikes, and phonetaps? In this afterword, I argue that orality is constructed around "technologies of presence" linked to state-sponsored surveillance, but the severing of my acoustic nerve has forced me to rethink the ease with which I use "voice" as an index for the way ideology speaks.

On a superficial level, having lost hearing on my left side means that in public spaces such as concert halls, restaurants, and classrooms I am forced to move "further to the left" in order to hear clearly. This provides me with a felicitous merging of physical and political positions that I hope is not only metaphoric. It also calls attention to the ways in which acoustic defamiliarization forces one to experience space as a flexible and porous phenomenon, not as a structural inevitability. Kant proposed that space is foundational for all perceptual acts; we inhabit it as individuals only because we assume an a priori experience of space shared by all others. But space is shared differently within hearing or non-hearing cultures. It is affected by acoustic, architectural, and electronic means that work to normalize an environment. When that acoustic space fails to normalize, its instrumentality is revealed, its ability to interpellate others made strange. When one steps off the curb and hears traffic approaching from the left as coming from the right, one's relations to rightness and leftness, causality and directionality, balance and verticality cease to be those of one's fellow pedestrian.

I say these things not to claim some special privilege as "hearing challenged." Compared to members of the deaf community I still inhabit a hearing culture, and my linguistic values still revolve around alphabetic script based on sound. But in speaking as I do about the invention of presence through orality I have perhaps treated too schematically what for many is a far more complex matter relating to the self-evident status of acoustic space. Orality, in its literary as well as philosophical senses, presumes an even distribution of speech acts among potential hearers. Even when listeners reconfigure the details of a well-known story or when speakers utilize gesture and mime to enhance their telling, it is understood that "the tale of the tribe" is intended to be heard. For those who cannot (or do not choose to) participate in such speech acts, their performative status can no longer be assumed. Thus, many of the claims for "voice" must be rewritten—or re-signed. I must rethink the circuitry of the oral imperative—its belief in an open conduit between speaker and hearer—as well as the circuitry of its critique. In a world where disinformation is parlayed through "sound bites," where "word of mouth" means lack of analysis, where "I hear what you're saying" confirms rather than rearticulates, the normativity of acoustic models of information dissolves.

If orality presumes open access among listeners, it also assumes a body prior to speech, a tympanum on which socially significant messages can be sounded. But one is not born a body; one becomes one. Upon entering the hospital to be manipulated toward health, one becomes subject to what Foucault calls the "medical gaze." In my case, I was seen by otolaryngologists, acoustic surgeons, speech therapists, anaesthesiologists, insurance agents, and hematologists through whom my ability to "speak" for my body (and to be "heard" accordingly) was ventriloquized. When speech becomes medicalized, it no longer possesses that spontaneity of expression accorded it by philosophers from Plato to Habermas; its ability, as Whitman says, to go after "what my eyes cannot reach" is restricted by institutional settings and discursive contexts that turn voice into text.

The medicalized body is the triumph of modernism, the end of a trajectory that begins in Machinery Hall in Philadelphia in 1876. Here, among the multitude of new labor-saving machines and whirring dynamos, one could see the palimtext in formation: the first typewriter, produced by the Remington Arms Company, Thomas Edison's new "multiplex" telegraph on which multiple messages could be contained on one wire, and Alexander Graham Bell's first telephone (Trachtenberg 41). In these three inventions, the private voice was decisively separated from the body in a surgical operation that left it in an odd epistemological limbo. Like the removal of the object from the labor process in Marx's discussion of the commodity, the voice could now attach itself to things and speak of desires formerly associated with humans. Or, alternately, technology could produce new hybrid identities in which to reconfigure agency. Whether this could lead to the emancipation of a new subject (the proletariat) in the nineteenth century or new gender categories (cyborg feminism, queer identities) in the late twentieth is still open for debate. What is clear is that the work of voice in an age of mechanical reproduction is neither a tapevoice nor a body, neither a construct nor an essence. The voice may not necessarily be heard in order to be heard or overheard in order to make sense. Sense is being made in new virtual realities where sound is only one among several options.

If this autobiographical anecdote has any relevance to the status of the material word, it is that my model of the palimtext is still locked in a spatial paradigm bequeathed by New Critical former teachers. In my new monophonic relationship to acoustic space, I see the text less as a thing (a page, an intertextual matrix) than as a relation among competing speech acts. To continue my acoustic metaphor, criticism could be regarded as what zoologists call "echo location" to describe the way in which bats "see" in the dark. Bats emit high frequency sounds ahead of them and orient themselves by means of reflected sound waves. By interpreting the reverberating sound as large (obstruction) or small (insect), they veer and feed in a digitalized hyperspace.

Applied to literature, we might say that criticism as echo location necessitates the treatment of texts as moving targets and critical acts as provisional trajectories. By this metaphor, we could also reverse the usual hermeneutic model and envision texts as having their own critical agency to which criticism must attend. I say this both as a poet and a critic at a moment when poetry as a form of significant intellectual discourse is in disfavor, in which a strong "narrative turn" has become the dominant mode. Just as I cannot separate my hearing body from acoustic models upon which poetics is based, so I cannot separate my critical relation *to* poetry from my productive role *within* it. The basis upon which the current antipoetic prejudice is formed is the modernist ideology of autonomy with which I began and which has reemerged in various forms of poststructuralism. Like the phantasmagoria of nineteenth-century consumer culture, this autonomy is a ghost that cannot be placated despite the attempts by poets discussed in this book to challenge its authority. The faint lines of the poet's critical engagement with social materiality are present in the interstices of the palimtext. Those lines might be all but invisible to Hegel's owl of Minerva, which exists in a posterior relation to history. To the blind postmodern bat, flying in a present being constructed moment by moment, those lines become a form of survival.

# Notes

## INTRODUCTION

1. It is perhaps appropriate to the derealizing function of the apparatus that the author of this handbook, *The Magic Lantern: How to Buy, and How to Use It*, is never named. On the title page the book is identified as having been written by "A Mere Phantom."

2. David Crowne reminds me that the Art Deco Métro stations of Paris where Pound witnessed his apparitions are themselves ghostly transformations of nature. It is not hard to understand why Pound associated faces in a crowd with petals on a black bough since the ornate metal gates and fences were—and remain—heavily decorated with organic shapes, leaves, and flowers. Walter Benjamin calls this retention of natural forms in modern architecture and design "wishful fantasies" or "wish-images" to speak of the way that forms of modern, industrial landscape (metro stations, public buildings) are linked back to precapitalist, agrarian modes of production and growth. See "Paris, Capital of the Nineteenth Century," in *Reflections* (148), and Buck-Morss (58–77).

3. On the multiple uses of phantasmagoria in Pound, see Bell in *Paideuma*, 361–85.

4. Ann Cvetkovich reads *Capital* as a sensationalist novel, mixing elements of melodrama and documentary to represent the worker's "body in pain" to "present in the flesh what might otherwise be abstract or invisible social processes" (168).

5. See Gertrude Stein, *Wars I Have Seen*, in *Selected Writings* (621).

6. On the nature of modernist genius and on Stein's particular relationship to authority, see Perelman (1–27, 129–69).

7. On Huyssen and Burger, see Perloff, *Radical Artifice* (5–10).

8. The metaphor of the palimpsest appears often in H.D.'s work, the most famous being that described in *Tribute to Freud*, in which she describes a series of "shadow or of light-pictures . . . projected on the wall of a hotel bedroom in the Ionian island of Corfu" in 1920 (41). In her analysis with Freud, the "Professor" treats this event as the most significant (or dangerous) symptom of her sessions with him. The palimpsest as a metaphor becomes the structural center of H.D.'s novel, *Palimpsest*, in which the same story is told three times at different moments in history.

9. Although she does not address H.D. or her critics per se, Teresa de Lauretis provides a lucid analysis of the limits of cultural feminist readings

based on a "'matristic' realm presided over by the Goddess, a realm of female tradition, marginal and subterranean and yet all positive and good, peaceloving, ecologically correct, matrilineal, matrifocal, non-Indo-European, and so forth; in short, a world untouched by ideology, class and racial struggle, television . . ." (20–21).

10. On Pound's use of Pre-Raphaelite design, see McGann, *Textual Condition* (129–52).

11. On Vorticism, see Perloff, *Futurist Moment* (162–93).

12. On Cubist poetry, see Brogan.

13. This remark and its pertinence for the evolution of Language-writing is discussed in Ron Silliman's preface to *In the American Tree*. I have discussed the same passage in "'Skewed by Design': From Act to Speech Act in Language-Writing."

14. One thinks, for example, of the endurance of Dada in a work such as Jerome Rothenberg's *That Dada Strain*, of Futurism in Marjorie Perloff's *The Futurist Moment*, and of Constructivism in the various forms of retro design in postmodern architecture.

15. On the "anxious object," see Rosenberg (89–96).

16. The Objectivists have had a particularly strong influence on poets in France. One of the first major recognitions of Zukofsky came from Anne-Marie Albiach, who translated the first part of "A"-9 in the journal *Siècle à mains* in 1970, a version that not only rendered Zukofsky's tortured syntax but maintained his convoluted rhyme scheme. Three books of George Oppen's have been translated by Yves di Manno, and various poems of the Objectivists have been translated in a range of French journals and anthologies. Claude Royet-Journoud comments on the influence of the Objectivists in an interview with Serge Gavronsky (121–22).

17. Many of Altieri's terms for the distinction between symbolist and immanent poetics within romanticism are developed in his book, *Enlarging the Temple*. It should be stressed that despite my caveats concerning Altieri's emphases, he is one of the few academic critics to see Objectivism's larger impact on postwar poetry and recognize its integrity as a continuum.

18. Peter Quartermain, who adopts a strategy of periodization similar to my own, notes that Objectivism is characterized by its resistance to a "preconstituted world 'out there'" and that, by stressing the poem-as-object, the Objectivists raised both the physical and socioeconomic world to center (1).

19. Alan Filreis observes that "At its most interesting, the radical poetry of the thirties inscribed its own sense of twenties formalism in *its* own form" (50). Filreis provides an excellent overview of the various ways that the formal models provided by Eliot and Pound were reworked during the 1930s to suit left-wing political agendas.

20. In discussing the political implications of form in modernism, it is always necessary to remember that there is no necessary relation between a specific practice—the use of montage or non sequitur, for example—and a particular political position. As I point out in chapter 4, the same poetics that articulated Pound's fascist views was enlisted in pursuit of socialist goals

among the Objectivists. Raymond Williams notes that the Futurists' break with the past led to rather different political solutions—with Marinetti supporting Italian Fascism and Mayakovsky "campaigning for popular Bolshevik culture" (58). When I refer to a politics of form I am not specifying *which* politics it may lead to, only that form is more than an inert base upon which a dynamic superstructure is welded.

21. For important revisions of 1930s literature, see Filreis; Kalaidjian; Nelson; and Nekola and Rabinowitz.

22. Filreis (50).

23. On Silliman's development of "third-phase objectivism," see his "Z-Sited Path" in *The New Sentence* (136–41).

24. For an excellent historical summary of small-press publishing during the period between 1960 and 1990, see Glazier (1–9). On technical aspects of offset printing, see Burke. On the larger context of letterpress printing, see Chappell (204–44).

25. Or Carl Orff. The *Los Angeles Times* (6 September 1995) reports the introduction of a new CD-ROM game called "Phantasmagoria" described as "a modern-day, gothic horror, interactive movie . . . that comes in seven discs." The article goes on to speak of the "Carl Orff–like theme music" that accompanies the game (Colker F1).

CHAPTER 1

1. The remark about Oakland appears in *Everybody's Autobiography* (189).

2. The W. C. Fields example suggests that Stein's work was recognizable enough in 1935 to satirize in a popular film. The reference to Stein goes considerably beyond Stein to the gendered context of much Hollywood humor in which comedians from Charlie Chaplin to the Marx Brothers to Eddie Murphy have gotten laughs by poking fun at the cultural pretensions of bourgeoise women. In the example from *The Man on the Flying Trapeze*, the wife's mindless endorsement of a piece of modernist nonsense (the fact that she calls it blank verse defines her cultural illiteracy) contrasts with the husband's more masculine pursuits (wrestling and drinking). Thus, Stein becomes the type of all obscurantist modern art being foisted upon a gullible (and largely female) public.

3. There is no direct evidence that Stein read the major works of this tradition, although her philosophical training at Radcliffe certainly would have prepared her. She was the secretary to the Philosophy Club, through which she met Josiah Royce, and she studied with George Santayana and William James. Her academic record shows that she took eight courses in philosophy, including Transcendentalism and Metaphysics, and received her highest grades therein. She may also have gained some insight into Kant through her friendship with Alfred North Whitehead, whose "philosophy of organism" in *Process and Reality* is Kantian in many respects. The point is not that Stein devoted formal study to Kant so much as that ideas of artistic disinterestedness, autonomy, and organic wholeness were very much part of her

generation's intellectual upbringing. On Stein's undergraduate relationship to philosophy, see Bridgeman (20–22).

4. See, for example, DeKoven, *Different Language* (13–16) and Weinstein (59).

5. On the gender of modernism, see DeKoven, *Rich and Strange*; Felski; Huyssen; Pollock; and Wolff.

6. See Janet Flanner's foreword to *Two: Gertrude Stein and Her Brother*, in which she comments on portraits such as "Bon Marché Weather" and "Flirting at the Bon Marché." In "And Now," Stein compares the pleasures of writing with those of spending money: "[Writing] is what I like best. I like it even better than spending money although there is no pleasure so sweet as the pleasure of spending money but the pleasure of writing is longer" (*How Writing Is Written* 64).

7. A 1911 letter from Mina Loy to Stein describes a ceramic "Black Madonna" sent by Loy from Florence and accompanied by a statue of a "gendarme" "to keep watch in case of attempted theft." Loy hopes that the madonna will find "an appropriate place in the manger of the Monte Nero quadruped you were pleased to take to Paris." I am grateful to Carolyn Burke for showing this letter to me.

8. See Bridgeman (290). See also Shirley Neuman, "'Would a Viper Have Stung Her If She Had Only Had One Name?': *Doctor Faustus Lights the Lights*," in Neuman and Nadel, eds. (168–93).

9. On Faust as the primordial myth for modernity, see Berman's *All That Is Solid Melts into Air*. For a critique of Berman's gendering of modernity, see Felski (1–4).

10. See, for example, Isaak in Kostelanetz, ed. (24–50).

11. For an extended discussion of Stein's relationship to male authority figures, see Ruddick.

12. DeKoven, *Different Language* (128). DeKoven's dismissal of "Patriarchal Poetry" is based partly upon her assumption that Stein's title overdetermines the text, forcing a feminist interpretation on a text that "defies reading." This seems an odd conclusion for someone trying to inscribe a gender narrative into the pragmatics of Stein's writing.

13. On Stein's use of the heterosexual frame of marriage, see Stimpson, "Gertrude Stein and the Transposition of Gender."

14. On the formalism of the *Autobiography*, see Perloff, "(Im)Personating Gertrude Stein," in Neuman and Nadel, eds. (61–80), and Schmitz, "Portrait Patriarchy Mythos: The Revenge of Gertrude Stein," in Kostelanetz, ed. (160–79). On the use of "open and public" to refer to the *Autobiography*, see Dydo, "Stanzas in Meditation," in *Gertrude Stein Advanced*, Kostelanetz, ed. (125, n. 2).

15. *Stanzas in Meditation* appeared posthumously in 1956 in the Yale University Press edition of Stein's works, which is now out of print. Citations in this essay refer to the reprint in Richard Kostelanetz's *The Yale Gertrude Stein*. Although Ulla Dydo has argued that the Yale text features numerous textual errors, I use it because it is the only complete edition in print. Dydo has provided a corrected text of several sections in *A Stein Reader*.

16. Dydo says that the early *Stanzas* were composed in uniform French school notebooks, each one containing one section of the poem, except for the first section, which filled two. Dydo notes that each section fits into a notebook, the last line ending on the last page, a challenge that kept the momentum of writing going. "Form has to do with how to shape a given space" ("*Stanzas in Meditation*" 117).

17. In Bridgeman (213–17).

18. On Stein's Jewishness, see Damon (202–35).

19. Ashbery's review originally appeared in *Poetry* 90.4 (July 1957): 250–54.

20. Stein acknowledges James's influence in several places, nowhere more succinctly than in her "Transatlantic Interview": "You see he made [the novel] sort of like an atmosphere, and it was not solely the realism of the characters but the realism of the composition which was the important thing, the realism of the composition of my thoughts" (17). The abrupt shift from third- to first-person pronoun indicates the degree of Stein's identification with him and with the James family in general.

21. On intransitive writing, see Barthes, "To Write: An Intransitive Verb?" in *The Rustle of Language* (11–21). Stein's writing is discussed in Lyotard's *The Differend: Phases in Dispute* (67–68).

CHAPTER 2

1. All references to George Oppen's papers are to the George Oppen Manuscript Collection at the Mandeville Department of Special Collections, University of California, San Diego.

2. To be historically accurate, the debate over genres is no longer "current," important work by Marjorie Perloff, Linda Hutcheon, Brian McHale, David Antin, Ihab Hassan, and others having been conducted between 1970 and 1980. What has superseded debate over genre more recently has been a powerful "narrative turn," marked most dramatically by the work of Fredric Jameson but visible in current trends in cultural studies, new historicism, and postcolonial studies. I discuss this shift in chapter 5.

3. Exceptions to this rule of reading Oppen's work as discrete poems are Joseph Conte's chapter on Oppen in *Unending Design* and Alan Golding's essay on "George Oppen's Serial Poems."

4. In earlier drafts of the poem, section 4 directly follows those which, in the published version, conclude section 2: "I have not and never did have any motive of poetry / But to achieve clarity."

5. Eric Mottram glosses these lines as stating that "Knowledge of boredom becomes a philosophic tool to ascertain what the facts are" ("Political Responsibilities of the Poet" 151).

6. The unusual convention of providing an oral script for one's reading is sustained by Oppen's colleague Charles Reznikoff. In the latter's papers, also housed in the Archive for New Poetry, can be found several such scripts for various venues, accompanied by written "offhand remarks" to the audience. A visual record of such practices can be seen in a video made of Reznikoff's

reading at San Francisco State University given in March 1973 and available through the Poetry Center, San Francisco State University, 1600 Holloway Ave., San Francisco, Calif., 94132, catalog number 36/28.

7. Many of the palimpsestic manuscripts had originally been pasted to the wall of Oppen's study, suggesting that he not only wrote *on* paper but lived quite literally *within* it.

8. I have edited a selection from Oppen's "daybooks" in *Ironwood* 26 (1985): 5–31. Excerpts appear, as well, in *Conjunctions* 10 (1987). Since many pages from his daybooks are early drafts of what became letters, it is worth looking at Rachel Blau DuPlessis's edition of *The Selected Letters of George Oppen*, which faithfully maintains the poet's spacing and typography.

9. In an interview in *The Difficulties*, Howe describes her work as a poet in ethnographic terms:

> I think that a poet is like an ethnographer. You open your mind and textual space to many voices, to an interplay and contradiction and complexity of voices.... Ethnographic data has generally been gathered by men from men telling their visions. So this is a complicated issue for women who sense silenced factions waiting to be part of any expression. (24)

10. "Why is wilderness called 'virgin'. I still have no idea. The answer must be deep in the structure of Language. And the mystery of that structure is a secret of poetry unsettled by history" (Howe, *The Difficulties* 26).

11. On Irigaray and French feminism in Howe, see *The Difficulties* (23).

12. This fragment is a draft of Shelley's "To Emilia Viviani," published in Mary Shelley's 1824 *Posthumous Poems*. Viviani was the nineteen-year-old daughter of Count Niccolo Viviani, the governor of Pisa. Shelley was pursuing her while she was incarcerated at the Convent of St. Anna, and several poems are dedicated to her, the most famous being "Epipsychidion." On Viviani, see Holmes (624 and *passim*).

13. On Mangan, see Lloyd, *Nationalism and Minor Literature: James Clarence Mangan and the Emergence of Irish Cultural Nationalism*.

14. Howe quotes from Louise I. Guiney, "James Clarence Mangan: A Study" (1897): "It is pleasant to think of the small blonde sprite of 1811 tripping in and out of the Derby Square school, who may have looked, more than once unawares, on Shelley's boyish self as he went crusading through the streets with Harriet" (*Nonconformist's Manual* 98).

15. Mitchel's remarks, quoted by Howe, establish a crucial connection between American and Irish culture against British:

> The comparative unacquaintance ... of Americans with these poems may be readily accounted for, when we remember how completely British criticism gives the law throughout the literary domain of that semi-barbarous tongue in which I have the honor to indite. For this Mangan was not only an Irishman,—not only an Irish papist,—not only an Irish papist rebel;—but throughout his whole literary life of twenty years, he never deigned to attorn to English criticism, never published a line in any English periodical, or through any English bookseller, never seemed to be aware that there was a British Public to please. (*Nonconformist's Manual* 106–7)

16. Some of this typographic display derives from Olson, who often utilized the possibilities of the typewriter to map his distractions and confusions. But Howe's background as a painter and collagist is equally influential in treating the page as a spatial field in which the rationalizing function of print as a "score for the voice" is thwarted.

17. Jerome McGann argues that, unlike many Language-writers, Howe is "more an absolutist of the word" and that her disruption of print conventions causes a "hyperawareness of 'the word (or the text) as such'" (*Black Riders* 104, 106). Yet he acknowledges that her materialization of the page offers a contemporary version of Brechtian epic theater that forces the reader to a "correspondent reflexive posture toward the scene of writing" (106).

18. See Paul de Man's essay "Triumph of Life" (Bloom 39–73). I have discussed the limits to deconstructive readings of Shelley in "Refiguring Shelley."

## CHAPTER 3

1. The best accounts of Pound's relationship to philology are several chapters in Hugh Kenner's *Pound Era*, especially those in the section titled "Toward the Vortex." See also Michael Andre Bernstein, *The Tale of the Tribe: Ezra Pound and the Modern Verse Epic*, chap. 4; John Peck, "Pound's Lexical Mythography"; Thomas Grieve, "Annotations to the Chinese in Section: Rock-Drill"; William Tay, "History as Poetry: The Chinese Past in Ezra Pound's *Rock-Drill Cantos*."

2. For a fascinating discussion of Pound's use of archival research in writing the Malatesta Cantos, see Rainey (64–70).

3. For a thorough study of citation in modern American poems, see Diepeveen. For a study of citationality in general, see Compagnon.

4. Pound continues his attacks against technical philology in the early cantos. In Canto 14—one of the "Hell" Cantos—Pound inveighs against

> usurers squeezing crab-lice, pandars to authority,
> pets-de-loup, sitting on piles of stone books,
> obscuring the texts with philology,
>     hiding them under their persons . . . (*Cantos* 63)

Here philology is aligned with usury as a practice that devalues the object by inflating its value. Usurers are not only moneylenders; they are "betrayers of language," like those Dante places in his tenth Bolgia, who have falsified the truth through their words. Philology, used only to hide texts under empty scholarship, is in this context no more worthwhile than the religious leaders and "perverts" Pound excoriates in the same canto. On Pound's reaction to German philology, see Rainey (64–75).

5. Guy Davenport's reading of this passage suggests that the ambiguity of the word in the original Greek is quite intentional: "Steisichorus felt the tension of opposing meanings in Ἄλιος as though it were a pun, and symbolized in his poem the double nature of the word, growing and ungrowing, light and dark, order and confusion" (quoted in Peck 6).

6. See Bernstein for a full development of this idea (147).

7. On the enduring fascism of *The Cantos*, see McGann, "The *Cantos* of Ezra Pound, the Truth in Contradiction," and Lauber.

8. For a full reading of this passage, see Witemeyer.

9. Maria Damon links Duncan's use of etymology to gay writing in general, which "derives its power and delight from a fine sense of interplay *between* surface and depth, 'appearance' and 'reality,' and even different states of consciousness and material being" (147). Damon points out that for Duncan etymology does not supply a "linear, two-dimensional history of the meanings of words but rather a multidimensional texture in which all meanings of all epochs live and interact any time a word is invoked" (147).

10. This objectivity is all the more important for a generation of poets that is, by and large, monolingual. Whereas Pound, Eliot, Stein, Joyce, and Beckett were relatively (if not totally) fluent in at least one other language, the postwar generation, with some exceptions (Gary Snyder, Nathaniel Tarn, John Ashbery), relies more on bilingual translations and dictionaries. I do not mean to suggest that Duncan or Olson lacks knowledge of French or German but that they lack the kind of fluency in languages that characterizes their predecessors.

11. On Olson's distinction between logos and mythos, see *The Special View of History*.

12. "A Syllabary for a Dancer" is dedicated to a male friend, Nataraj Vashi, who taught dance at Black Mountain. Olson's use of the masculine pronoun, his stress on "will" and "force," and his disparaging remarks about other women suggest that dance, even if performed by women, is gendered masculine. He sees Martha Graham's violent, atavistic dance as embodying a rape fantasy. Graham is a "monster" "who is so far back she craves to be scalped and dragged over the ground and so, because nobody has dragged her, she has everybody do it, she does it, she makes dance an enemy" ("Syllabary" 14). The lines about being "dragged" are included in "Tyrian Business" and are linked to references to Madame Chiang Kai-shek, "that international doll."

13. Robert von Hallberg calls "Tyrian Business" a "logographic poem," based on a series of "etymological puns" (155). See also George Butterick's useful detailing of the poem's sources in his *Guide* (57–65).

CHAPTER 4

1. On alternate canons of modernism, see Baker; Honey; Nekola and Rabinowitz; and Nelson.

2. Both the New Formalism and Language-writing could be placed under this agenda, but the political and cultural concerns for each are vastly different. The New Formalists have adopted much the same stance as their formalist counterparts in the early 1950s, treating form as a test of sensibility. But as Alan Golding points out, New Formalist rhetoric often stresses the very depth psychology and expressivism that were the hallmark of open-

form verse during the 1960s. Robert Richman, in the introduction to his anthology of New Formalist verse, *The Direction of Poetry*, admits that the "rehabilitation" of metered verse "should never be undertaken because it is deemed to be sufficient in itself," but he goes on to say that the poets in his book employ meter "because it allows them to probe deeper into the experience or emotion they are exploring in their poems" (xvii). Language-writing, on the other hand, has appropriated the formalist position advanced by Zukofsky in which the use of procedures or numbered series serves specific critical functions. The Fibonacci series in Ron Silliman's *Tjanting* or the regularized sentences in Lyn Hejinian's *My Life* represent ways of recontextualizing elements, thus generating new meanings out of repeated materials.

3. Reprinted in *Prepositions* (12–18).

4. My use of the phrase "ideology of form" is similar to Fredric Jameson's discussion of ideological analysis in Kenneth Burke. Jameson points out that Burke's theory of symbolic action, by stressing the strategic features of language, does not thereby validate an intrinsic or antireferential text. Rather, symbolic action takes place "as a gesture and a response to a determinate situation" (*Ideologies of Theory* 139). Jameson then goes on to state that by speaking of text and "determinate situation" he does not mean to replicate the older model of text and context:

> This is why it has seemed more satisfactory to me to describe ideological analysis as the . . . rewriting or restructuration of a prior ideological or historical subtext, provided it is understood that the latter—what we used to call the "context"—must always be (re)constructed after the fact, for the purposes of the analysis. (141)

The text, in Jameson's model, exists in an active relationship to the real, interpreting and bracketing it as something "produced" or "represented" as (and in) a text. In terms of the Objectivists, such bracketing implies not only that poets "respond" to the political climate of the 1930s but that they regard their formalism as a material agent within the social. Formalism does not stand over against ideology but is a means by which the illusions of materialist culture can be revealed.

5. A more sympathetic account of Zukofsky's politics of form can be found in Norman O. Brown's "Revisioning Historical Identities." I was not aware of this essay until after my own was published, but it tends to support my view that Zukofsky was engaged in acts of rewriting and rearticulation of Marxist tenets and that his use of the sestina was "a kind of thinking," not a form of aesthetic escape. I am grateful to Professor Brown for alerting me to his essay.

6. On Oppen's twenty-five-year "silence," see his interview in *Contemporary Literature*. See also my "Forms of Refusal: George Oppen's 'Distant Life'" and DuPlessis, "'The Familiar / Becomes Extreme': George Oppen and Silence."

7. Carolyn Porter has studied this alienated vantage as it emerges in four American writers: Emerson, James, Adams, and Faulkner. She has also rec-

ognized the paradox of defining modernity with Lukácsian tools since he was to repudiate that movement as well as his own early work for its idealist tendencies. Porter's response is to speak of a need to "rescue a set of tools for other uses than those to which Lukács himself limited them in his own literary criticism," a task with which I am obviously in accord (281). There are, needless to say, vast differences between the narratives Porter considers and poetry of a late modernist such as Zukofsky.

8. I am using "production" here in the sense that it is used by Louis Althusser and Pierre Machery, specifically as the way that the artwork enables us to see by creating (producing) an "internal distanciation" from the ideology in which that art is produced. In Althusser (who discusses Balzac and Solzhenitsyn), this distancing is a relatively passive act, distinct from active scientific knowledge. I would contend that Zukofsky, by reminding us of his own susceptibility to reification, accomplishes just such scientific self-consciousness as Althusser denies the artist. See Althusser (221–27) and Machery.

9. See Zukofsky's sequence, "I's (Pronounced *Eyes*)" in *All* (217–20).

10. Norman O. Brown claims that "*A*"-9 is a reply to Pound's *ABC of Economics*, published in 1933, although one could say that, based on their correspondence during this period, there were many other factors leading to Zukofsky's disaffection (*Apocalypse* 169).

11. In a letter of 1933, Pound comments on Charles Reznikoff's work as published in *The Active Anthology:* "Possibly by pickin' out the Hebe element we can get something that will arouse interest" (*Letters* 144). In a letter from 1938, Pound writes that "the neschekers [usurious Jews] are gittin UN=pupular. A nice anti=neschek boom wd/ conduce to the amenities/ I mean FROM a semetic [sic] source . . ." (*Letters* 195). And in 1940, Pound seems to feel that he has responded to charges of anti-Semitism by claiming that "I've finally found a quotation from Chas. Mordecai Marx on Rothschild etc/ that will stop off Bull Bublle WillieYams [Williams] from tellin the woild I am an anti=semite" (Pound and Zukofsky 201).

12. Pound's contributions are by no means slighted in *First Half of "A"-9*. Zukofsky clearly admires Pound's translations and understands how they participate in the larger scope of a historical poetics. But he is also concerned that his Cavalcanti not serve history in the same way. In a letter that included an early draft of "*A*"-9, Zukofsky remarks, "The local small fry would no doubt accuse me of being a fascist for having lived with the Guido as basis day in & day out for the last two years. You will probably see how far gone I am on the Marx side of it, & attribute all my faults to the influence of his unenlightened use of language" (Pound and Zukofsky 199).

13. Marx reappears several more times in the poem, prominently in "*A*"-12, but in this instance, the author of *Capital* has been reduced to writing "fugues/ On a theme of Aristotle," reflective of Zukofsky's musical concerns. Politics returns most directly in "*A*"-18, a section that deals primarily with the Vietnam War. I am grateful to Bob Perelman for reminding me of these passages.

14. On the use of incarnation as a metaphor in "*A*"-9, see Quartermain (215).

15. One might say that this is the agenda of all formalisms—from Wyatt and Shakespeare to Marilyn Hacker—but to say this is to ignore the historical meaning of formalism at any given period and to treat the nature of "things" as timeless, divorced from a specific mode of production.

## CHAPTER 5

1. Some of these titles are taken from panels at recent Modern Language Association annual meetings: "Is Talk about Poetry Still Important to Us?" (1991: #264); "Do We Still Talk about Poetry?" (1991: #717); "Are the Pleasures of Experimental Poetry Important and When?" (1992: #152); "Personal Poetry amid the Skeptics" (1992: #409); "But What Is the Reader to Make of This? The Audience for Poetry" (1993: #366). *Can Poetry Matter?* is Dana Gioia's attempt to shore up poetry written in traditional forms in an age of academic specialization. "What Happened to Poetics?" is the subtitle of Peter Brooks's essay on the decline of poetics in an era of new historicisms of various sorts. An important intervention into this debate is Bob Perelman's *The Marginalization of Poetry: Language Writing and Literary History*, which acknowledges poetry's minority status within postmodernism while studying the political implications of marginalization within a specific movement.

2. In using the term "postcolonialism," I am aware that there is a significant debate over its usefulness in describing a wide range of critical discourses involving questions of nationality, imperialism, and colonialism. One of the major points of contestation is the fact that the use of "post" implies (1) that colonization is a thing of the past and (2) that theories of decolonization and social movements are therefore written within the very temporality of nation-formation they contest. On the debate over terminology, see McClintock (1994) and Shohat (1992).

3. On "internal distanciation," see Althusser (222–23). Jameson's essay "Third World Literature in the Era of Multinational Capitalism" has been the subject of several essays critical of his generalization of third-world literature and his inscription of national allegory within the political category of "the nation" and nationalism. See especially Ahmad.

4. Jameson recognizes the dominance of this modernist ideology in his essay on "Modernism and Imperialism." The aesthetic features of autonomous art "are part of the baggage of an older modernist ideology which any contemporary theory of the modern will wish to scrutinize and to dismantle. But there is something to be said in the present context, for beginning with the formalist stereotype of the modern, if only to demonstrate with greater force the informing presence of the extraliterary, of the political and the economic within it" (45). By basing his study of imperialism on a stereotype of aesthetic modernism, Jameson permits it to organize the terms under which the "extraliterary" (the political context of colonialism) is contained within the "literary." The "spatial poetry" of Forester's prose, for instance,

becomes the marker of this containment, a recognition of the cultural effects of the colonial encounter.

5. Jameson's one major foray into poetry is "Baudelaire as Modernist and Postmodernist," but here Baudelaire is read less as a poet than as a precursor to current critical theories of urbanism and modernization for which the poet is a kind of symptom.

6. In another context, New Americanists such as Donald Pease and Jonathan Arac regard the ideal of a national narrative—a totalizing story of American exceptionalism, for example—as dominating American studies, replicating in the aesthetic field marginalizations in the social. Against a monolithic national narrative (and in the light of new developments in transnational capitalism, the breakup of the former Soviet Union, the challenges posed by new social movements), Pease posits *post*national identities defined by "multiple interpellations: their different identifications with the disciplinary apparatuses in the new American Studies, as well as with social movements comprised of the 'disenfranchised groups'" (3). On postnational identities and American studies, see Pease (1992) and Arac.

7. Rukeyser's line may also represent her unease as an activist, but closeted, lesbian writer for the more openly lesbian salons of Natalie Barney or Gertrude Stein. This society, which Shari Benstock has called "sapphic modernism," is hardly congruent with Rukeyser's more proletarian visions of community during the 1930s.

8. As William Alexander points out, the list of board members for Frontier Films reads like a who's who of "fellow travelers, liberal adherents to the popular front, and Communist Party members" (146). The board included Paul Strand, Leo Hurwitz, Ralph Steiner, Bernard Reis, Elia Kazan, David Wolff (Ben Maddow), Joris Ivens, Irving Lerner, Margaret Murray, and Willard Van Dyke. The advisory board featured Aaron Copland, Malcolm Cowley, John Dos Passos, Waldo Frank, Lillian Hellman, Josephine Herbst, Max Lerner, Archibald MacLeish, Clifford Odets, Edwin Rolf, and Genevieve Taggard, as well as Rukeyser.

9. As Paula Rabinowitz points out, Rukeyser's work in film is a sign of mobility provided by the Depression for middle-class women to escape traditional female roles, permitting them to travel as "journalists, photographers, organizers, and teachers" (66). At the same time, it was precisely Rukeyser's violation of gender roles that caused Willard Maas to attack "The Book of the Dead" because in it she neglected her lyric gifts, becoming "a Carrie Nation with a political hatchet on a Cook's tour" (quoted in Thurston 205).

10. For thorough summaries of the poem and its reception, see Kertesz (98–113), Kalaidjian (160–75), and Thurston (201–49).

11. According to Botha's memoir, the film was to feature himself as director, music by Hanns Eisler, and the acting of Paul Robeson, Franchot Tone, and John Garfield (211).

12. Naumberg's own documentaries included *Sheriffed* (1934) with James Guy (on farmers' struggles against mortgage foreclosures) and *Taxi* (1934)

(on the New York taxi strike). In Naumberg's films, newsreel footage was combined with dramatized material using a cast made up of members of the communities being depicted. On Naumberg, see Campbell (82–87).

13. In a note at the back of *U.S. 1*, Rukeyser provides a citation for the hearings: "An Investigation Relating to Health Conditions of Workers Employed in the Construction and Maintenance of Public Utilities. Hearings before a Subcommittee of the Committee of Labor. House of Representatives, Seventy-fourth Congress, Second Session, on H.J. Res. 449, January 16, 17, 20, 21, 22, 27, 28, 29 and February 4, 1936. United States Printing Office. Washington: 1936" (146).

14. On WPA road construction, see Kalaidjian (166).

15. It is worth mentioning that Reznikoff's most famous remark concerning Objectivism did not emerge spontaneously in response to L. S. Dembo's question but from a page of quotations to which the poet referred throughout the interview. Thus, even Reznikoff's own "spontaneous" testimony is taken from a prior transcript.

16. Kathryn Shevelow points out that in manuscript drafts of *Testimony* Reznikoff refers to himself as the poem's "editor" (292).

17. For a history of the West reporter system, see Cohen and Berring, chaps. 2 and 3.

18. The task of translation informs all of Reznikoff's work, beginning with his rewriting of biblical stories in *Uriel Accosta* (1921) and *Jerusalem the Golden* (1934) through *Inscriptions* (1959) and *Jews in Babylonia* (1969). In *Holocaust* (1973), he draws upon testimony from the Nuremberg and Eichmann trials much as he translated court cases into verse in *Testimony*. *Family Chronicle* (1963), as Peg Syverson documents, is a complicated series of translations, first from his father's and mother's Yiddish memoirs into autobiographical novels (*By the Waters of Manhattan* and *Early History of a Sewing Machine Operator*) and finally into a section of "Early History of a Writer," written in verse. On Reznikoff's processes of transcription and translation, see Syverson; Shevelow; and Simon.

19. On the verse versions of *Testimony*, see Shevelow; Chilton; Holsapple; Simon; and Hindus.

CHAPTER 6

1. "Rethinking Borders." San Diego Museum of Contemporary Art, 9 October 1990–14 May 1991.

2. Although Baudrillard is not mentioned by name, Jameson in *Postmodernism, or the Cultural Logic of Late Capitalism* describes the "new spatial logic of the simulacrum" in distinctly Baudrillardian terms. For Jameson, postmodernism implies the destruction of all models of depth, including the cartographical one. Utilizing Kevin Lynch's concept of "cognitive mapping," Jameson speaks of the alienated space of postmodern cities as one "in which people are unable to map (in their minds) either their own positions or the urban totality in which they find themselves" (51). Elsewhere in the book,

Jameson describes postmodern space, using Baudrillard's term "hyperreality," as a reality impossible to represent, a reality produced by codes and models.

3. I have discussed this cultish aspect of Duncan's poetics in *The San Francisco Renaissance,* chaps. 4 and 5.

4. This project was tentatively titled *Gleanings* and had, as its primary impulse, "the studio work of writing writing and learning my letters before the decade of publishing 1960–1970" (1). *Gleanings* would be "a record issued of work in progress for certain friends as readers before publication, passages from notebooks, drawings, inventions, the ground work of what I now see is to be calld *Ground Work*—speculations and appreciations, associations, rantings if need be, phantasies, lectures, nocturnes and mind soul and spirit dances and inventions" (1). True to Duncan's word, *Gleanings* is printed from the poet's typewritten copy with occasional notations in holograph. Individual issues of *Gleanings* were stapled at the upper left-hand corner and mailed on an occasional basis to a list of friends. Several poems that were subsequently published in *Ground Work: Before the War* appeared in this series ("Santa Cruz Propositions"; "A Seventeenth Century Suite").

5. The use of typewriter copy could also suggest holographic features of the text that would otherwise be lost in a typeset version. In its published version, for example, lines from the opening of "The Missionaries" are printed as follows

> Nor to recover rime
> nor to cover but to discover among you
> that *you* all resonance addresses
> that *I* I address goest time presses on [ghost]
> the key:
> 
> (*Ground Work* 135)

The (apparently mistaken) addition of "t" to "goes" is retained from his holographic copy along with the word "ghost," which Duncan added in parentheses underneath. The slip-of-pen provides a nice verification of those unanticipated "resonances" discovered in writing. By retaining the effaced "t," Duncan may also suggest the "ghost" time that orders the measure—the "rime"—of his poem. Typesetting could, of course, render these holographic intentions perfectly well, but the typewriter copy makes the slip-of-pen more immediate.

6. I have discussed the role of homosocial bonding and postwar literary communities in "Compulsory Homosociality."

7. See, for instance, Bernstein ("Robert Duncan") and my *San Francisco Renaissance* (127–31).

8. The strongest precedent for Duncan's use of margins to inscribe homosexual meanings would be Hart Crane's "The Harbor Dawn" from *The Bridge.* Here Crane describes a scene of waking with a lover ("And you beside me blessed now while sirens / Sing to us, stealthily weave us into day—") whose gender is left indistinct. The homosexual nature of the awak-

ening, however, is given force by Crane's inclusion of a companion poem written in the margins of "The Harbor Dawn" that translates the local, urban awakening into something larger: "*400 years and / more . . . or is / it from the / soundless shore / of sleep that / time // recalls you to / your love, / there in a / waking dream / to merge / your seed / —with whom?*" (55–57). The question of "with whom" the speaker merges is answered by another question: "*Who is the / woman with / us in the / dawn?*" Thomas Yingling interprets this seeming substitution of a heterosexual "answer" to the question as implying that "the woman here is not the beloved; she is 'with' the lovers only as an official argument of the epic, a literally marginal presence who remains trapped within an unanswered question" (201).

As the poem progresses, it is clear that the marginal poem represents Crane's attempt to give epic scope to a more localized, potentially erotic scene involving homosocial, working-class male society. Using Koestenbaum's arguments in *Double Talk*, however, we could see Crane constructing a homoerotic dialogue not only with "Rail-squatters" and "Hobo-trekkers" but with T. S. Eliot, whose tone and cadence are repeated here: "Behind / My father's cannery works I used to see / Rail-squatters ranged in nomad raillery, / The Ancient men—wifeless or runaway / Hobo-trekkers that forever search / An empire wilderness of freight and rails" (64).

9. This is the burden of Duncan's essay "Man's Fulfillment in Order and Strife."

10. "In Blood's Domaine" was first published in *Sulfur* 3 (1982), and because the lines were so long the publishers printed it lengthwise. Duncan's writing practice during this period involved using both sides of a 8½-by-11-inch spiral notebook, the lines often extending across the binding.

## CHAPTER 7

1. Marjorie Perloff points out that when poets of the 1950s and 1960s speak of "common speech," it is not that of the common man, as invoked by poets from Wordsworth to Eliot, but "the making present, via the breath, of internal energy . . . *this* speech, *my* speech" (*Radical Artifice* 34). Perloff traces the growing skepticism about this personalist ethos to the importance of mass cultural phenomena such as television talk shows and political sound bites in which the illusion of "common speech" is presented as actual, in which Baudrillard's "hyperreal" replaces the rhetoric of feeling, depth, affectivity.

2. The best standard accounts of postwar poetry are Altieri (1979); Breslin; and Molesworth.

3. The important exception is the collection of essays on sound, radio, and magnetic recording edited by Douglas Kahn and Gregory Whitehead, *Wireless Imagination*. The editors rightly recognize that modernism was formed around a visualist imperative. Their anthology is an attempt to show the vitality and range of experimentation utilizing new acoustic technologies in everything from Futurism and Dada to the cut-up novels of William Burroughs.

4. On postmodernism as anti-ocularcentric, see Jay.

5. My initiative in extending Foucault's thesis regarding the production of sexuality through specific social and ideological practices is inspired by Teresa de Lauretis's *Technologies of Gender: Essays on Theory, Film, and Fiction* (35–38).

6. On Burroughs' use of the tape recorder, see Lydenberg, "Sound Identity Fading Out: William Burroughs' Tape Experiments," in Kahn (409–37).

7. In this chapter, I am focusing only on magnetic recording in which the storage medium is wire or tape. Mechanical systems of sound storage were developed in the Edison labs during the late nineteenth century. In these early forms of recording, sound waves were mechanically inscribed on a rotating disk or a cylinder. In the first version of this machine, developed by Edison in 1877, sound waves were recorded on a tin-lined cylinder by means of a stylus. Playback required a second stylus that responded to the undulations—the "hill and dale" effect—of those inscribed sound waves. Although the development of phonographic technology runs parallel to that of magnetic recording, the recording apparatus was—and remains—more bulky and costly, necessitating the use of a recording studio and relatively stable microphones. The early dictaphones and tape recorders were obviously much more portable and inexpensive and thus could be used more easily for on-the-spot recording.

8. On the history of magnetic recording, see Engel; "Sound"; and Thiele.

9. Max Horkheimer and Theodor Adorno in "The Culture Industry" remark that electronic media, like the radio and wireless, contributed to the creation of Hitler's "metaphysical charisma." "The gigantic fact that the speech penetrates everywhere replaces its content, just as the benefaction of the Toscanini broadcast takes the place of the symphony. No listener can grasp its true meaning any longer, while the Führer's speech is lies anyway. The inherent tendency of radio is to make the speaker's word, the false commandment, absolute" (159).

10. On surveillance technology, see Brenton; Donner; Lapidus; Long; Miller; and Packard.

11. *Olmstead v. United States*, 277 U.S. 438, 48 S. Ct. 564, 72 L.Ed. 944 (1928).

12. Quoted in Lapidus (17).

13. "Despite repeated refusals of Congress to legalize eavesdropping, over sixty executive agencies were reported to have extensive electronic monitoring hardware which they used in investigations. The Internal Revenue Service of the Treasury Department conducted a seven-week course for agents in electronic eavesdropping, installing microphones, and monitoring calls. The Department of Justice in 1962 created an Organized Crime Division and authorized investigations to be made by use of electronic equipment" (Lapidus 12).

14. Nixon was not the first president to bug his office. Franklin Roosevelt installed a secret recording device, which Truman subsequently removed (McCullough 403).

15. I have discussed *Visions of Cody* and its use of the tape recorder in *The San Francisco Renaissance* (73-76).

16. These tapes—over five hundred of them—are housed at the Archive for New Poetry at the University of California, San Diego, Central Library.

17. On Antin's talk pieces, see Altieri; Perloff; and Sayre.

18. See Austin (24-27) and Levinson (229-31, 238-40).

19. This scenario is at the core of Horkheimer and Adorno's criticism of radio in "The Culture Industry." The difference between a telephone and a radio, Adorno contends, is that "the former [allows] the subscriber to play the *role* of the subject" while the latter is democratic: "it turns all participants into listeners and authoritatively subjects them to broadcast programs which are all exactly the same" (122). Antin challenges the unidirectional format of radio by permitting the listener to "play the role of subject." But it is still a "role" that the listener plays since she/he is really not permitted a response. What Adorno fails to see (or at least could not have anticipated when the essay was written in the 1940s) is the degree to which certain forms of radio (talk shows, consumer channels, call-in formats) provide the listener with possibilities for interaction and debate.

20. On the "choric," see Kristeva, who defines this phenomenon as "a nonexpressive totality formed by the drives and their stases in a motility that is as full of movement as it is regulated" (25-30).

21. Parts of *United States* can be heard on a Warner Brothers' recording, *Big Science* (1982), and seen in a book, *United States* (1984). Several sections of the opera are represented on *Collected Videos*. References to the text will refer to the book, although since it is not paginated, reference will be made to individual sections listed in the book's contents page.

22. The ambiguity of such assertions (you are alone in space; you are not alone in being paranoid) is matched visually by Anderson's use of dissolving images in the video. At one point, she raises her arms to imitate the wings of an airplane, but the shape dissolves into a meditating Buddha against a red background. We do not know if we are seeing an image of ominous power (jet planes) or images of peaceful spirituality. Are her "arms" threatening or nurturing? At one point, she asks her "mom" to hold her in her "long arms," but she quickly changes the lyrics to say "in your long arms, in your electronic arms, in your military arms, in your petrochemical arms."

23. For a résumé of critical responses to *United States* along with an interview with Laurie Anderson, see Dery.

24. In a performance at 80 Langton Street in San Francisco, Benson says that in reading from his journals he tries to "negate every sentence and turn the sentence into saying the opposite of what it seemed to be saying." In conversation, Benson elaborated on this remark, saying that such negations and transformations represent ways of keeping the performance situation alive and mobile. Instead of providing "filler" while the tape is rewinding, these journal readings provide another occasion for response. Steve Benson. Reading at 80 Langton Street, audiotape, rec. 1981. University of California, San Diego, Archive for New Poetry, L-714.

# Works Cited

Adorno, Theodor. *Aesthetic Theory*. Trans. C. Lenhardt. Ed. Gretel Adorno and Rolf Tiedemann. London: Routledge and Kegan Paul, 1984.
Ahearn, Barry. *Zukofsky's "A": An Introduction*. Berkeley: U of California Press, 1983.
Ahmad, Aijaz. "Jameson's Rhetoric of Otherness and the 'National Allegory.'" *Social Text* 15 (1986): 3–25.
Alcott, David. "Gertrude Stein Revised: There's a There There." *Oakland Tribune* 24 Jan. 1986: A-1+.
Alexander, William. *Film on the Left: American Documentary Film from 1931 to 1942*. Princeton: Princeton U Press, 1981.
Althusser, Louis. *Lenin and Philosophy*. Trans. Ben Brewster. New York: Monthly Review Press, 1971.
Altieri, Charles. *Enlarging the Temple: New Directions in American Poetry during the 1960s*. Lewisburg: Bucknell U Press, 1979.
———. "The Objectivist Tradition." *Chicago Review* 30.3 (Winter 1979): 5–22.
———. "The Postmodernism of David Antin's *Tuning*." *College English* 48.1 (Jan. 1986): 9–26.
*American Tobacco Co. v. Strickling*. 41 A 1083. Md. Ct. of App. 1898.
Anderson, Benedict. *Imagined Communities: Reflections on the Origin and Spread of Nationalism*. London: Verso, 1983.
Anderson, Laurie. *Collected Videos*. Los Angeles: Warner Reprise, 1990.
———. *United States*. New York: Harper and Row, 1984.
Angus, Robert. "History of Magnetic Recording," parts 1 and 2. *Audio* 68.8 (Aug. 1984): 27–33, 96–7; 68.9 (Sept. 1984): 33–39.
*An Anthology of Concrete Poetry*. Ed. Emmett Williams. New York: Something Else Press, 1967.
Antin, David. "Some Questions about Modernism." *Occident* n.s., 8 (Spring 1974): 7–38.
———. "Whos Listening out There." In *Tuning*. New York: New Directions, 1984. 269–96.
Arac, Jonathan. "Hypercanonization and *Huckleberry Finn*." *Boundary 2* 19.1 (1992): 14–33.
Ashbery, John. "The Impossible." In *Critical Essays on Gertrude Stein*. Ed. Daniel J. Hoffman. Boston: G. K. Hall, 1986.
Austin, J. L. *How to Do Things with Words*. Cambridge: Harvard U Press, 1975.
Baker, Houston A., Jr. *Modernism and the Harlem Renaissance*. Chicago: U of Chicago Press, 1987.

Bakhtin, M. M. *The Dialogic Imagination*. Ed. Michael Holquist. Trans. Caryl Emerson and Michael Holquist. Austin: U of Texas Press, 1981.
Banta, Martha. *Taylored Lives: Narrative Productions in the Age of Taylor, Veblen, and Ford*. Chicago: U of Chicago Press, 1993.
Barthes, Roland. *The Rustle of Language*. Trans. Richard Howard. New York: Hill and Wang, 1986.
———. *Writing Degree Zero*. Trans. Annette Lavers and Colin Smith. New York: Hill and Wang, 1977.
Baudelaire, Charles. *Oeuvres complètes*. Paris: Seuil, 1968.
Bell, Ian. "The Phantasmagoria of Hugh Selwyn Mauberley." *Paideuma* 5.3 (Winter 1976): 361–85.
Benjamin, Walter. *Reflections: Essays, Aphorisms, Autobiographical Writings*. Trans. Edmund Jephcott. New York: Harcourt Brace Jovanovich, 1978.
———. "The Work of Art in the Age of Mechanical Reproduction." In *Illuminations*. Ed. Hannah Arendt. New York: Schocken Books, 1969.
Benson, Steve. *Blindspots*. Cambridge: Whale Cloth, 1981.
Benstock, Shari. *Women of the Left Bank: Paris, 1900–1940*. Austin: U of Texas Press, 1986.
Berman, Marshall. *All That Is Solid Melts into Air: The Experience of Modernity*. New York: Penguin, 1988.
Bernstein, Michael André. "Robert Duncan: Talent and the Individual Tradition." *Sagetrieb* 2/3 (Fall/Winter 1982): 177–90.
———. *The Tale of the Tribe: Ezra Pound and the Modern Verse Epic*. Princeton: Princeton U Press, 1980.
Bhabha, Homi. *The Location of Culture*. London: Routledge, 1994.
Bloom, Harold, ed. *Deconstruction and Criticism*. New York: Seabury Press, 1979.
Botha, Paul. *Documentary Diary: An Informal History of the British Documentary Film, 1928–1939*. New York: Hill and Wang, 1973.
Brenton, Myron. *The Privacy Invaders*. New York: Coward-McCann, Inc., 1964.
Breslin, James E. B. *From Modern to Contemporary: American Poetry 1945–1965*. Chicago: U of Chicago Press, 1984.
Bridgeman, Richard. *Gertrude Stein in Pieces*. New York: Oxford U Press, 1970.
Brogan, Jacqueline Vaught. *Part of the Climate: American Cubist Poetry*. Berkeley: U of California Press, 1991.
Brooks, Peter. "Aesthetics and Ideology: What Happened to Poetics?" *Critical Inquiry* 20 (1994): 509–23.
Brown, Norman O. "Revisioning Historical Identities." *Apocalypse and/or Metamorphosis*. Berkeley: U of California Press, 1991.
Buck-Morss, Susan. *The Dialectics of Seeing: Walter Benjamin and the Arcades Project*. Cambridge, Mass.: MIT Press, 1991.
Burger, Peter. *Theory of the Avant-Garde*. Trans. Michel Shaw. Minneapolis: U of Minnesota Press, 1984.
Burke, Clifford. *Printing It: A Guide to Graphic Techniques for the Impecunious*. Berkeley: Wingbow Press, 1972.

Burroughs, William. *The Ticket That Exploded*. New York: Grove Press, 1967.
Butterick, George F. *A Guide to* The Maximus Poems *of Charles Olson*. Berkeley: U of California Press, 1978.
Campbell, Russell. *Cinema Strikes Back: Radical Filmmaking in the United States 1930–1942*. Ann Arbor: UMI Research Press, 1982.
Castle, Terry. *The Female Thermometer: Eighteenth-Century Culture and the Invention of the Uncanny*. New York: Oxford U Press, 1995.
Chappell, Warren. *A Short History of the Printed Word*. New York: Alfred A. Knopf, 1970.
Chilton, Randolph. "Charles Reznikoff: Objectivist Witness." In *Charles Reznikoff: Man and Poet*. Ed. Milton Hindus. Orono: National Poetry Foundation, 1984.
Cohen, Morris L., and Robert G. Berring. *How to Find the Law*. 8th ed. St. Paul: West Publishing Co., 1983.
Colker, David. "Rocky Digital Picture Show: 'Phantasmagoria' Sets New Standards in Size and Gore." *Los Angeles Times* 6 Sept. 1995: F1+.
Compagnon, Antoine. *La Seconde main: Ou le travail de la citation*. Paris: Seuil, 1979.
Conte, Joseph. *Unending Design: The Forms of Postmodern Poetry*. Ithaca: Cornell U Press, 1991.
Cowen, Walker. *Melville's Marginalia*, Vol. 1. New York: Garland, 1987.
Crane, Hart. *The Complete Poems and Selected Letters and Prose*. Ed. Brom Weber. New York: Liveright, 1966.
Crary, Jonathan. "Eclipse of the Spectacle." In *Art after Modernism: Rethinking Representation*. Ed. Brian Wallis. Boston: David Godine, 1984.
Creeley, Robert. *The Collected Poems of Robert Creeley: 1945–1975*. Berkeley: U of California Press, 1982.
———. *Contexts of Poetry: Interviews, 1961–1971*. Bolinas, Calif.: Four Seasons, 1973.
———. "An Interview with Robert Creeley." In *The Poetics of the New American Poetry*. Ed. Donald Allen and Warren Tallman. New York: Grove Press, 1973.
Cvetkovich, Ann. *Mixed Feelings: Feminism, Mass Culture, and Victorian Sensationalism*. New Brunswick, N.J.: Rutgers U Press, 1992.
Damon, Maria. *The Dark End of the Street: Margins in American Vanguard Poetry*. Minneapolis: U of Minnesota Press, 1993.
Davidson, Michael. "'By Ear, He Sd': Audio-Tapes and Contemporary Criticism." *Credences* n.s., 1.1 (n.d.): 105–20.
———. "Compulsory Homosociality: Charles Olson, Jack Spicer, and the Gender of Poetics." In *Cruising the Performative: Interventions into the Representation of Ethnicity, Nationality, and Sexuality*. Ed. Sue-Ellen Case, Philip Brett, and Susan Leigh Foster. Bloomington: Indiana U Press, 1995.
———. "Forms of Refusal: George Oppen's 'Distant Life.'" *Sulfur* 26 (1990): 127–34.
———. "Refiguring Shelley: Postmodern Recuperations of Romanticism." *Keats-Shelley Journal* 42 (1993): 48–57.

———. *The San Francisco Renaissance: Poetics and Community at Mid-Century.* Cambridge: Cambridge U Press, 1989.

———. "'Skewed by Design': From Act to Speech Act in Language-Writing." *Aerial* 8 (1995): 241–46.

de Lauretis, Teresa. *Technologies of Gender: Essays on Theory, Film, and Fiction.* Bloomington: Indiana U Press, 1987.

Deleuze, Gilles, and Félix Guattari. *Kafka: Toward a Minor Literature.* Minneapolis: U of Minnesota Press, 1991.

DeKoven, Marianne. *A Different Language: Gertrude Stein's Experimental Writing.* Madison: U of Wisconsin Press, 1983.

———. *Rich and Strange: Gender, History, Modernism.* Princeton: Princeton U Press, 1991.

De Man, Paul. *Blindness and Insight: Essays in the Rhetoric of Contemporary Criticism.* New York: Oxford U Press, 1971.

Dembo, L. S. "The 'Objectivist' Poet: Four Interviews." *Contemporary Literature* 10.2 (Spring 1969): 193–202.

Dery, Mark. "Signposts on the Road to Nowhere: Laurie Anderson's Crisis of Meaning." *South Atlantic Quarterly* 90 (1991): 785–801.

Dickinson, Emily. *The Complete Poems of Emily Dickinson.* Ed. Thomas H. Johnson. Boston: Little, Brown, 1960.

———. *The Letters of Emily Dickinson.* Ed. Thomas H. Johnson. Cambridge, Mass.: Harvard U Press, 1958.

Diepeveen, Leonard. *Changing Voices: The Modern Quoting Poem.* Ann Arbor: U of Michigan Press, 1993.

DiPrima, Diane, and LeRoi Jones, eds. *The Floating Bear: A Newsletter, 1961–1969.* La Jolla, Calif.: Laurence McGilvery, 1973.

———. *Revolutionary Letters.* N.p.: n.p., 1968.

Donner, Frank J. *The Age of Surveillance: The Aims and Methods of America's Political Intelligence System.* New York: Alfred A. Knopf, 1980.

Doolittle, H. [H.D.] *Helen in Egypt.* New York: New Directions, 1961.

———. *Palimpsest.* Carbondale: Southern Illinois U Press, 1968.

———. *Tribute to Freud.* Boston: David Godine, 1974.

Dreiser, Theodore. *Sister Carrie.* Ed. Donald Pizer. New York: Norton, 1991.

Drucker, Johanna. "Against Fiction." *Leonardo.* 17.1 (1984): 50–60.

———. *The Visible Word: Experimental Typography and Modern Art, 1909–1923.* Chicago: U of Chicago Press, 1994.

Duncan, Robert. *Bending the Bow.* New York: New Directions, 1968.

———. *Gleanings.* N.p.: privately printed, n.d.

———. *Ground Work: Before the War.* New York: New Directions, 1984.

———. *Ground Work II: In the Dark.* New York: New Directions, 1987.

———. "The Homosexual in Society." *Politics* 1.7 (Aug. 1944): 209–11. Also in Faas, 319–22.

———. "Interview with Robert Duncan." *Gay Sunshine* 40/41 (Summer/Fall 1979): 1–8.

———. "Man's Fulfillment in Order and Strife." *Fictive Certainties: Essays by Robert Duncan.* New York: New Directions, 1985.

———. *The Opening of the Field*. New York: Grove, 1960.
———. "Pages from a Notebook." *The Artist's View* 5 (July 1953): n.p.
———. "A Pre-Face." *Maps* 6 (1974): 1–16.
———. *Roots and Branches*. New York: New Directions, 1964.
———. *Tribunals: Passages 31–35*. Los Angeles: Black Sparrow Press, 1970.
———. *The Years as Catches: First Poems (1939–1946) by Robert Duncan*. Berkeley: Oyez, 1966.
DuPlessis, Rachel Blau. "'The Familiar / Becomes Extreme': George Oppen and Silence." *North Dakota Quarterly* 55.4 (1987): 18–36.
Dydo, Ulla. "Composition as Meditation." In *Gertrude Stein and the Making of Literature*. Ed. Shirley Neuman and Ira B. Nadel. Boston: Northeastern U Press, 1988. 42–60.
———. "*Stanzas in Meditation*: The Other Autobiography." In *Gertrude Stein Advanced: An Anthology of Criticism*. Ed. Richard Kostelanetz. Jefferson: McFarland, 1990.
Eagleton, Terry. *The Ideology of the Aesthetic*. Oxford: Basil Blackwell, 1990.
Eagleton, Terry, et al., eds. *Nationalism, Colonialism, and Literature*. Minneapolis: U of Minnesota Press, 1990.
Easthorpe, Anthony. *Poetry as Discourse*. London: Methuen, 1983.
Eliot, T. S. *The Complete Poems and Plays, 1909–1950*. New York: Harcourt, Brace and World, Inc., 1962.
Emerson, Ralph Waldo. "The Poet." In *Selections from Ralph Waldo Emerson*. Ed. Stephen E. Whicher. Boston: Riverside-Houghton, 1960.
Engel, Friedrich Karl. "Magnetic Tape: From the Early Days to the Present." *AES: Journal of the Audio Engineering Society* 36 (1988): 606–16.
Faas, Ekbert. *Young Robert Duncan: Portrait of the Poet as Homosexual in Society*. Santa Barbara: Black Sparrow, 1983.
Fabian, Johannes. *Language and Colonial Power: The Appropriation of Swahili in the Former Belgian Congo 1880–1938*. Berkeley: U of California Press, 1986.
Felman, Shoshana, and Dori Laub. *Testimony: Crises of Witnessing in Literature, Psychoanalysis, and History*. New York: Routledge, 1992.
Felski, Rita. *The Gender of Modernity*. Cambridge, Mass.: Harvard U Press, 1995.
Fenollosa, Ernest. *The Chinese Written Character as a Medium for Poetry*. San Francisco: City Lights, 1936.
Fierstein, Frederick. *Expansive Poetry*. Santa Cruz, Calif.: Story Line Press, 1989.
Filreis, Alan. *Modernism from Right to Left: Wallace Stevens, the Thirties, and Literary Radicalism*. Cambridge: Cambridge U Press, 1994.
Flanner, Janet. Foreword. In *Two: Gertrude Stein and Her Brother and Other Portraits*. New Haven: Yale U Press, 1951.
Foucault, Michel. *The Birth of the Clinic: An Archaeology of Medical Perception*. Trans. A. M. Sheridan Smith. New York: Random House, Vintage Books, 1994.
———. *The History of Sexuality*, Vol. 1, *An Introduction*. Trans. Robert Hurley. New York: Random House, Vintage Books, 1980.

———. *Language, Counter-Memory, Practice: Selected Essays and Interviews by Michel Foucault.* Trans. Donald Bouchard and Sherry Simon. Ed. Donald F. Bouchard. Ithaca: Cornell U Press, 1977.

———. *The Order of Things: An Archaeology of the Human Sciences.* New York: Pantheon, 1970.

Friedman, Susan Stanford. "Creating a Women's Mythology: H.D.'s *Helen in Egypt.*" In *Signets: Reading H.D.* Ed. Susan Stanford Friedman and Rachel Blau DuPlessis. Madison: U of Wisconsin Press, 1990.

Friedman, Susan Stanford, and Rachel Blau DuPlessis, eds. *Signets: Reading H.D.* Madison: U of Wisconsin Press, 1990.

Ginsberg, Allen. *Collected Poems, 1947–1980.* New York: Harper and Row, 1984.

Gioia, Dana. *Can Poetry Matter? Essays on Poetry and American Culture.* St. Paul: Graywolf Press, 1992.

Glazier, Loss Pequeno. *Small Press: An Annotated Guide.* Westport, Conn.: Greenwood Press, 1992.

Golding, Alan. "George Oppen's Serial Poems." *Contemporary Literature* 29 (1988): 221–40.

———. "Openness, Closure, and Avant-Garde Rhetoric." American Literature Association Conference. San Diego, 1 June 1990.

Grenier, Robert. *What I Believe. Abacus* 37 (October 1988).

Grieve, Thomas. "Annotations to the Chinese in *Section: Rock-Drill.*" *Paideuma* 4 (1975): 362–85.

Gunn, Thom. *Moly.* London: Faber and Faber, 1971.

Haraway, Donna J. "A Cyborg Manifesto: Science, Technology, and Socialist-Feminism in the Late Twentieth Century." In *Simians, Cyborgs, and Women: The Reinvention of Nature.* New York: Routledge, 1991.

Harris, Neil. *Cultural Excursions: Marketing Appetites and Cultural Tastes in Modern America.* Chicago: U of Chicago Press, 1990.

Hindus, Milton, ed. *Charles Reznikoff: Man and Poet.* Orono: National Poetry Foundation, 1984.

Hindus, Milton. "Epic, 'Action-Poem,' Cartoon: Charles Reznikoff's *Testimony: The United States: 1885–1915.*" In *Charles Reznikoff: Man and Poet.* Ed. Milton Hindus. Orono: National Poetry Foundation, 1984.

Holmes, Richard. *Shelley: The Pursuit.* New York: Viking Penguin, 1987.

Holsapple, Bruce. "Poetic Design in Reznikoff's *Testimony.*" *Sagetrieb* 13.1–2 (1994): 123–46.

Honey, Maureen, ed. *Shadowed Dreams: Women's Poetry of the Harlem Renaissance.* New Brunswick, N.J.: Rutgers U Press, 1989.

Horkheimer, Max, and Theodor Adorno. "The Culture Industry: Enlightenment as Mass Deception." In *Dialectic of Enlightenment.* New York: Seabury: 1972.

Howe, Susan. ———. *The Birth-mark: Unsettling the Wilderness in American Literary History.* Hanover: Wesleyan U Press, 1993.

———. *Defenestration of Prague.* New York: Kulchur Foundation, 1983.

———. Interview. *The Difficulties* 3.2 (1989): 17–42.

———. *My Emily Dickinson*. Berkeley: North Atlantic Books, 1985.
———. *The Nonconformist's Memorial*. New York: New Directions, 1993.
———. "Women and Their Effect in the Distance." *Ironwood* 14.2 (1986): 58–91.
Huyssen, Andreas. *After the Great Divide: Modernism, Mass Culture, Postmodernism*. Bloomington: Indiana U Press, 1986.
Isaak, Jo-Anna. "The Revolutionary Power of a Woman's Laughter." In *Gertrude Stein Advanced: An Anthology of Criticism*. Ed. Richard Kostelanetz. Jefferson, N.C.: McFarland, 1990.
James, Henry. *The Ambassadors*. New York: Norton, 1994.
———. *The Golden Bowl*. Harmondsworth: Penguin Books, 1973.
Jameson, Fredric. "Baudelaire as Modernist and Postmodernist: The Dissolution of the Referent and the Artificial 'Sublime.'" *Lyric Poetry: Beyond New Criticism*. Ed. Chaviva Hosek and Patricia Parker. Ithaca: Cornell U Press, 1985.
———. *The Ideologies of Theory: Essays 1971–1986*. Vol 1. Minneapolis: U of Minnesota Press, 1988.
———. "Modernism and Imperialism." In *Nationalism, Colonialism, and Literature*. Ed. Terry Eagleton et al. Minneapolis: U of Minnesota Press, 1990.
———. *The Political Unconscious: Narrative as a Socially Symbolic Act*. Ithaca: Cornell U Press, 1981.
———. *Postmodernism, or The Cultural Logic of Late Capitalism*. Durham: Duke U Press, 1991.
———. "Third World Literature in the Era of Multinational Capitalism." *Social Text* 15 (1986): 65–88.
Jardine, Alice A. *Gynesis: Configurations of Woman and Modernity*. Ithaca: Cornell U Press, 1985.
Jay, Martin. *Downcast Eyes: The Denigration of Vision in Twentieth-Century French Thought*. Berkeley: U of California Press, 1993.
Kahn, Douglas. *Wireless Imagination: Sound, Radio and the Avant-Garde*. Cambridge, Mass.: MIT Press, 1992.
Kalaidjian, Walter. *American Culture between the Wars: Revisionary Modernism and Postmodern Critique*. New York: Columbia U Press, 1993.
Kant, Immanuel. *Critique of Judgement*. Trans. J. H. Bernard. New York: Hafner Publishing, 1972.
Kaplan, Alice Yaeger. *Reproductions of Banality: Fascism, Literature, and French Intellectual Life*. Minneapolis: U of Minnesota Press, 1986.
Kenner, Hugh. "*Drafts & Fragments* and the Structure of *The Cantos*." *Agenda* 8 (Autumn/Winter 1970): 7–18.
———. *The Pound Era*. Berkeley: U of California Press, 1974.
Kerouac, Jack. *Visions of Cody*. New York: McGraw-Hill, 1972.
Kertesz, Louise. *The Poetic Vision of Muriel Rukeyser*. Baton Rouge: Louisiana State U Press, 1980.
Knight, Alan R. "Masterpieces, Manifestoes, and the Business of Living: Gertrude Stein Lecturing." In *Gertrude Stein and the Making of Literature*. Ed. Shirley Neuman and Ira B. Nadel. Boston: Northeastern U Press, 1988.

Koestenbaum, Wayne. *Double Talk: The Erotics of Male Literary Collaboration.* New York: Routledge, 1989.

Kostelanetz, Richard, ed. *Gertrude Stein Advanced: An Anthology of Criticism.* Jefferson, N.C.: McFarland, 1990.

———. *Text-Sound Texts.* New York: William Morrow, 1980.

Kristeva, Julia. *Revolution in Poetic Language.* Trans. Margaret Waller. New York: Columbia U Press, 1984.

Lanham, Richard. *The Electronic Word: Democracy, Technology, and the Arts.* Chicago: U of Chicago Press, 1993.

Lapidus, Edith J. *Eavesdropping on Trial.* Rochelle Park, N.J.: Hayden Book Co., 1974.

Lauber, John. "Pound's *Cantos*: A Fascist Epic." *Journal of American Studies* 12 (1978): 3–21.

Layoun, Mary. "Telling Spaces: Palestinian Women and the Engendering of National Narratives." *Nationalisms and Sexualities.* Ed. Andrew Parker, Mary Russo, Doris Sommer, and Patricia Yaeger. New York: Routledge, 1992.

Levinson, Stephen. *Pragmatics.* Cambridge: Cambridge U Press, 1985.

Lloyd, David. *Nationalism and Minor Literature: James Clarence Mangan and the Emergence of Irish Cultural Nationalism.* Berkeley: U of California Press, 1987.

Long, Edward V. *The Intruders: The Invasion of Privacy by Government and Industry.* New York: Frederick A. Praeger, 1967.

Loy, Mina. Letter to Gertrude Stein. 2 Dec. 1911. Gertrude Stein Papers. Beinecke Library, Yale University.

Luhan, Mabel Dodge. *European Experiences.* Vol. 2 of *Intimate Memories.* New York: Harcourt, Brace, 1935.

Lukács, Georg. *History and Class Consciousness: Studies in Marxist Dialectics.* Trans. Rodney Livingstone. Cambridge, Mass.: MIT Press, 1976.

Lyotard, Jean-François. *The Differend: Phases in Dispute.* Trans. Georges Van Den Abbeele. Minneapolis: U of Minnesota Press, 1988.

———. *The Postmodern Condition: A Report on Knowledge.* Trans. Geoff Bennington and Brian Massumi. Minneapolis: U of Minnesota Press, 1984.

Macherey, Pierre. *A Theory of Literary Production.* Trans. Geoffrey Wall. London: Routledge and Kegan Paul, 1978.

*The Magic Lantern: How to Buy and How to Use It . . . by "A Mere Phantom."* London: Houlston and Wright, 1866.

Mallarmé, Stéphane. *Oeuvres complètes.* Paris: Gallimard, 1965.

Marx, Karl. *Capital: A Critique of Political Economy.* Vol. 1. Trans. Ben Fowkes. New York: Random House, Vintage Books, 1977.

Marx, Karl, and Frederick Engels. *The German Ideology.* Ed. C. J. Arthur. New York: International Publishers, 1970.

McClintock, Anne. "The Angel of Progress: Pitfalls of the Term 'Post-Colonialism.'" *Colonial Discourse and Post-Colonial Theory: A Reader.* Ed. Patrick Williams and Laura Chrisman. New York: Columbia U Press, 1994.

McCullough, David. *Truman*. New York: Simon and Schuster, 1992.
McGann, Jerome. *Black Riders: The Visible Language of Modernism*. Princeton: Princeton U Press, 1993.
———. "The *Cantos* of Ezra Pound, the Truth in Contradiction." *Critical Inquiry* 15.1 (Autumn 1988): 1–25.
———. *A Critique of Modern Textual Criticism*. Chicago: University of Chicago Press, 1983.
———. *The Textual Condition*. Princeton: Princeton U Press, 1991.
Miles, Barry. *Ginsberg: A Biography*. New York: Simon and Schuster, 1989.
Miller, Arthur R. *The Assault on Privacy: Computers, Data Banks, and Dossiers*. Ann Arbor: U of Michigan Press, 1971.
Molesworth, Charles. *The Fierce Embrace: A Study of Contemporary American Poetry*. Columbia: U of Missouri Press, 1979.
Mottram, Eric. "1924–1951: Politics and Form in Zukofsky." *Maps* 5 (1978): 76–103.
———. "The Political Responsibilities of the Poet: George Oppen." In *George Oppen Man and Poet*. Ed. Burton Hatlon. Orono: National Poetry Foundation, Inc., 1981.
Nekola, Charlotte, and Paula Rabinowitz, eds. *Writing Red: An Anthology of American Women Writers, 1930–1940*. New York: Feminist Press, 1987.
Nelson, Cary. *Repression and Recovery: Modern American Poetry and the Politics of Cultural Memory, 1910–1945*. Madison: U of Wisconsin Press, 1989.
Neuman, Shirley, and Ira B. Nadel. *Gertrude Stein and the Making of Literature*. Boston: Northeastern U Press, 1988.
"Notes on Contributors." *New Directions: 1938*. Norfolk, Conn.: New Directions, 1938.
O'Hara, Frank. "Personism." *The Collected Poems of Frank O'Hara*. Ed. Donald Allen. New York: Alfred A. Knopf, 1971.
Olson, Charles. "Against Wisdom as Such." *Human Universe and Other Essays*. Ed. Donald Allen. New York: Grove Press, 1967.
———. *The Collected Poems of Charles Olson*. Ed. George F. Butterick. Berkeley: U of California Press, 1987.
———. *The Maximus Poems of Charles Olson*. Ed. George Butterick. Berkeley: U of California Press, 1983.
———. *The Selected Writings of Charles Olson*. Ed. Robert Creeley. New York: New Directions, 1966.
———. *The Special View of History*. Berkeley: Oyez, 1970.
———. "A Syllabary for a Dancer." *Maps* 4 (n.d.): 9–15.
Ong, Walter J. *Orality and Literacy: The Technologizing of the Word*. London: Methuen, 1982.
Oppen, George. *Collected Poems*. New York: New Directions, 1975.
———. Interview with L. S. Dembo. *Contemporary Literature* 10.2 (Spring 1969): 159–77.
———. "Letters to Rachel Blau DuPlessis." *Ironwood* 24 (Fall 1984): 119–38.
———. *The Selected Letters of George Oppen*. Ed. Rachel Blau DuPlessis. Durham: Duke U Press, 1990.

Owens, Craig. "Amplifications: Laurie Anderson." *Art in America* (March 1981): 121–23.
Packard, Vance. *The Naked Society*. New York: David McKay Co., 1964.
Pease, Donald. "National Identities, Postmodern Artifacts, and Postnational Narratives." *Boundary 2* 19.1 (1992): 1–13.
Peck, John. "Pound's Lexical Mythography: King's Journey and Queen's Eye." *Paideuma* 1 (1972): 3–36.
Perelman, Bob. *The Marginalization of Poetry: Language Writing and Literary History*. Princeton: Princeton U Press, 1996.
———. *The Trouble with Genius: Reading Pound, Joyce, Stein, and Zukofsky*. Berkeley: U of California Press, 1994.
Perloff, Marjorie. *The Futurist Moment: Avant-Garde, Avant Guerre, and the Language of Rupture*. Chicago: U of Chicago Press, 1986.
———. *The Poetics of Indeterminacy: Rimbaud to Cage*. Princeton: Princeton U Press, 1981.
———. *Radical Artifice: Writing Poetry in the Age of Media*. Chicago: U of Chicago Press, 1991.
Pollock, Griselda. *Vision and Difference: Femininity, Feminism, and the Histories of Art*. New York: Routledge, 1988.
Porter, Carolyn. *Seeing and Being: The Plight of the Participant Observer in Emerson, James, Adams, and Faulkner*. Middletown: Wesleyan U Press, 1981.
Pound, Ezra. *ABC of Reading*. New York: New Directions, 1987.
———. *The Cantos of Ezra Pound*. New York: New Directions, 1973.
———. *The Letters of Ezra Pound: 1907–1941*. Ed. D. D. Paige. New York: Harcourt, 1950.
———. *Literary Essays of Ezra Pound*. New York: New Directions, n.d.
———. *The Spirit of Romance*. New York: New Directions, n.d.
Pound, Ezra, and Louis Zukofsky. *Pound/Zukofsky: Selected Letters of Ezra Pound and Louis Zukofsky*. Ed. Barry Ahearn. New York: New Directions, 1987.
Quartermain, Peter. *Disjunctive Poetics: From Gertrude Stein and Louis Zukofsky to Susan Howe*. Cambridge: Cambridge U Press, 1992.
Rabinowitz, Paula. *They Must Be Represented: The Politics of Documentary*. London: Verso, 1994.
Rainey, Lawrence S. *Ezra Pound and the Monument of Culture: Text, History, and the Malatesta Cantos*. Chicago: U of Chicago Press, 1991.
Reznikoff, Charles. "My Country 'Tis of Thee." *Contact* 1.2 (May 1932): 99–108.
———. "A Talk with L. S. Dembo." In *Charles Reznikoff: Man and Poet*. Orono: National Poetry Foundation, 1984.
———. *Testimony*. New York: Objectivist Press, 1934.
———. *Testimony*. Vol. 1: *The United States (1885–1915) Recitative*. Santa Barbara: Black Sparrow, 1978.
Richman, Robert. *The Direction of Poetry*. New York: Houghton, 1988.
Rosenberg, Harold. *The Anxious Object: Art Today and Its Audience*. New York: Collier Books, 1964.

Royet-Journoud, Claude. Interview. Serge Gavronsky, ed. *Toward a New Poetics: Contemporary Writing in France*. Berkeley: U of California Press, 1994.
Ruddick, Lisa. *Reading Gertrude Stein: Body, Text, Gnosis*. Ithaca: Cornell U Press, 1990.
Rukeyser, Muriel. *The Life of Poetry*. New York: A. A. Wyn, 1949.
———. "Poem out of Childhood." *Theory of Flight*. New Haven: Yale U Press, 1935.
———. *U.S. 1*. New York: Covici and Friede, 1938.
Ruthven, K. K. *A Guide to Ezra Pound's* Personae *(1926)*. Berkeley: U of California Press, 1969.
Said, Edward. *Orientalism*. New York: Random House, 1979.
———. "Yeats and Decolonization." In *Nationalism, Colonialism, and Literature*. Ed. Terry Eagleton, Fredric Jameson, and Edward Said. Minneapolis: U of Minnesota Press, 1990.
Sayre, Henry. *The Object of Performance: The American Avant-Garde since 1970*. Chicago: U of Chicago Press, 1989.
Scalapino, Leslie. *Objects in the Terrifying Tense Longing from Taking Place*. New York: Roof Books, 1993.
Sennett, Richard. *The Fall of Public Man*. New York: Norton, 1976.
Shevelow, Kathryn. "History and Objectification in Charles Reznikoff's Documentary Poems, *Testimony* and *Holocaust*." *Sagetrieb* 1.2 (1982): 290–306.
Shohat, Ella. "Notes on the 'Post-Colonial.'" *Social Text* 31/32 (1992): 99–113.
Silliman, Ron, ed. *In the American Tree*. Orono: National Poetry Foundation, 1986.
———. *The New Sentence*. New York: Roof Books, 1987.
Silverman, Kaja. *The Acoustic Mirror: The Female Voice in Psychoanalysis and Cinema*. Bloomington: Indiana U Press, 1988.
Simon, Linda. "Reznikoff: The Poet as Witness." In *Charles Reznikoff: Man and Poet*. Ed. Milton Hindus. Orono: National Poetry Foundation, 1984.
Smith, Terry. *Making the Modern: Industry, Art and Design in America*. Chicago: U of Chicago Press, 1993.
Snyder, Gary. *Regarding Wave*. New York: New Directions, 1970.
———. "The Blue Sky." *Six Sections from Mountains and Rivers without End*. San Francisco: Four Seasons Foundation, 1970.
Spicer, Jack. *The Collected Books of Jack Spicer*. Ed. Robin Blaser. Los Angeles: Black Sparrow Press, 1975.
Stein, Gertrude. *The Autobiography of Alice B. Toklas*. In *Selected Writings of Gertrude Stein*. Ed. Carl Van Vechten. New York: Random House, 1962.
———. *Doctor Faustus Lights the Lights*. In *A Gertrude Stein Reader*. Ed. Ulla Dydo. Evanston: Northwestern U Press, 1993.
———. *Everybody's Autobiography*. New York: Random House, 1964.
———. *The Geographical History of America or the Relation of Human Nature to the Human Mind*. New York: Random House, 1973.
———. *How Writing Is Written*. Vol. 2 of *Previously Uncollected Writings of*

*Gertrude Stein*. Ed. Robert Bartlett Haas. Los Angeles: Black Sparrow, 1974.
———. *Lectures in America*. New York: Random House, 1962.
———. "Patriarchal Poetry." In *The Yale Gertrude Stein*. Ed. Richard Kostelanetz. New Haven: Yale U Press, 1980.
———. *Selected Writings of Gertrude Stein*. Ed. Carl Van Vechten. New York: Random House, Vintage Books, 1962.
———. *Stanzas in Meditation*. In *The Yale Gertrude Stein*. Ed. Richard Kostelanetz. New Haven: Yale U Press, 1980.
———. *A Stein Reader: Gertrude Stein*. Ed. Ulla Dydo. Evanston: Northwestern U Press, 1993.
———. "Transatlantic Interview." *A Primer for the Gradual Understanding of Gertrude Stein*. Ed. Robert Bartlett Haas. Los Angeles: Black Sparrow, 1971.
———. *Two: Gertrude Stein and Her Brother and Other Portraits*. New Haven: Yale U Press, 1951.
———. *Useful Knowledge*. Barrytown, N.Y.: Station Hill, 1988.
———. "What Are Masterpieces." *Gertrude Stein: Writings and Lectures 1909–1945*. Ed. Patricia Meyerowitz. Harmondsworth: Penguin, 1967.
———. *Writings and Lectures 1909–1945*. Ed. Patricia Meyerowitz. Harmondsworth: Penguin, 1971.
Stevens, Wallace. *The Collected Poems of Wallace Stevens*. New York: Alfred A. Knopf, 1968.
———. *Wallace Stevens Reading His Poems*. LP Caedmon Records TC 1068.
Stimpson, Catherine R. "Gertrude Stein and the Transposition of Gender." In *The Poetics of Gender*. Ed. Nancy K. Miller. New York: Columbia U Press, 1986.
———. "The Somagrams of Gertrude Stein." In *Critical Essays on Gertrude Stein*. Ed. Michael J. Hoffman. Boston: G. K. Hall, 1986.
Surette, Leon. *A Light from Eleusis*. Oxford: Clarendon, 1979.
Syverson, M. A. "The Community of Memory: A Reznikoff Family Chronicle." *Sagetrieb* 11.1–2 (1992): 127–70.
Taggart, John. "Deep Jewels: Oppen's *Seascape: Needle's Eye*." *Ironwood* 26 (Fall 1985): 252–62.
Tay, William. "History as Poetry: The Chinese Past in Ezra Pound's *Rock-Drill Cantos*." *Tamkang Review* 10 (Autumn/Winter 1979): 97–125.
"Sound." *Encyclopedia Britannica: Macropoedia*. 1992.
Thiele, Heinz H. K. "Magnetic Sound Recording in Europe up to 1945." *AES: Journal of the Audio Engineering Society* 36.5 (1988): 396–408.
Thurston, Michael. *Engaging Aesthetics: American Poetry and Politics, 1925–1950*. Diss. U of Illinois. 1994.
Tichi, Cecelia. *Shifting Gears: Technology, Literature, Culture in Modernist America*. Chapel Hill: U of North Carolina Press, 1987.
Trachtenberg, Alan. *The Incorporation of America: Culture and Society in the Gilded Age*. New York: Hill and Wang, 1982.

von Hallberg, Robert. *Charles Olson: The Scholar's Art.* Cambridge, Mass.: Harvard U Press, 1978.
Watten, Barrett. "Total Syntax: The Work in the World." *Total Syntax.* Carbondale: Southern Illinois U Press, 1985.
Weinstein, Norman. *Gertrude Stein and the Literature of the Modern Consciousness.* New York: Frederick Ungar, 1970.
Whalen, Philip. "The Education Continues Along." *On Bear's Head.* New York: Harcourt, 1969.
Williams, Emmett. *An Anthology of Concrete Poetry.* New York: Something Else Press, 1967.
Williams, Raymond. *The Politics of Modernism: Against the New Conformists.* Ed. Tony Pinkney. London: Verso, 1989.
Williams, William Carlos. *The Collected Poems of William Carlos Williams,* Vol. 1. Ed. A. Walton Litz and Christopher MacGowan. New York: New Directions, 1986.
Witemeyer, Hugh. "The Flame-style King." *Paideuma* 4 (1975): 333–35.
Wolff, Janet. *Feminine Sentences: Essays on Women and Culture.* Berkeley: U of California Press, 1990.
Yingling, Thomas. *Hart Crane and the Homosexual Text: New Thresholds, New Anatomies.* Chicago: U of Chicago Press, 1990.
Zola, Émile. *The Ladies' Paradise.* Berkeley: U of California Press, 1992.
Zukofsky, Louis. *"A."* Berkeley: U of California Press, 1978.
———. *All the Collected Short Poems, 1923–1964.* New York: Norton, 1971.
———. *First Half of "A"-9.* New York: Author, 1940.
———. Interview with L. S. Dembo. *Contemporary Literature* 10 (1969): 202–19.
———. *Prepositions: The Collected Essays of Louis Zukofsky.* Berkeley: U of California Press, 1981.

# Index

Abrams, M. H., 138
Adams, Henry, 48, 163; *The Education of Henry Adams*, 130
Adamson, Robert, 180
Adorno, Theodor, xii, 134, 137; *Aesthetic Theory*, 35, 41; on autonomy theory, 6, 62. *See also* "The Culture Industry"
Aesthetic, the, 88; as flawed, 40, 62–63; and left-wing politics, 117, 122; as masculine, 45; and Stein, 35–63; and theories of spatialization, 168. *See also* Autonomy theory
Agee, James, and Walker Evans: *Let Us Now Praise Famous Men*, 138, 140
Ahearn, Barry, 129
AIDS, 192, 194
Alcott, David, 35
Allen, H. Stanley: *Electrons and Waves: An Introduction to Atomic Physics*, 125, 129
Althusser, Louis, 240n.8
Altieri, Charles: *Enlarging the Temple*, 232n.17; "The Objectivist Tradition," 24
Ampex, 203
Anderson, Benedict, 135, 170
Anderson, Laurie, 213–19, 223, 247n.22; *Collected Videos*, 213; "Language of the Future," 215–16; "O Superman (For Massenet)," 216–17
Antebellum South, 147, 163–67. *See also* Slavery
Antin, David: and magnetic recording, 199, 207, 218, 223; on professionalism and amateurism, 211–13; on radio, 209–13; on voice, 207–8, 214. Works: "Some Questions," 62; *Talking at the Boundaries*, 208; *Tuning*, 208; *What It Means to Be Avant Garde*, 208; "whos listening out there," 209–13
Anti-Semitism, 97, 117, 124–25. *See also* World War II
*Anvil*, 25
Anzaldúa, Gloria, 27

Apollinaire: *Calligrammes*, 13; "Il Pleut," 16
Archive for New Poetry at the University of California, San Diego, xii–xiii, 66, 76–79
Archives: and gender, 82; literary, 5, 32–33, 93; as poetic source, 79–80; tape recorder as, 207
Arensberg, Walter Conrad, 13
Aristotle, 208
Arnold, Matthew, 86, 89–90
Arts and Crafts Movement, 179
Ashbery, John, 15, 55, 61
*Atlantic Reporter*, 153
Atom bomb, 150
Auden, W. H., 138–39
Auschwitz, 150. *See also* World War II
Autonomy theory, 6–8, 38–41, 62, 117, 127, 137, 226, 230. *See also* Aesthetic
Avant-garde: American, 13, 21, 133; and politics, 8; and technologies, 28

Bach, Johann Sebastian, 129, 133
Bakhtin, M. M., 6; and stylistics, 135
Balzac, Honoré de, 47
Banta, Martha, 5
Baraka, Amiri. *See* Jones, LeRoi
Barnes, Djuna, 29
Barreto-Rivera, Rafael, 18
Barthes, Roland, 6, 93
Baudelaire, Charles: in Duncan, 179, 191; in Eliot, 98, 141; and *ennui*, 72; and *flaneur*, 44; *Les Fleurs de mal*, 192; *Oeuvres complètes*, 192; and urban life, 68
Baudrillard, Jean, 243n.2; on commodity culture, 171–72, 195
Beat poets, 203
Beckett, Samuel, 6, 199, 222
Belknap Press (Harvard University), 80
Bell, Alexander Graham, 229
Bell Laboratories, 203
Benjamin, Walter, 30, 68, 140, 200
Benson, Steve, 219–23; magnetic recording, 199, 218–22, 247n.24

## Index

Bercovich, Sacvan, 81
Berlioz, Hector, 33
Berman, Russell, 45
Berryman, John, 78
Beyond Baroque, 30
Bhabha, Homi, 135, 168; "Dissemination," 136
Bible, 75, 164. *See also* Christianity
Bishop, Elizabeth: "The Fish," 78
Black Mountain poets, 194
Black Sparrow Press, 156
Blackburn, Paul: and magnetic recording, 207
Blake, William, 14, 93, 179
Blaser, Robin, 174
*Blast*, 12
Bloom, Harold, 138
*Blow Out*, 202
Boccioni, Umberto, 12
Bodleian Library (Oxford), 82–83
*Book of the Dead* (Egyptian), 147, 150
Bopp, Franz, 95
Borges, Jorge Luis, 28, 33
Boulez, Pierre: *Pli selon Pli*, 176–77
Brainard, Joe, 15
Brancusi, Constantin, 180
Brathwaite, Edward: *Middle Passage*, 137
Brautigan, Richard: *Please Plant This Book*, 32
Braque, Georges, 12
Bridgeman, Richard, 57
Broadside, 30
*Broom*, 163
Brown, Bob, 22
Brown, John, 147
Brown, Norman O., 239 n.5
Brown, Robert Carleton, 29
Browning, Robert, 138
Bunting, Basil, 23
Burger, Peter, 7
Burke, Kenneth, 150, 163, 167
Burnshaw, Stanley, 27
Burroughs, William, 199, 214, 223; *Naked Lunch*, 204; *The Ticket That Exploded*, 203–4
Byzantium, 103–4

Cage, John, 207, 219
Caldwell, Erskine and Margaret Bourke White: *You Have Seen Their Faces*, 138
Calvinism, 82
Camera obscura, 3–4
*Camera Work*, 36
Cassady, Neal, 203
Castle, Terry, 2

Cavalcanti, Guido: "Donni mi priegha," 26, 117, 124–27, 132
Celan, Paul, 179
Cézanne, Paul, 41
Cha, Theresa Hak Kyung, xii, 27
Charlemagne, 105
Chiang Kai-shek ("Mei-ling"), 112
Chopin, Kate: "A Pair of Gloves," 45
Chosroes III (king), 104
*Chou King*, 102
Christianity, 50–51. *See also* Bible
CIA (Central Intelligence Agency), 201
Cinema. *See* Technology
City Lights Press and Bookstore, 30
Civil War, 149
Cobbing, Bob: "Worm," 16–17
Cold War: as anti-ideological, 115; paranoia, 202; and surveillance, 200–203. *See also* Watergate
Coleridge, Samuel Taylor, 80
Colonialism, 81, 96–97, 117, 136; in Howe; and narrative turn, 135, 168, 170; and phantasmagoria, 2, 33, 241 nn.2–4
Commodity: artwork as, 6–7, 22, 41, 62, 117, 127; culture, 38, 48, 120–21, 131, 171–72, 230; as fetish, 33, 45, 118, 127; labor power as, 118–19; of language, xiii; in Marx, 3–4, 124–25, 128, 229; speaking as, 225
Concrete poetry, 13, 15–16, 18
Confucianism, 100–103
Conrad, Joseph, 137
Constructivism, 15
Consumerism, 44, 45–47, 148. *See also* Commodity
*Contact*, 156, 158, 161, 163
Contact Editions, 29
Coolidge, Clark, 15
Cooney, Seamus, 156
Copland, Aaron, 142
Coppola, Francis Ford: *The Conversation*, 202
*Corpus Juris*, 151
Cortez, Jayne, 27, 197
Couvreur, Père Séraphine. *See Chou King*
Cowen, Wilson Walker. *See Melville's Marginalia*
Cowley, Malcolm, 26
Crane, Hart, 81, 245 n.8; *The Bridge*, 12, 138, 149, 244 n.8; "The River," 29
Cranium, 30
Crary, Jonathan, 172
Crawford, John, 71
Creeley, Robert, 14, 24, 133; "Collected

Poems," 196; *Contexts*, xi; "An Interview," 70
*Crisis*, 142
Cuala Press, 28
Cubism, 7, 11–13, 41, 45, 49
"The Culture Industry" (Adorno and Horkheimer), 246n.9, 247n.19
cummings, e. e., 12–13, 197
Cvetkovich, Ann, 3

Dadaism, 7, 11–13, 16, 49, 139, 207
Damon, Maria, 238n.9
Daniel, Arnaut, 119
Dante Alighieri, 98, 141, 179–80, 191, 221; *Vita Nuova*, 122
Darrah, Tina, 106
Davidson, Michael: "By Ear," 198; *San Francisco Renaissance*, 11
Deaf culture, 228. *See also* Orality
Deconstructionism, 91, 137, 198–99
*The Defense of Madrid*, 141
DeKoven, Marianne, 52; *Different Language*, 37, 234n.12
De Lauretis, Teresa, 218, 231n
Deleuze, Gilles, and Félix Guattari, 67, 86, 135
De Man, Paul, 91, 168
Del Mar, Alexander: *History of Monetary Systems*, 103–4
Dembo, L. S., 23, 151
Depression, 4, 26, 138, 150, 163, 226
De Stijl, 180
DIA (Defense Intelligence Agency), 201
Dick, A. B., 30
Dickinson, Emily, 29, 80–81, 93; *Collected Poems*, 79; *Letters*, 80
Diepeveen, Leonard: *Changing Voices*, 97–98
Dioce, 106
DiPrima, Diane: *Revolutionary Letters*, 31. *See also The Floating Bear*
Dobbs, Stephen, 35
Documentary culture, 135–70
Doolittle, Hilda, 7, 40; *Helen in Egypt*, 1, 4, 8, 38, 96; *Palimpsest*, 231n.8
Dos Passos, John: *U.S.A.* trilogy, 138
Dreiser, Theodore: *Sister Carrie*, 225
Drucker, Johanna, 29, 106; *Against Fiction*, 18–19; *Visible Word*, 7
Duchamp, Marcel, 7, 13
Dulles, John Foster, 105
Duncan, Robert, 5, 14–15, 80; cessation of publication, 9, 177–78, 190; and etymology, 238n.9; family background, 174–75, 187–89; on homophobia, 172;
homosexuality of, 179, 181, 188–89, 190–95; and homosociality, 181, 195; interview in *Gay Sunshine*, 189; and lexical insert, 94–95, 106; in *Maps*, 178–79; and marginality as fetish, 173; and margins of page, 176, 179–95, 245n.10; on Pound, 180–81; and sadomasochism, 174, 186; and scene of instruction, 175–76, 192–93; and scene of invasion, 192–93; and violence, 174–75, 181, 188, 190, 194. Works: "An African Elegy," 173–74; "Against Wisdom," 174; "An Alternate Life," 190 *Bending the Bow*, 94, 98–99, 108, 175, 177–78; "In Blood's Domaine," 192; *Dante Etudes*, 179–81; *Gleanings*, 244n.4; *Ground Work: Before the War*, 179–80, 186; *Ground Work II: In the Dark*, 179, 190–91; "The Homosexual in Society," 172–74; "An Interlude of Winter Light," 176–77; "A Lammas Tiding," 175; "At the Loom," 94–95; "To Master Baudelaire," 191–92; *Medieval Scenes*, 175; "The Missionaries," 244n.5; "My Mother Would Be a Falconress," 175; "Near Circe's House," 183–84; *Opening of the Field*, 175, 194; "Out of the Cradle, Endlessly Rocking," 188; "Passages," 108, 178; "A Poem Beginning with a Line by Pindar," 175–76, 190; "Poems Written in the Margins of Thom Gunn's *Moly*," 181–90; "Pre-Face," 178; "Projective Verse," 178; "Rites of Passage: I," 185; *Roots and Branches*, 175; "Spelling," 108; *Tribunals*, 178; "Two Presentations," 175
DuPlessis, Rachel Blau, 26, 70–71
Dutton, Paul, 18
Dydo, Ulla, 55–56, 234n.15; 235n.16

Eagleton, Terry, 40–41, 49
Easthorpe, Anthony, 25
Eckhart, Meister, 71
Edison, Thomas, 48, 229
Eisenstein, Sergei, 141
Eisler, Hanns, 142
Eliot, George, 80
Eliot, T. S., 38, 72, 98, 138, 147, 196: and allusion; and *ennui*; impersonality, cult of, 23, 125; "The Love Song of J. Alfred Prufrock," 3, 37; *The Waste Land*, 12, 36, 96, 141
Emerson, Ralph Waldo, 95, 100, 109
Empedocles, 179

## Index

Ephemerality, 28, 68; textual, 5, 32–33
Ethnopoetics, 197
Etymology. *See* Philology
Euclidean mathematics, 129
Evans, Walker. *See* Agee, James
Existentialism, 66, 114
Expressivism, 197. *See also* Personalism

Faas, Ekbert, 174
Fabian, Johannes, 96
FAP (Federal Arts Project), 140
Fascism. *See* Pound, Ezra; World War II
Federal agencies. *See individual agencies*
Federal Communications Act, 201
Felman, Shoshana, 149
Feminism, 5, 8, 37, 81; and cyborg identities, 214–15, 229
Fenollosa, Ernst, 11; *Chinese Written Character*, 100
Ferlinghetti, Lawrence, 15
Fields, W. C.: "The Man on the Flying Trapeze," 36, 63, 233 n.2
Fierstein, Frederick, 148
Film and Photo League, 141, 143
Filreis, Alan, 226
Finlay, Ian Hamilton: "Acrobat," 15
Flanner, Janet, 45
Flaubert, Gustave: *Madame Bovary*, 33; *The Temptation of St. Anthony*, 33–34
*The Floating Bear*, 31
Fordism, 49
Formalism, 241 n.15; high modernist, 139; and ideology of modernism, xiii, 232 n.20; and instability, 129; New, 238 n.2; of 1930s, 5, 117–18, 133–34, 232 n.19, 239 n.4; and Objectivism, 24–27; politics of, 233 n.20; Russian, 4, 6, 133
Foucault, Michel, 218, 223, 228; *History of Sexuality*, 199; *Language, Counter-Memory, Practice*, 33–34; *Order of Things*, 6–7
Four Horsemen, 18
Fourth Amendment, 201
Freud, Sigmund, 1, 8, 22, 135, 137, 174
Friedman, Susan Stanford, 8
Frontier Films, 141, 242 n.8
Frost, Robert, 139
FSA (Farm Security Administration), 140
Futurism, 7, 11, 13, 15–16, 47; Russian, 12, 20. *See also* Zaum language
FWP (Federal Writers' Project), 149

Gaudier-Brzeska, Henri, 12
*Gay Sunshine*, 189
*Geisteswissenschaften*: cultural criticism, 96
Gemisto (Gemisthus Plethon), 101
Gender, 49, 50, 215–18; stereotypes of, 38, 107
Genre, 67–68, 69
Ginsberg, Allen, xi, 14, 70, 197, 223; and contemporaries, 203, 206–7; *The Fall of America*, 204–5; "Howl," 199, 218; "Wichita Vortex Sutra," 204–5
Gissing, George Robert, 137
Gothic, 1, 3
Gounod, Charles, 33
Graham, Martha, 110
Grahn, Judy, 27
Greenberg, Clement, 63
Grenier, Robert, 19–21
Gris, Juan, 41
Guattari, Félix. *See* Deleuze, Gilles, and Félix Guattari
Gunn, Thom: *Moly*, 5, 179, 181–84, 186–88; "Rites of Passage," 185
Guston, Philip, 15
Gutenberg, Johann, 29

H.D. *See* Doolittle, Hilda
Habermas, Jürgen, 228
Hackman, Gene, 202
Hagedorn, Jessica, 27
Hamaday, Walter, 30
Haraway, Donna, 214
Harlem Renaissance, 117, 136
Harpers Ferry, 147
Harris, Neil, 5
Havelock, Eric, 199
Hawthorne, Nathaniel, 167
*Heart of Spain*, 142
Hegel, Georg Wilhelm Friedrich, 78, 100, 132, 163, 230
Heidegger, Martin, 70, 96
Hejinian, Lyn, 18
Henderson, David, 197
Heraclius, 104
Herbert, George, 187
Herder, J. G., 95
Hitler, Adolf, 173, 178, 179, 200, 246 n.9; conspiracy with Stalin, 131, 134. *See also* World War II
Hogarth Press, 178
Hollander, John, 21
Hollywood: culture industry, 141–42
Holocaust, 150. *See also* World War II
Homer, 1, 97, 99, 141
Homophobia, 172, 173–74
Homosexuality, and marginalization,

172, 174, 179, 244 n.8. *See also* Lesbianism
Homosociality, 181, 244 nn.6,8. *See also* Homosexuality
Hoover Commission Task Force on Intelligence, 201
Horkheimer, Max. *See* "The Culture Industry"
House Un-American Activities Committee, 201
Howe, Susan, xii, xiii, 92; and archives, 5, 80; and dictionary, 106; and marginal voices, 68, 80–81; and materiality of page, 68, 79, 237 nn.16,17; on Shelley, 82–92; and textual errors, 90–91. Works: *The Birth-mark*, 82, 90; *The Difficulties* (interviewed in), 236 nn.9,10,11; "Melville's Marginalia," 84–92; *My Emily Dickinson*, 80–81; *Nonconformist's Manual*, 84, 87, 92, 236 nn.14, 15; "Women and Their Effect," 82
Hoyem, Andrew, 30
Hughes, Langston: *Montage of a Dream Deferred*, 29, 138–39
Humboldt, Baron Wilhelm von, 95
Humphrey, Hubert, 206
Hurwitz, Leo, 141
Hutchinson, Anne, 81
Huyssen, Andreas, 8, 38
Hypertext. *See* Technology

IAC (Intelligence Advisory Committee), 201
Ideogram. *See* Pound, Ezra
Ideology: of form, 5, 25, 117, 133–34, 239 n.4; of modernism, xiii, 8, 21, 24, 27, 226; poetry as, xi–xii
Imagism, 3, 10, 24–25; and George Oppen, 64, 70–71, 78
Intersection, 30
Irigaray, Luce, 81
Ivans, Joris, 141

James, Henry, 1, 56, 63, 235 n.20; *The Ambassadors*, 2; *The Golden Bowl*, 61–62; *Wings of the Dove*, 61
Jameson, Fredric, 22, 172, 239 n.4; "Modernism and Imperialism," 241 n.4; and narrative turn, 135–36, 242 n.5; and political unconscious, 137; *Postmodernism*, 137, 243 n.2; "Third World Literature," 137, 241 n.3
Jardine, Alice, 81
Jed, Stephanie, xiii

Jeffers, Robinson, 139
Jesperson, Otto, *A Modern English Grammar on Historical Principles*, 108
Jewish heritage: and the Objectivists, 25, 49, 59, 117, 121 132, 173
Johnson, Lyndon, 206
Johnson, Philip, 23
Johnson, Thomas, 80
Jones, LeRoi (pseud. Amiri Baraka), 15, 197, 207. *See also The Floating Bear*
Joyce, James, 33, 38, 86, 137; *Ulysses*, 36, 96
Jung, Carl Gustav, 78

Kahn, Douglas. *See Wireless Imagination*
Kahnweiler, Daniel, 41–42
Kafka, Franz, 33
Kalaidjian, Walter, 143, 148
Kant, Immanuel, 6, 9, 41, 49, 60, 119, 227; and aesthetics, 24, 38–39, 57–58, 61–62
Kaplan, Alice, xiii, 200
Karlgren, Bernard, 100
Katz, Alex, 15
Kelly, Robert, 106, 207
Kelmscott, 28
Kenner, Hugh: "Drafts," 101; *Pound Era*, 96
*Kenyon Review*, 173–74
Kerouac, Jack, 15, 197, 199; "Imitation of the Tape," 203; *Visions of Cody*, 203
Kertesz, Louise, 143
Kierkegaard, Søren, 71
Kim Chi Ha, 149
Kinglake, A. W.: *The Invasion of the Crimea*, 89
Knight, Alan, 39
Koestenbaum, Wayne, 181
Kooning, Willem de, 23
Kostelanetz, Richard, 16, 55
Kreymborg, Alfred: *Others*, 13
Kristeva, Julia, 81, 93, 214, 247 n.20

LSD, 186
Lacan, Jacques, 49
Language Writing, 18, 22, 27, 92, 133, 218, 232 n.13; 238 n.2
Lanham, Richard, 28
Lantern shows, 2, 4. *See also* Phantasmagoria
Larsen, Nella: *Passing*, 45
Lawrence, D. H., 32
Layoun, Mary, 136
Leger, Fernand, 12
Lenin, Nikolai (Vladimir Ilich Ulynov), 226

## Index

Legge, James, 100–101
Lesbianism, 8, 39, 49, 242 n.7. *See also* Homosexuality
Levertov, Denise, 14, 24, 174; organic form, 197
Lew, Walter, 27
Lewis, Wyndham, 12
Lexical insert, 94, 95, 98, 102, 106. *See also* Philology
Lippard, George, 89
Lloyd, David, 85–86
Lomax, Alan, 207
Lord, Albert, 199
Loringhoven, Elsa von Freytag (Baroness), 13
Lowell, Robert: "Skunk Hour," 78
Loy, Mina, 12–13, 22, 45, 234 n. 7
Luhan, Mabel Dodge, 46
Lukács, Georg, 118–19, 120–21, 127
Lyotard, Jean-François, 135, 169; *Postmodern Condition*, 62–63

MacDiarmid, Hugh, 138
MacLow, Jackson, 133, 207, 219; "Gathas," 16
Maddow, Ben, 141
Magnetic recording: as archive, 207; and global communications, 204–6; invention of, 199–200, 246 n. 7; the Magnetophone, 200; and material text, xi; and Nazi propaganda, 200, 246 n. 9; in 1930s, 198; in 1950s and 1960s, 206–7; in 1970s, 207–8; in 1980s, 208–22; as agent in composition, 218–22; and postmodernism, 223; and surveillance, 200–204, 246 nn.13,14; and typewriter, 197–98
Mailla, Père de Moyriac, *Histoire générale de la Chine*, 102
Mallarmé, Stéphane, 2, 67, 133; and Duncan, 176–77, 179, 193; *Le Livre*, 33; *Ouvres complètes*, 2; Oxford lectures (1894), 168
*The Man from U.N.C.L.E.*, 204
*The Manchurian Candidate*, 202
Manet, Edouard, *Gare Saint-Lazare*, 44
Mangan, James Clarence, 85–88, 90
*Maps*, 178
Marginalization, 172, 173, 174, 179; material and textual, 181, 194–95
Marinetti, Filippo Tommaso, 12
Martin, John, 178
Marx, Karl, 26, 117, 129, 130, 132–33, 143, 163; *Capital*, 3, 48, 118, 125–28, 231 n. 4, 240 n. 13; *The German Ideology*, 3–4; *Grunderisse*, 132;. *See also* Commodity; Marxism
Marxism, xi–xii, 7, 25, 45, 123, 226
Mass culture, 8, 40–41, 45, 88, 97
*The Masses*, 25
Massinger, Philip, 86
Materiality 33,,, 79, 93, 95, 104, 109, 148; aesthetic, xiii, 4, 6; of language, 34, 38, 49; of sign, 111, 116; social, xii, 4–5, 23, 27, 230; social and textual, 25, 64, 96, 156, 226; textual, xi–xiii, 6–9, 32–33, 66, 69, 79, 92–93, 175, 192, 207, 226
Matisse, Henri, 41
Mathews, R. H.: *Chinese-English Dictionary*, 102, 105
Maximus of Tyre, 110
McAlmon, Robert, 13, 29
McCaffery, Steve, 16, 18
McCarthy Committee, 201, 203
McClure, Michael, 197
McGann, Jerome, xiii; *Black Riders*, 11, 28–29, 237 n. 17; *Critique of Modern Textual Criticism*, 69; *Textual Condition*, 9
McIntosh, Graham, 178
Melville, 81, 205; and Howe, 84–92. Works: "Bartleby the Scrivener," 85, 88; *Melville's Marginalia* (ed. Cowen), 84–85, 88–92; *Moby-Dick*, 89, 123; *Omoo*, 88; *Pierre*, 89; *Typhoo*, 88
*Melville's Marginalia*, 84–92
Metaphysical poets, 179, 187
Migne, J. P., *Patrologiae*, 103
Miller, Perry, 81
Milton, John, 82, 187
Minimalism, 26
Mitchel, John, 85
Modernisms, 22, 69, 97, 94–115, 117–18, 138–39, 180–81, 198; and gender, 8, 38, 44–45, 79
Moore, Marianne, xii; "Marriage," 45; pastiche poems, 138; "When I Buy Pictures," 45
Morris, William, 11
Mottram, Eric, 118, 122
Multilith, 30
Mussolini, Benito, 103, 117, 120, 124. *See also* World War II

Narcissus, 90, 222–23
Narrative poetry, 18, 138–70
Narrative turn, xi, 135–38, 230, 235 n. 2. *See also* Nationalism
Nationalism, 136–38, 146–47, 168–70, 242 n. 6

Native Land, 142
Naumberg, Nancy, 143, 149, 242n. 12
Nazi propaganda, 200. See also World War II
NEA (National Endowment for the Arts), 30
Nelson, Cary, 27
Neoplatonic Philosophy, 100–101, 110, 132
Neruda, Pablo: Canto General, 137
New Americanists, 26, 135, 242n. 6
New Criticism, xi, 6, 23, 133, 137, 229; and disinterested reading, 173, 197
New Deal, 169
New Directions Press, 179
New Historicism, 135
The New Masses, 117, 163
New York School, 15, 32
New Yorker, The, 27
NIA (National Intelligence Agency), 201
Nichol, bp, 18
Nietzsche, Friedrich, 96, 192
Night Mail, 142
Nixon, Richard, 202–3
NSA (National Security Agency), 201

Oakland Tribune, 35
Objective correlative, 9, 138, 186
Objectivism, 3, 5, 21–27, 133–34, 232n. 16; and materialist poetics, 116–17, 150–51, 239n.4; Oppen and, 64, 77, 92; political efficacy of, 24–27
The Objectivist Anthology, 27, 156
Objectivist Press, 29, 156, 158
Odysseus, 101, 186, 188–89
Offset printing. See Technology
O'Hara, Frank, 15, 28, 197, 218
Olmstead v. US, 201
Olson, Charles, xii, 27, 78, 90, 106, 109–11, 196, 237n.16; and archaeology, 109–10; field politics, 24, 31, 194; and history in poetry, 112, 114; and masculinity, 111, 238n.12; and orality, 9, 109, 207, 218; poetics and dance, 110–13, 238n.12. Works: "Letter, May 2, 1959," 14; "The Librarian," 110; The Maximus Poems, 14, 111, 113, 196, 199; "Pages from a Notebook," 174; "Projective Verse," 3, 14, 197–98; Selected Writings, 14, 109–11, 197; The Special View of History, 70
Omnibus Crime Control and Safe Streets Act of 1968, 202
Ong, Walter, 198
Oppen, George, 12, 29, 69–70, 72–75, 77–78, 140; and archives, 5, 32, 76–77; and daybooks, 236n.8; and Imagism, 64, 70–71; and Objectivism, 64, 79, 92; and "palimpsestic" manuscripts, 236n.7; and politics, 25, 68, 117–18; and textual materiality, 64–66, 92–93. Works: Discrete Series, 26, 71; Of Being Numerous, 71; The Collected Poems, 67, 71–72, 79; "Interview," 71–72; "The Little Pin," 77; The Materials, 27, 77; "Party on Shipboard," 71; "Rembrandt's Old Woman Cutting Her Nails," 64–66; "Route," 71–72; "Women see no purpose . . ." 72–75
Orality, 109, 196–223, 197, 204–6, 213–15, 227–28; and modernist voice, 9, 225; in 1950s, 14, 199; and technology, 209–11, 217. See also Magnetic recording; Sound poetry
Orwell, George: 1984, 202, 215
OSS (Office of Strategic Studies), 200
Ovid, 223
Owen, Craig, 214
Oxford English Dictionary, 94, 99

Padget, Ron, 15
Palimpsest, xii–xiii, 1, 8–9, 77–78, 231n.8
Palimtext, 28, 33, 64–93, 229, 230; writing as, 9–10, 67–68, 92, 156, 176
Paris, 45, 68
Paris Commune of 1871, xii
Parry, Milman, 199
The Partisan Review, 117, 143
Patchen, Kenneth, 15
Paul the Deacon, 104
Pauthier, M. G., 100
Peck, John, 102
Peirce, C. S., 96
Performance poetry, 197
Perelman, Bob, 241n.1; "China," 137
Perloff, Marjorie, 12; Poetics of Indeterminacy, 37
Persian Gulf War, 218
Persky, Stan: Open Space, 31
Personalism, 15–16, 28, 32. See also Expressivism
Phantasmagoriá, 3–4, 230; in literature, 1–4, 33, 231nn.2,3; poem as, xii, 225
Phenomenology, 114
Phillips, M. Norbese, 27
Philology, 94–115, 176
Picabia, Francis, 13
Picasso, Pablo, 12, 41, 50; Demoiselles d'Avignon, 44; portrait of Gertrude Stein, 37, 42

Pindar: first Pythian ode, 175–76, 190
Pivert de Senancour, Étienne, 88
Plain Editions, 29
Plato, 71, 78, 212, 228; *The Symposium*, 65–66
Poe, Edgar Allen, 85, 89; "The Fall of the House of Usher," 2; "Ligeia," 2
*Poetry*, 27
*Politics*, 173
Pollock, Jackson, 19
Pop Art, 15
Popular Front, 169
Porphyry, 101
Porter, Carolyn, 239n.7
Postcolonial criticism, 136. *See also* Colonialism
Postmodernism, 6, 21, 67, 98, 108–9, 135–38; modernist, 198–99, 223; and transgression, 171, 195. *See also* Jameson, Fredric
Pound, Ezra, 24, 33, 40, 69, 100, 103–4, 148, 196; and anti-Semitism, 97, 124–25, 240n.11; and Confucianism, 102–3, 139; and facism, 25, 103, 106, 117, 120, 132, 139; and ideograms, 117, 206; on the Mediterranean virtu, 106, 207; and Neoplatonic philosophy, 100–101; and Objectivism, 23, 26, 28, 117; and patriarchal modernism, 8, 38; and phantasmagoria, xii, 1, 231 n.2; at Pisa, 101–3, 106; and philology, 97–106, 114, 237n.4; and print technology, 13–14, 197; and St. Elizabeth's period, 102, 106; and Zukofsky, 119–20, 124–25, 133–34, 240n.12. Works: *Cantos*, 9–12, 78, 96–106, 137–39; Canto 14, 237n.4; Canto 23, 101; Canto 35, 124; Canto 36, 124; Canto 39, 99; Canto 51, 100; Cantos 52–71, 102; Canto 91, 11; Canto 96, 103; Adams Cantos, 138; Chinese History Cantos, 102; Dynastic Cantos, 138; Malatesta Cantos, 99; *Hugh Selwyn Mauberley*, 180; "In a Station of the Metro," 3, 10, 231n.2; *Letters*, 105; *Literary Essays*, 3, 10, 124; *Lustra*, 180; *Rock-Drill*, 101–3, 105; *The Spirit of Romance*, 99, 119; *Thrones*, 101–3, 105; translation of Calvalcanti's canzone, 125–26
Poststructuralism, 67, 230
Poulsen, Vlademar, 199
Print culture, 12–13, 28, 170
Projectivism: and "deep image" theories, 207

Psellos, 101
Pynchon, Thomas, 214

Quartermain, Peter, 80, 86, 126, 129
Quintilian (Marcus Fabius Quintilianus), 208
Queer identity, 229

Racism: and homophobia, 172; and sexuality, 158, 163–65. *See also* Slavery
Rainey, Lawrence, 99
Rakosi, Carl, 29
Ransom, John Crowe, 63, 138. See also *Kenyon Review*
Ray, Man, 13
Red scare, 201
Reiman, Donald H., and Reiman, Hélène Dworzan, 82–84
Reisman, Jerry, 126
Remington Arms Company, 229
Renan, Ernest, 95; *Histoire générale*, 97
"Rethinking Borders" (museum lecture series), 171
Rexroth, Kenneth, 15, 139
Reznikoff, Charles, 29, 71, 150–51, 156–57, 158–59, 160, 163–66, 167, 168; in *Contact*, 158, 161; and legal language, 23, 155; and nationalism, 5, 139–40, 169–70; and orality, 235 n.6; and originality, 155; and "Ring around the rosy," 154; and translation, 153, 243nn.15, 18; and witnesses, multiple, 140, 160. Works: "Depression," 158, 160; "Hands," 166; "Machine Age," 153; "Of Murder," 158; "My Country 'Tis of Thee," 156–59; "Prolegomena," 151–52; "Rivers and Seas, Harbors and Ports," 166–67; "Sailing Ships and Steamers," 165–66; "Of Slaves," 158; "Southerners and Slaves," 163; "A Talk," 151; *Testimony*, 26, 138–39, 150–67, 169–70
Richman, Robert, 239n.2
Ricoeur, Paul, 135
Riding, Laura, 22
Rilke, Rainer Maria, 40, 192
Rimbaud, Arthur, xii, 2
Rivers, Larry, 15
Rosenberg, Harold, 22
Ross, Kristen, xii
Rossetti, Christina, 209
Rotha, Paul, 141–42
Rothenberg, Jerome, 207
Roussel, Raymond, 33

Rowlandson, Mary, 81–82
Rukeyser, Muriel, 5, 9, 144, 146–148, 163, 242n.7; and *Book of the Dead (Egyptian)*, 147, 150; and cinema, 141–42, 143; and documentary culture, 138, 140, 142–49, 156; and Gauley's Junction tragedy, 142–49, 169; and materiality, textual, 148; and narration, 145–46, 148; and phantasmagoria, xii; and photojournalism, 138, 140–41, 169, 242n.9; and silenced voices, 145, 168; and South, history of, 147, 149; and testimonies, 144, 149, 169. Works: "The Book of the Dead," 135, 139–40, 142–49; "The Gates," 149; *The Life of Poetry*, 141–42; "Mediterranean," 149; "Poem out of Childhood," 138; *U.S. 1*, 140, 142–49

Sacco-Vanzetti trial, 138
Said, Edward: *Orientalism*, 95, 97; "Yeats and Decolonization," 136
Sappho, 138
Sanchez, Sonia, 197
Sandberg, Carl, 139
Sanders, Ed: *Fuck You: A Magazine of the Arts*, 31
San Francisco, 35, 186
Saussure, Ferdinand de, 96, 171
Scalapino, Leslie, 21
Schlegel, August Wilhelm von, 95
Schoenberg, Arnold, 6
Schwerner, Armand, 71, 207
Scottsboro trial, 158
Semiotics, 96, 135
Sennett, Richard, 45
Shakespeare, William, 82, 93
Shelley, Percy Bysshe, 90–92, 180; "Address to the Irish People," 85–86; Howe on, 84–92; "Mask of Anarchy," 138; *Prometheus Unbound*, 91–92; "To Emilia Viviani," 236n.12; *The Triumph of Life*, 91. *See also* Reiman, Donald H.
Shevelow, Kathryn, 155–56
Silliman, Ron, 18, 26–27
Silverman, Kaja, 202
Slavery, 163–66. *See also* Racism
Smith, Terry, 5
Snyder, Gary, 56, 106; "The Blue Sky," 108; *Mountains and Rivers Without End*, 108; *Regarding Wave*, 107; "Wave," 107
Social Credit, 120, 134
Socialism, 122
Socrates, 187, 208, 212

Sound poetry, 16, 18, 67, 197
Spanish Civil War, 141
*Spanish Earth*, 142
Speech act theory, 210
Spengler, Oswald, 150
Spenser, Edmund, 98
Spicer, Jack, 27, 31, 93, 174, 194
Spinoza, Baruch, 127, 131–33
Spivak, Gayatri Chakravorty, 135
*St. Matthew Passion* (Bach), 116, 133
St. Marks Poetry Project, 30
Stalin, Joseph, 173; conspiracy with Hitler, 131, 134
Steiglitz, Alfred: *291*, 12; *Camera Work*, 12
Stein, Gertrude, 24, 47, 49, 53–54, 54–55, 81, 233n.3, 235n.20; as abstractionist, 39, 43, 49, 58; and the aesthetic, 35–64; and autonomy theory, 6, 226; biography of, 36–37; and consumerism, 5, 9, 38, 41–41, 45–46, 61–63, 68, 234n.6; and Cubism, 12, 41, 45, 49; and difference, 37, 55; landscape, interest in, 56–58, 61; and language, 49–54; as object, 35–37, 40; parodies of, 36, 233n.2; and technologies, 38, 47–48. Works: "Apple," 42; *The Autobiography of Alice B. Toklas*, 36, 45–46, 54–56, 58; "A Box," 42; "A Chair," 43–44; *Doctor Faustus Lights the Lights*, 48, 68; "Flirting at the Bon Marché," 46–47; *The Geographical History of America*, 39, 50, 56; *How to Write*, 36; "An Instant Answer to a Hundred Prominent Men," 60; *Lectures in America*, 39, 41, 47; "Lifting Belly," 39; *Lucy Church Amiably*, 29, 36; *The Making of Americans*, 50; "And Now," 234n.6; "Patriarchal Poetry," 50–54, 234n.12; "Pink Melon Joy," 39; portraits, 36, 41–44, 46–47, 50; "Susie Asado," 37, 52; "Rooms," 44; *Stanzas in Meditation*, 55–62, 235n.16; *Tender Buttons*, 36, 42, 44, 46, 52; *Three Lives*, 50; *Useful Knowledge*, 60; "What Are Masterpieces," 38–39; *Writings and Lectures*, 50
Stein, Leo, 50, 54
Steisichorus, 101
Stevens, Wallace, 9, 27, 223, 225–27; "Mozart, 1935," 226; on phantasmagoria, xii; "Sunday Morning," 226
Stimpson, Catherine: "Somagrams of Gertrude Stein," 37
Strand, Paul, 141
Structuralism, 135

Surette, Leon, 105
Surrealism, 24, 139
Surveillance ideology, 200–201; and electronic surveillance, 201–3; and orality, 227; and poetry, 203, 215–16, 218, 223. *See also* Cold War; Nixon, Richard
Swift, Jonathan, 192
Symbolism, 10, 24, 61–62, 133, 168

Taggart, John, 78. *See also Maps*
Technology, 4–5, 8, 21, 28, 179; cinema, 47–48, 142–43; new, 33, 339; offset printing, 15, 29–30, 197. *See also* Magnetic recording; Print culture
Tanselle, Thomas, xiii
Taylor, Edward: *Preparatory Meditations*, 60
Thaew, Celia, 131
Theocritus, 99
*These Are the Men*, 142
*They Must All Be Represented*, 140
Thomas, Dylan, 21
Thompson, E. P., xii
Thomson, Virgil, 142
Thurston, Michael, 146
Traherne, Thomas: *Centuries of Meditations*, 60
Tichi, Cecelia, 5
TO press, 29
Toklas, Alice B., 29, 35, 40, 54–56, 62
Twombly, Cy, 21

Union Carbide, 142–49
U.S. 1 (road), 149

Valéry, Paul, 40
Van Vliet, Claire, 30
Vancouver Poetry Conference (1963), xi
Veblen, Thorstein, 44
Vietnam War, 179, 193, 202, 204–6
Visual Poetry. *See* Concrete Poetry
Vorticism, 11–12, 133
Vygotsky, Lev Semenovich, 222

Waldman, Anne: *The World*, 31–32
*Walk East on Beacon*, 202
Wang, David, 105
Wang Wei, 105
Warner Communications, 172
Watergate, 202–3. *See also* Cold War
Watten, Barrett, 218
*Webster's Fifth Collegiate Dictionary*, 110–12

West Publishing Company, 151
Whalen, Philip, 15, 106; "The Education Continues Along," 108
Wharton, Edith: *The House of Mirth*, 45
Wheelwright, Philip, 143
White, Hayden: on historiography, 135
White, Margaret Bourke. *See* Caldwell, Erskine
Whitehead, Alfred North, 71
Whitehead, Gregory. See *Wireless Imagination*
Whitman, Walt, 14, 32, 71, 166, 180, 192, 204–5, 228; "Democratic Vistas," 206; *Leaves of Grass*, 29; "Out of the Cradle, Endlessly Rocking," 167, 188
Williams, Emmett, 15
Williams, Raymond, xii
Williams, William Carlos, 12, 13, 148; "The Attic Which Is Desire," 29; *Contact*, 156; and Objectivism, 23–24, 26, 117; *Paterson*, 138, 149; and print technology, 14, 28, 197; *Spring and All*, 12
*Wireless Imagination*, 245 n.3
Wittgenstein, Ludwig: *Philosophical Investigations*, 44
Woolf, Janet, 44
Woolf, Leonard, 178
Woolf, Virginia, 178; *Mrs. Dalloway*, 45; *Three Guineas*, 178–79
Wordsworth, William, 53, 56
World War II, 131, 150, 173, 179. *See also* Anti-Semitism; Auschwitz; Fascism; Hitler; Holocaust; Mussolini; Nazi propaganda
WPA (Works Projects Administration), 140, 149

Yeats, William Butler, 1, 28, 99, 110, 136; "Meditations in Time of Civil War," 138
Youngman, Henny, 208

Zaum language, 23, 49
Zola, Émile: *The Ladies' Paradise*, 2–3
Zukofsky, Louis, 106, 117, 125, 126, 127, 130, 131; on alienation, 119, 121, 125; on commodity culture, 120–21, 124–25, 127, 134, 140; critiqued, 118, 122; and formalism, 118, 126–29, 134, 239 n.5; Jewish ethnicity, 121, 125, 132; and politics, 117–34, 240 n.13; and Objectivism, 3, 5; as postmodern and post-Marxist, 123–24, 128; and Pound, critique of, 119–20, 124, 133–34, 240 nn.10, 12; and science and mathe-

matics, 126, 129–30, 133; on writing as production, 127, 133–34. Works: "A," 25–26, 123; "A"-1, 133; "A"-7, 116, 134; "A"-8, 126–27, 130, 132, 134; "A"-9, 117–18, 124–34, 140; "D.R.," 127; "During the Passaic Strike of 1926," 127; *First Half,* 125–29; "For My Son When He Can Read," 133; "Interview," 116; "Mantis" (sestina), 118–23, 127–28, 131–34; "'Mantis,' an Interpretation," 122–24; "Memory of V. I. Ulianov," 127; "Notes on Contributors," 133; "Poem Beginning 'The,'" 123; *Poetry* (essay, 1931), 117; *Prepositions,* 23, 69, 117, 130, 133–34, 226

Compositor: G&S Typesetters, Inc.
Text: 10/13 Palatino
Display: Palatino

www.ingramcontent.com/pod-product-compliance
Lightning Source LLC
Chambersburg PA
CBHW021655230426
43668CB00008B/631